nal dynamics. The authors, with their extensive experi-
ence in alternative movements, were able to talk in
depth with the Greens, who were freer and more self-
critical in these discussions than they have been with
journalists. The result is a book of unprecedented depth
and insightfulness, a realistic look at the Greens' global
promise for an imaginative alternative to "politics
as usual."

FRITJOF CAPRA is the author of two international best
sellers, *The Tao of Physics* and *The Turning Point.* He
lectures widely in the United States and Europe on the
philosophical, social, and political implications of modern science.

CHARLENE SPRETNAK is the author of "Naming the Cultural
Forces that Push Us toward War" (*Journal of Humanistic
Psychology*), editor of *The Politics of Women's Spir-
ituality,* and author of *Lost Goddesses of Early Greece.*
She lectures in the United States and Europe on issues in
peace work, spirituality, and feminism.

GREEN POLITICS

E. P. DUTTON, INC.   NEW YORK

GREEN POLITICS

Fritjof Capra and Charlene Spretnak

In collaboration with Rüdiger Lutz

Published in the United States by E.P. Dutton, Inc.,
2 Park Avenue, New York, N.Y. 10016

Library of Congress Cataloging in Publication Data

Capra, Fritjof.
  Green politics.
    1. Grünen (Political party) I. Spretnak, Charlene.
II. Lutz, Wulf-Rüdiger.   III. Title.
JN3971.A98G7232 1984   324.243'07   83–27474
ISBN 0-525-24231-7

Published simultaneously in Canada by Fitzhenry & Whiteside Limited,
Toronto

COBE

10 9 8 7 6 5 4 3 2 1
First Edition

Acknowledgments

We would like to express our deep gratitude to the many people in West Germany who kindly aided us in our research for this book, and especially to Rüdiger Lutz, director of *Zukunftswerkstatt* (Future Lab), who facilitated our initial contacts with many of the Greens and expanded our understanding of recent political events in his country.

We are extremely grateful to the following members of the Green party for generously giving us extensive interviews, often in the midst of highly demanding schedules:

from the national executive committee: Rudolf Bahro, Wilhelm Knabe, Manon Maren-Grisebach, and Rainer Trampert;

from the national steering committee: Christine Schröter;

at the national party headquarters: Lukas Beckmann; we also thank Wolfgang Clabbers and Renate Lang for assistance;

from the parliamentarians in the Bundestag: Sabine Bard, Gert Bastian, Marieluise Beck-Oberdorf, Erika Hickel, Gert Jannsen, Petra Kelly, Joachim Müller, Gabi Potthast, Christa

Reetz, Jürgen Reents, Otto Schily, Waltraud Schoppe, Walter Schwenninger, Heinz Suhr, and Roland Vogt;

from the special assistants to the parliamentarians in the Bundestag: Alfred Horn, Sarah Jansen, Martha Kremer, Renate Mohr, and Connie Sauer.

We are also grateful to the following Greens in villages, towns, suburbs, and cities for giving us interviews and, in many cases, extending their gracious hospitality to us, and we thank Lukas Beckmann and Roland Vogt for kindly preparing a letter of introduction and contact lists of key Greens:

from Baden-Württemberg: Roland Görger, Wolf-Dieter Hasenclever, Jürgen Maier, Emilie Meyer, Thomas Schaller, Gisela von Kügelgen, and Beate Orgonas; we also thank Thomas Kleine-Brockhoff, Karl Mennicken, and Gert Meyer for their assistance;

from Bavaria: Anton Betzler, Gisela Erler, August Haussleiter, Bernhard Kölbl, Gabi Kloske, and Klaus Peter Morawski; we also thank Nanna Michael and Erika Wisselink for their assistance;

from the city-state of Bremen: Dagmar Eder, Bernd Schorn, and Helga Truepel;

from the city-state of Hamburg: Thomas Ebermann;

from Hesse: Chris Boppel, Thomas Gröbner, Klaus Kallenbach, Irene Khateek, Regina Maier, Marion Papaczek, Monika Scheffler, Frank Schwalba-Hoth, and Werner Wenz; special thanks to Alfred Horn for his assistance;

from Lower Saxony: Helmut Lippelt, Sylvia Müller, and Jürgen Paeger;

from North Rhine-Westphalia: Dieter Brandt and Udo Henke;

from Rhineland-Pfalz: Thomas Pensel;

from Schleswig-Holstein: Helga Fritzsche.

We are greatly indebted to the following members of Green or Green-oriented parties and organizations in other European countries for long conversations and correspondence: Erich Kitzmüller in Austria; Cécile Delbascourt, Dirk Janssens, Jean-Marie Pierlot, and François Roelants in Belgium; Jonathan Porritt in England; Michel Delore, Edouard Kressmann, and Armand Petitjean in France; Grazia Borrini and Franco La Cecla in

Italy; Pieter Mors and Hans Verstraaten in The Netherlands; and Stephan Wik in Sweden. We also thank Eva Quisdorp of Berlin for conversations about the international peace movement. It is our special pleasure to acknowledge telephone interviews with our Canadian "neighbors" Adrian Carr and Wally Thomas, members of the Green party of British Columbia.

In the United States we received valuable advice and assistance from many friends and colleagues to whom we are deeply grateful. We especially wish to thank our two consultants: Hazel Henderson, who made time for many discussions on global Green politics even though she was hard at work producing her television program, "Creating Alternative Futures," and Mark Satin, editor of *New Options,* who gave us many hours of his time in detailed discussions of possibilities for Green politics in the United States. Mark also read the entire manuscript and offered many helpful suggestions. A third person to whom we are very grateful for his advice, especially in the early stages of this project, is Byron Kennard.

We thank the following people for reading parts or all of the manuscript and offering valuable comments: Janet and Robert Aldridge, Walter Truett Anderson, Judy and Peter Berg, Michael Closson, Leonard Duhl, Daniel Ellsberg, David Haenke, Willis Harman, Barbara Huber, Michael Koetting, Kay Lawson, John McClaughry, Ute and Helmut Milz, Laura Nader, Janice Perlman, Kirkpatrick Sale, Nikki Spretnak, Keith Thompson, and Dana Ullman.

For research assistance we are grateful to Paula Gunn Allen, Ward Ashman, Chip Berlet, Sigi Brauner, Lina Hayward, Michael Helm, Phil Hill, Florentin Krause, Michael Marien, Gary Ruchwarger, and Philip Spielman. We also thank Renate and Robert Holub and Patrick Murphy for assisting us in translating a large number of Green publications. Special thanks go to Nettie Hammond, Nesta Lowenberg, and Alma Taylor for secretarial work and typing.

Above all, we are deeply grateful for the support from our families and close friends: Sheila Ballantyne, Jacqueline Capra, Pamela Crawford, Michael Duden, Barbara Green, Michael Koetting, Patricia Leonetti, Lissa Merkel, Maria Monroe, and

Judith Todd. We also appreciate the kindness of John Eastman, Carolyn Shafer, and Eleanor Vincent.

Finally, we are indebted to our editor at E.P. Dutton, Bill Whitehead, and we wish to acknowledge the work of our agents, Frances Goldin and John Brockman.

Contents

Preface

A ritual procession of twenty-seven people—including a nurse, a shop steward, a former general, a mason, several teachers, a veterinarian, a retired computer programmer, three engineers and a scientist, a bookseller, an architect, a journalist, a professor of agriculture, and a lawyer—walked through the streets of West Germany's capital on 22 March 1983 with a huge rubber globe and a branch of a tree that was dying from pollution in the Black Forest. They were accompanied by representatives from various citizens' movements and from other countries. They entered the lower chamber of their national assembly, the Bundestag, and took seats as the first new party to be elected in more than thirty years. The new parliamentarians insisted on being seated in between the conservative party (Christian Democrats), who sat on the right side of the chamber, and the liberal-left party (Social Democrats). They called themselves simply *die Grünen,* the Greens.

Our interest in the Greens began in 1982 during our respective lecture tours in West Germany. We learned that many of the ideas explored in our recently published books, *The Turning Point* (Bantam Books, 1983) and *The Politics of Women's Spirituality* (Anchor/Doubleday, 1982), were closely related to the programs of this new party, which was winning seats in city councils, county assemblies, and state legislatures. They declared themselves an antiparty party, the political voice of the various citizens' movements. The Greens proposed an integrated approach to the current ecological, economic, and political crises, which they stressed are interrelated and global in nature. They spoke of the "spiritual impoverishment" of industrialized societies. They asked questions that neither of the major parties nor the government could answer and they amplified with playful humor the ironies that resulted. Next to the starched white shirts in the assemblies, the Greens looked unconventional, as their innovative proposals cut through the traditional boundaries of left and right.

Because of our own work, we felt an immediate resonance with Green politics. Moreover, we were intrigued with the diverse yet successful composition of the party: ecologists and peace activists, holistic theorists and anti-nuclear-power activists, feminists and Third World activists, value-conservatives and converts from radical-left groups. The Greens introduced a new style of politics into the electoral system. While other politicians spoke with pompous and evasive rhetoric, the Greens used simple, direct language and coined new phrases. The conventional parties were all led by men; the Greens had a striking proportion of women in leading positions. The old-style politicians dressed in suits and ties; the Greens wore casual clothes.

After we returned to the United States, we were surprised to find that American media coverage of the Greens' activities was extremely biased. Rather than reporting the analyses and proposals of the Greens, journalists usually filed dramatically negative articles, referring, for example, to ". . . the disruptive emergence of the so-called Green protest movement. A jumbled alliance of ecologists, romantic far-leftists, Communists, and enemies of nuclear weapons, the Greens sapped the strength of the Social Democrats and spread panic among Genscher's Free Democrats by threatening their very existence" (*New York Times* wire release, 20 September 1982). The Greens' opposition to deployment of the new NATO missiles in Europe was often equated by the press with being "anti-American," even though they have close ties with the American peace movement and call on both East and West to end the arms race. The *New York Times'* bureau chief in Bonn explained to Americans that the Greens are "volatile" (13 February 1983), "messianic" (27 February 1983), and "far left," a charge he included in nearly every article even though the Greens emphatically reject the programs suggested by the left wing of the Social Democrats, let alone the Communist groups—all of whom embrace the fetish of open-ended growth as blindly as do the conservatives.

When the Greens published a thirty-nine-page economic program during the national election campaign in the spring of 1983, which included substantive proposals for an ecologically balanced, appropriately scaled, self-organized (not state-controlled!) economy, the American media reported either that the Greens' ideas are merely "outlandish" (*Washington Post,* 2 March 1983) or that the Greens "offer virtually nothing" on this issue *(New York Times,* 13 February 1983). Readers of *Time* were informed that the Greens are "inchoate and unrealistic" and driven by "romantic and dangerously simplistic longing" (28 February 1983). CBS's "Sixty Minutes" (27 February 1983) featured a segment on the Greens that showed them looking as bizarre as possible because it was filmed partially at one of the costume parties held all over Germany on *Fasching,* or Mardi Gras.

This is not to say that a conspiracy against the Greens exists among American journalists. Their negative and inaccurate reporting is due, for the most part, to the usual lack of comprehension that new ideas encounter. For instance, political journalists accustomed to thinking in terms of a linear spectrum from left to right continue to misunderstand the concepts of the Greens. Perhaps more important, we began to see that the journalists were writing to suit the expectations of the Establishment media for whom they work. We were quite surprised to learn from one of the Greens in Bonn that the American journalist who had written the most consistently negative articles professes a deep personal commitment to the peace movement and handed out leaflets with the Greens at Krefeld when Vice-

President Bush made a speech there. Perhaps a cynically prejudiced voice is helpful in keeping one's job as a chief correspondent for a major newspaper. (By August 1983, it should be noted in fairness, that journalist did file an impartially worded article in which he conceded that the Greens "have shown a capacity to articulate issues.") After the Greens' July 1983 visit to Washington, D.C., the *Washington Post* featured a column in which the writer was moved to praise the Greens as "a serious movement with a prevailing dedication to nonviolent protest"; however, he concluded that the reason they should be respected is not their moral impetus but, rather, that "they constitute a potent and potentially dangerous force" because violent protesters might join their demonstrations. Perhaps it would have been too "soft" to admire the Greens for their Gandhian approach and moral goals; a more acceptable equation in this culture is the frequent association of respect with that which must be feared.

With the help of friends in many parts of the country, we monitored the media coverage of the Greens from September 1982 through October 1983; to our knowledge, the single positive editorial in a major American newspaper appeared in the *Boston Globe* after the Greens' peace demonstration in East Berlin (14 May 1983), and the only impartially insightful article on them was a guest column in the *Los Angeles Times* by Gordon A. Craig, the distinguished American historian of the modern German era (6 April 1983). However, the accuracy and substance of articles on the Greens improved during September and October 1983, when three Green leaders—Rudolf Bahro, Gert Bastian, and Petra Kelly—made lecture tours of the United States and presented Green politics in numerous newspaper interviews, and when *Vanity Fair* published an impressionistic but largely accurate article on the Greens by Ronald Steel.

In the alternative press, the coverage was not much better. A leftist newspaper published in New York, *The Guardian,* ran a series of articles on the Greens, but their journalist presented the relatively small radical-left faction as being the most important part of the party. In fact, as we discuss in this book, the role of the left in the Green party is extremely complicated and by no means do they characterize the entire party. When we mentioned a few of the distortions in those articles to Greens in

Bonn, they laughed and said, "Oh, yes, that journalist has a lot of friends in Hamburg!" (Hamburg and West Berlin are the strongest centers of the radical left within the Greens.) Two articles published in *Radical America* (January–February 1983), a leftist journal published in Boston, were more balanced.

By October 1982 it was clear to us that the breadth and accuracy of information we were seeking would not be forthcoming in the media. When we decided to write this book, the response from our friends and colleagues reflected the prejudices of the media coverage: "Why are you studying the Greens?" they asked. "Aren't they Communists?" "Aren't they neo-Nazis?" "Aren't they just naïve protesters?"

In 1983 we returned to Europe on separate six-week trips with a dual purpose: to conduct interviews and gather information on the Greens, and to give lectures and seminars on our own work. We both gathered research and conducted interviews on the composition and history of the Greens (Chapter 1) and on their political principles (Chapter 2). Charlene conducted most of the interviews on their politics of peace (Chapter 3), social issues (Chapter 5), grassroots electoral politics (Chapter 6), the evaluation of their first four years (Chapter 7), and their party structure and operation (Appendix A). In addition, she compiled most of the research for the American chapter (Chapter 9). Fritjof conducted most of the interviews on the Greens' economic program (Chapter 4) and on the global network of Green movements (Chapter 8). He also studied the relationship between Green politics and science, particularly systems theory. Rüdiger Lutz, who was associated with the Green movement from its beginning and knows many of its leaders personally, served as our liaison in West Germany, introducing us to the Greens in an informal way and helping us with the logistics of the interviews. He also contributed background information on German politics and on the peace, ecology, and alternative movements, as well as material on the postwar developments that led to the formation of the Greens, on which a section of Chapter 1 is partially based. The major portion of the text was written by Charlene.

Unlike the journalists who had previously questioned the Greens, we brought to our interviews an understanding of the holistic political theory informing their work, which provided a basis for our inquiries, skepticism, and enthusiasm. The Greens themselves were extremely generous in the time they gave us for interviews and discussions. In addition, they were much more frank and self-critical than we had expected. We interviewed the three speakers and the general manager of the national party, numerous Green parliamentarians in the Bundestag, and dozens of other officeholders and party activists in nearly all parts of West Germany. We also analyzed their major position papers and numerous publications. Because West Germany is an affluent, industrialized society with a central position in the politics of nuclear deterrence, many of the problems the Greens are addressing are similar to those in the United States. It is those issues we focus on. Our book, then, provides an introduction to Green political thought, both in West Germany and in its global manifestations, and it explores the impact that a similar movement could have in the United States.

The starting point of Green politics is the recognition that we find ourselves in a multifaceted, global crisis that touches every aspect of our lives: our health and livelihood, the quality of our environment and our social relationships, our economy, technology, our politics—our very survival on this planet. The nations of the world have stockpiled more than 50,000 nuclear warheads, enough to destroy the entire world several times over, and the arms race continues at undiminished speed. While worldwide military spending is more than one billion dollars a day, more than fifteen million people die of starvation annually—thirty-two every minute, most of them children. Developing countries spend more than three times as much on armaments as on healthcare. Thirty-five percent of humanity lacks safe drinking water, while nearly half of its scientists and engineers are engaged in the technology of making weapons. Economists are obsessed with building economies based on unlimited growth, while our finite resources are rapidly dwindling; industrial corporations dump toxic wastes somewhere else, rather than neutralizing them, without caring that in an ecosystem there is no "somewhere else." Modern medicine often endangers our health, and the Defense Department itself has become a threat to our national security.

Our politicians no longer know where to turn to minimize the damage. They argue about priorities and about the relative merits of short-term technological and economic "fixes" without realizing that the major problems of our time are simply different facets of a single crisis. They are systemic problems, which means that they are closely interconnected and interdependent. They cannot be understood through the fragmented approaches pursued by our academic disciplines and government agencies. Rather than solving any of our difficulties, such approaches merely shift them around in the complex web of social and ecological relations. A resolution can be found only if the structure of the web itself is changed, and this will involve profound transformations of our social and political institutions, values, and ideas.

The first step in overcoming the crisis is to recognize a new "paradigm"—a new vision of reality. The beginnings of this change are already visible and are likely to dominate the entire decade. The paradigm that is now beginning to recede has dominated our culture for several hundred years, during which it has shaped our modern Western society and has significantly influenced the rest of the world. This paradigm, or world view, consists of a number of ideas and values, among them the belief in the universe as a mechanical system composed of elementary material building blocks, the view of the human body as a machine, the view of life in society as a competitive struggle for existence, the belief in unlimited material progress to be achieved through economic and technological growth, and— last, not least—the belief that a society in which the female is everywhere subsumed under the male is one that follows a basic law of nature. During recent decades all of these assumptions have been found severely limited and in need of radical revision.

The emergence of Green politics in many countries is part of that revision. It is an ecological, holistic, and feminist movement that transcends the old political framework of left versus right. It emphasizes the interconnectedness and interdependence of all phenomena, as well as the embeddedness of individuals and societies in the cyclical processes of nature. It addresses the unjust and destructive dynamics of patriarchy. It calls for social responsibility and a sound, sustainable economic system, one that is ecological, decentralized, equitable, and comprised of flexible institutions, one in which people have significant control over their lives. In advocating a cooperative world order, Green politics rejects all forms of exploitation—of nature, individuals, social groups, and countries. It is committed to nonviolence at all levels. It encourages a rich cultural life that respects the pluralism within a society, and it honors the inner growth that leads to wisdom and compassion. Green politics, in short, is the political manifestation of the cultural shift to the new paradigm.

Many of the same forces that created Green politics in Europe are on the rise in North America. In fact, the evolution of the Green party in West Germany included a number of direct connections with political events in the United States. We were often told that three of the basic principles of Green politics—ecology, grassroots democracy, and nonviolence—were inspired in large part by citizens' movements in America, especially the civil rights and environmental movements. Many Greens have been influenced by the ecological wisdom of the Native Americans, and they cite the examples of Thoreau and Martin Luther King in their nonviolent resistance to military escalation. The core symbol of the Greens itself, the sunflower, is not native to Germany but to North America. The Greens certainly drew on other antecedents as well, but their impressive achievement was grown from partially American seeds. The German Greens have preceded their American counterparts in transforming holistic theory into political practice, and we can learn a great deal from their successes and errors.

In developing Green politics, no one country can serve as a fixed model for others—and, indeed, we distinguish several aspects of the West German situation that are quite different from the American—but the success of the German Greens in introducing new-paradigm thinking into electoral politics makes them a fascinating case study. In this country a broad spectrum of people have grown frustrated with the sorry ritual we stage every four years, in which the Democrats and Republicans attack each other's performance, appeal with slick media campaigns to our desires for a better society, and sell us old-paradigm solutions to our problems that are gravely ineffectual. Rather than a coherent program with a long-term vision of sustainability and the quality of life, we are offered the marketing of a hero figure with his empty rhetoric and promises of short-term fixes.

The liberal/conservative stalemate is blocking a great deal of creative thinking that could guide our society within a sound framework based on holistic insights and ecological imperatives. What we need is a new dimension of politics altogether. Green politics offers such a dimension, a politics that is neither left nor right but in front.

FRITJOF CAPRA and CHARLENE SPRETNAK

Berkeley, January 1984

Part One

Green Politics in West Germany

Chapter 1

Who Are
the Greens?

On 22 March 1983 newspapers around the world published photographs of a new political force entering history. Twenty-seven recently elected parliamentarians from the Green party took their seats in West Germany's national assembly, the Bundestag, forming a river of colorful sweaters, shirts, and dresses that flowed down the middle of the chamber between the tiers of black-and-white-suited politicians of the conservative Christian Democrats (*Christlich Demokratische Union*, CDU) on one side and the liberal-left Social Democrats (*Sozialdemokratische Partei Deutschlands*, SPD) on the other. The new parliamentarians had refused to be seated to the left of the Social Democrats, whose party consists of a left wing as well as the dominant liberal wing. In calling for an ecological, nonviolent, nonexploitative society, the Greens *(die Grünen)* transcend the linear span of left-to-right.

The Greens consider themselves the political voice of the citizens' movements, that is, ecology, anti-nuclear-power, peace, feminist, and others. Most members of the Green party are also activists in one or more of those movements, and this diverse orientation is reflected in the wings, or factions, of the party: the visionary/holistic Greens, the Eco-Greens, the peace-movement Greens, and the radical-left Greens. A great deal of overlapping occurs with any categorizing of Green identities and some people say there are no actual factions, but clearly there are different priorities among the four clusters.

The visionary/holistic Greens have as their central concern and guiding principle the evolution of a new society based on ways of thinking and being that reflect the interconnected nature of all phenomena. They want people to move beyond the mechanistic world view that has dominated Western thinking for the past three hundred years to a fuller understanding of the subtle relationships and dynamic flux that comprise life on Earth. They call for more sensible, postpatriarchal ways of interacting with nature, individuals, groups, and other countries. They question *what* the economy should produce in addition to how and how much. These people are sometimes called the "moral" or "ideological Greens." They are concerned with inner development as well as a comprehensive politics.

The Eco-Greens, or "green Greens," focus their efforts primarily on protecting the natural world from toxic wastes, radiation, air pollution, and other hazards, as well as promoting "ecodevelopment," that is, the use of renewable-resource technologies for energy and industry. This cluster includes the "value conservatives," who see the need for far-reaching changes in many government policies but insist on preserving the traditional values. The value conservatives often live in rural areas and are somewhat comparable to the Republican populists in the United States today. Also in this cluster are the "ecological reformists," who come from a liberal background.

The peace-movement Greens concentrate primarily on garnering public support for the Green party's peace program, working closely with the larger West German peace movement, and networking with peace activists in other countries. Many of these people came into the Greens from the antimissile movement, that is, the activism aimed specifically at halting deployment of the 108 Pershing II missiles and the 96 cruise missiles in West Germany as part of the NATO defense system. However, the peace proposals of the Greens extend far beyond this one issue; they include bloc-free thinking, phases of demilitarization, social defense, and a regionalized global community.

The radical-left, or Marxist-oriented, Greens are those who entered the Green party from various Communist groups. In a more narrow sense, these terms refer to those Greens who are former members of the Communist Alliance (*Kommunistischer Bund* or KB), especially those in Hamburg, who united to form "Group Z" within the Green party. Numerically the radical-left cluster is much smaller than any of the other three, but it is influential in certain areas, as we shall discuss. Although Group Z members are in frequent contact with one another, they have not met formally since 1982 and seem to be moving toward becoming a more loosely defined socialist faction. These people emphasize effecting social change by working with the trade unions although ironically many leftist trade unionists reject these "red Greens" as having become too ecologically oriented at the expense of class struggle and unqualified economic growth.

Sometimes the Greens are also classified according to their position on political strategy. They have drawn some votes from the Christian Democrats and are expected to increase that trend as more conservatives realize that the corporate interests of the CDU often conflict with their own desires for an unpolluted environment and a community-based economy. It is the Social Democrats, however, with whom the Greens are more compatible, although there are numerous points of departure in their programs. The question that is continually debated among the Greens is whether their small party of 30,000 members should form a coalition with the Social Democrats. In West German politics a coalition does not entail bloc voting but, rather, agreeing on major issues and forming a combined majority in a legislative body until the next election, which is generally held every four years. The smaller partner then becomes part of the ruling majority and receives some of the government appointments, such as cabinet-level ministers. Those Greens who feel that the integrity of their positions would be compromised and eventually destroyed by a general coalition are called the "fundamental oppositionists" or simply "fundamentalists." Those who favor a coalition, usually with specific conditions, call themselves the "realists."

The ages of Green party members fall mainly between twenty and forty-five. We were told that the West Germans who are now over sixty are the "economic-miracle generation," who rebuilt their country from the postwar rubble into affluence. They and their children feel they have been served well by the industrial and political mechanisms of modern "progress" and are not interested in questioning its problematic aspects. However, the Greens do attract some members from the over-sixty-five group specifically because they remember life before heavy pollution, industrially processed food, dying forests, and nuclear missiles. The Greens are not starry-eyed romantics attempting to turn back the clock, but the older Greens' experiences of a prewar childhood enable them to gauge environmental damage and agree with the call for an ecologically wise society.

As we traveled around West Germany talking with Green party officials and legislators in villages, university towns, suburbs, and cities, we noticed a refreshing contrast to political parties in the United States: the Green party is not run by lawyers! Just imagine. The broad range of occupations represented by the Green parliamentarians in the Bundestag (see Preface) is typical of all their elected officials. For example, the Greens in the state legislature of Hesse consisted in 1983 of four teachers, four sociologists, two social workers, a minister, a nurse who was formerly a nun, a former priest, a psychologist, a translator, a writer, a salesman—and one lawyer. (This group of eighteen includes the nine legislators and their nine successors under the Greens' rotation system, which we explain in Chapter 2.) The Green party's executive committee in that state is comprised of two university students, a teacher, a business consultant, a sales trainee, and a social worker. The Green city council members in the university town of Freiburg consist of two homemakers, one of whom is a grandmother and formerly a farmer; an architect; and a sociologist. The profession with the largest representation in the Greens is probably teaching, and religious studies was often cited as the area of specialization among Green teachers. In addition to their wide range of occupations, the warmth, humor, and spontaneity of the Greens' style make them unique in West German politics.

Throughout this book we introduce dozens of Green activists, but the one who is best known in America is Petra Kelly. In 1983 she made two trips here, along with other Greens, and presented Green political positions on nationally broadcast television programs: "Meet the Press," "The Today Show," and "The MacNeil-Lehrer Report." In addition, she accepted a longstanding invitation to address the Foreign Relations Council in New York and the National War College in Washington, D.C., as well as delivering numerous lectures on campuses, at conferences, and for peace groups' fundraising events in San Francisco and Los Angeles. In Philadelphia she was presented with the Woman of the Year Award by the Women's Strike for Peace. Kelly has been profiled in many American newspapers and magazines as the Green leader with the American connection: her stepfather is a retired U.S. Army officer, and the family lived in Georgia and Virginia while she attended high school and then earned a degree from American University's School of International Service in Washington.

Petra Karin Kelly was born of German parents in Bavaria in 1947. After their divorce she was raised by her mother and grandmother and spent six years in a convent school. Although her parents and half-brother now live in Virginia, Kelly's grandmother has remained in Nuremberg and the two are very close. Kelly's half-sister died at age ten from cancer in one eye, and Kelly feels her death was the result of excessive radiation during treatments in the late 1960s which caused her to lose her nose and nearly an ear. Kelly subsequently founded and chairs the Grace P. Kelly Association for the Support of Cancer Research in Children, a European group that studies the relationship between children's cancer and environmental factors, especially radiation.

During her college years in Washington, Kelly worked in the presidential campaign of Robert Kennedy and became friends with Hubert Humphrey. She was also drawn to the civil rights movement and the tactics of nonviolent civil disobedience called for by Martin Luther King. By the time she returned to Europe in 1970 Kelly had been involved for years in the antiwar movement and had also been influenced by the feminist movement. She earned a Master of Arts degree in political science from the University of Amsterdam before taking the position of administrator in European health and social policy questions with the European Economic Community (the Common Market) in Brussels. Kelly held that post from 1972 until her election to the Bundestag, which necessitated countless all-night commutes to various cities in West Germany for her central participation in founding the Greens and achieving their electoral victories.

It was during her years at the European Economic Community that Kelly began to develop a systemic, or new-paradigm, mode of analyzing societal problems. Kelly joined the Social Democratic party—where she encountered "so many men who knew so little"—and became involved with the Union of German Ecological Citizens' Groups (*Bundesverband der Bürgerinitiativen Umweltschutz* or BBU), which promoted ecological consciousness on a large scale and was the first organization to structure a grassroots movement. Throughout the 1970s she lectured in Japan and Australia as well as Europe on antinuclear and feminist issues. Like so many others who felt the need for a new politics, Kelly left the Social Democrats at the beginning of 1979; however, unlike other people she sent a personal letter to the Chancellor and head of the party, Helmut Schmidt, informing him of her departure.

Many journalists who describe Kelly compare her to Joan of Arc. They note her short, sandy hair and attractive features, her deep engagement, her urgent speech . . . and her air of a martyr. They say she is humorless and driven. She does indeed seem almost possessed at moments when she brilliantly condenses complicated Green political positions into the tight constraints of an interview, gazing over the dark circles of fatigue that always rim her eyes and speaking at so rapid a clip that the need for breathing seems hardly indulged. Yet there is another side to her: warm, caring, and laughing easily. We saw these traits during the times she invited us to spend with her in Bonn and when she passed through San Francisco on her lecture tour in September 1983.

When we began researching this book, we wondered about the paradox of the role of Petra Kelly and the Greens' rejection of the idea of strong, charismatic leaders. The answer, we discovered to our surprise, is that Kelly is appreciated very little within the Greens. The major complaint is that she is too enamored of personal publicity. "But if she didn't give the interviews," we pointed out, "Americans and others would have learned nothing about the Greens except through the often sensationalist and inaccurate media coverage. Don't you see her interviews and first-rate performances on news programs as being good for the Greens?" Shrugs. She could share the spotlight more, they countered. That may be true, but whether she does or not will not exempt her from the ill will often directed toward women in public positions of power: resentment from men and jealousy from women. A national conference of Green women in June 1983 resolved that Kelly is "not really feminist, only when it suits her purposes." Recalling all the strong feminist positions she has expounded in her writings, her interviews, her speeches, and her parliamentary work, we asked if even one person in the hall had stood up to defend her. No, we were told, no one did.

"Petra Kelly's deepest layer seems to be an extremely ambitious Catholicism, although not in an ecclesiastical sense," we were informed by Rudolf Bahro. The context of Bahro's statement is that he was raised on the Lutheran turf of northern Germany and is a great admirer of Luther. Moreover, he himself is no stranger to ambition, having produced a stream of lectures and articles since leaving East Germany, as we subsequently discuss. Except for that apparently irresistible Protestant jibe, however, Bahro does not speak ill of Kelly and professes "a deep loyalty" to her. In that, he is quite unusual among the men in the Greens who come from a leftist background. Many of them consider Kelly an irritation for two reasons: Her heroes are Gandhi, Martin Luther King, and the Berrigan brothers rather than Marx, and she includes spiritual values in politics. One of the Green parliamentarians who was formerly a Communist told us that the Bundestag is not the proper place for Kelly specifically because she has "a certain religious tendency in her politics" and therefore is not pragmatic enough. We found that a rather astounding position since many of the Greens told us of their sense of a spiritual dimension to Green politics and since Kelly's pragmatism is wanting only from a Marxist perspective. "To push her out of the forum of power because you don't believe there is such a thing as the spiritual dimension in life would be an ideological purge," we responded. He then asserted that Petra is someone who can "rouse the masses" but that such talent is not necessarily suitable for the Bundestag. Another man told us simply, "While it is probably true that the Green party is still too patriarchal, it may also be too Petra-archical."

Some Greens complained that Kelly is "too individualistic" and rigidly demanding. More common, though, was talk of her allegedly spending all of her time giving interviews. In fact, she rejects most requests for interviews and spends most of her time, along with four assistants, trying to deal with the two hundred letters per day she usually receives—some addressed merely "Petra Kelly, Germany"—and doing peace work and mobilization on behalf of the Greens. The resentment toward Kelly is nearly relentless, but many Greens suggested that certain of her traits exacerbate the friction: she is considered a high-strung genius, a loner, an impatient theoretician, a bearer of the world's burdens who is always embroiled in several crisis situations simultaneously.

Perhaps the Greens' "Petra paradox" can best be summarized by juxtaposing Kelly's own perception—"I have no personal life. I am almost married to the Greens"—with a typical response from a member of the Greens' national executive committee: "Petra Kelly was very important in the formative stages of the party because charismatic personalities are necessary to create stability and to establish the new ideas in the public's consciousness. However, that function is no longer needed."

How the Greens address the tensions between Kelly and other key members will be one of the most intriguing internal dynamics to watch over the next few years. She is certainly as frustrated with the party as it is with her. Will the Greens find a meaningful role for someone with such unique talents and widespread public appeal even though she can be difficult to work with—or will the party forfeit her contributions?

The cultural and political forces that led to the formation of the Green party have been the subject of much speculation in this country. Several publications have asserted that forming Green-type movements is simply something German youth do every few decades. They compare the Greens to the romantic *Wandervögel* of the late nineteenth century and even to the Nazi youth groups, who were taught that nature—within German borders—is sacred. A second common assumption is that the

Greens have their roots "in the counterculture of the 1960s" (*Los Angeles Times*, 18 September 1983). That is a projection of the American experience. While Amsterdam, London, and San Francisco were inundated with the colors, music, flowers, blind trust (of people under thirty!), and surging optimism of the hippies, West German youth were enmeshed in the angry, Marxist-dominated student revolt of 1968 and its aftermath. It is true that one can connect certain aspects of Green politics to strains in German culture such as regionalism and a romantic love of nature. However, the Greens must be understood as a postwar phenomenon because their roots, their context, and their memories lie on this side of the great trauma that severed the continuity of the German experience: the Nazi era.

The majority of the Greens were born during the fifteen years following World War II. The collapse of the "Thousand Year Reich," which fortunately lasted "only" for twelve, destroyed all the ideologies and values that had guided the culture, leaving a void and a shocked aftermath. History and tradition were put under the carpet because they could no longer be shown—not to other countries, not to other people, not to one's own children. Adults threw themselves into the task of rebuilding an industrialized Germany and reflected little on the Holocaust. Their children grew up in a world without a past, knowing only that their parents had done something wrong.

By the 1960s a youth rebellion had erupted to challenge the older economic-miracle *(Wirtschaftswunder)* generation, which had lost its authority because of its Nazi past. The young people censured their parents for their cooperation during the Nazi regime, and they chided them for their obsession with material accumulation. They grew up hypercritical, resisting every attempt to ideologize or moralize or mystify their social context and development. They felt betrayed because the continuity of their tradition and their existence as a people had been broken by their parents' generation, which had allowed the Third Reich to prevail. The "angry young Germans," as they became known, were rebels with a cause.

In school these young people were educated to be objective, critical, and skeptical. Official policy supported a version of democratization that provoked students to distrust authorities, social institutions, and hierarchical ordering. Only by critiquing everything was it believed that a nightmare like the Nazi regime could never happen again. The generational conflict grew more intense as the students identified their parents' characteristics as products of Nazi socialization: to be dutiful, tidy, obedient, and production-oriented. When these postwar children reached the universities in the mid-1960s, they were brimming with revolutionary fervor looking for a form.

The German university system they encountered was perhaps the only institution that had resisted the postwar democratization. It consisted of an authoritarian hierarchy of 5,000 full professors nationwide, accorded great esteem by the public, and making every possible decision over the pyramid of faculty underlings and, below them, the 300,000 students. The students demanded democratic reforms in that elitist system. As the momentum of their protests gathered, they often disrupted lectures and faculty meetings. Some protesters shocked the German public by throwing eggs, tomatoes, and paint at the professors. During the upheavals, many of the students experimented with self-organized learning in collective structures and other new forms.

Like the student movement in the United States during those years (which had begun with opposition to the Vietnam War), the German student rebellion soon became dominated by Marxist thinking; it also maintained close ties with the French student revolt of May 1968. However, unlike the American situation with four separate but overlapping anti-Establishment movements—the New Left, the antiwar movement, the feminist movement, and the counterculture—Marxism was practically the only game in town. It continued to dominate German university life (its forms as well as the contents of many courses) and much of alternative politics from the violent protesters of 1968 until around 1976. Therefore, most of the Greens under forty with whom we spoke, no matter how far from Marxist thought they had moved, had in common the experience of learning the Marxist vocabulary during their university years and believing then that it was the only "scientific" and "objective" tool for critical discussion. (The only Green leader who did not share that experience is Petra Kelly, who spent the 1960s in the American antiwar movement.) In retrospect, many people told us that the Marxist student movement had been rigid and tightly disciplined, rarely acknowledging personal realities because of its "historical task" of becoming the revolutionary vanguard who would supposedly lead the proletariat into open class struggle. The workers, however, were not interested in the plan, and the movement suffered attrition because its ideal of the coldly "objective" man excluded many enthusiasts from full participation.

After 1969 the Marxist/student movement splintered into dozens of Communist groups, or *K-Gruppen,* which can be categorized as either the "dogmatic left" (adhering to the Communist party lines of the Soviet Union, China, or Albania) or the "nondogmatic left" (unaffiliated and slightly less doctrinaire Marxists). Among the latter are the *Spontis,* that is, spontaneous movements, who call for "personal emancipation" in addition to the traditional Marxist formula. Urban communes were formed in which property, privacy, and monogamy were eschewed. Some people joined what Rudi Dutschke labeled "the march through institutions," entering social and political institutions in an attempt to change the system from within. Some people became impatient and went underground, surfacing in the mid-1970s as terrorists, of which the Baader-Meinhof gang was the most famous—or infamous. However, most people left the movement to become apolitical (either inside or outside the Establishment) or to seek a form of political development that would be more comprehensive and vital than the "intellectual dialectical form." Many of them took part in what was called the "inner migration," focusing on personal growth, spiritual work, and group dynamics. They made trips to India, Africa, and other Third World countries as well as discovering books from the American counterculture.

From 1974 on, the radical-left avant-garde found themselves surrounded by—and largely ignored by—the burgeoning citizens' movements against environmental destruction and the proliferation of nuclear power plants. From the student protests, the citizens had learned the possibility of questioning the underpinnings of "Model Germany." For the first time, a broad range of "good Germans" who were socialized to be obedient and loyal to the dream of the economic miracle questioned the government's plans for more freeways, more high-rise-oriented urban renewal, more plutonium-producing power plants, and more pollution of the rivers and the air. No longer could authorities plan in the dark as public awareness of government machinations grew dramatically throughout the 1970s. It is true that some groups in the ecology movement attracted "brown" elements, that is, reactionary people who had been raised with Hitler's notion of *Blut und Boden* (Blood and Soil), which located sanctity specifically in Germans and Germany. However, most people in the ecological protest movements were apolitical or politically moderate. They had become materially comfortable enough to pause and question the ongoing destruction they saw around them.

We were told by many Greens that the ecological concerns being formulated during those years were given a focus by the widely read *Limits to Growth*, published by the Club of Rome (Universe Books, 1974), and later by *Ein Planet wird geplündert (A Planet Is Plundered*, Fischer Verlag, 1978) by Herbert Gruhl, a conservative politician who subsequently became a founder of the Greens. Also popular were Ivan Illich's books and his articles on institutions. By the late 1970s, many Marxist groups had begun to work with the citizens' movements primarily because the Marxist women convinced the men that people's everyday concerns are as valid as abstract rationalism. The major lesson in the extremely heterogeneous citizens' movements was the importance of tolerance and compromise and the possibility of unifying diverse perspectives, a process that continues today within the Greens.

By the mid-1970s another movement arose that was related to the student protests, the citizens' movements, and the "inner migration" phenomenon: the alternative movement. Very much influenced by the counterculture in the United States and England, these people focus on addressing the practical needs of an alternative culture, for example, appropriate technology, renewable-resource energy systems, organic agriculture, and holistic healthcare. They were particularly inspired by E. F. Schumacher's *Small Is Beautiful: Economics As If People Mattered* (Harper & Row, 1973) and Ernest Callenbach's novel *Ecotopia* (Bantam Books, 1977). More than 4,000 of them joined the Self-Help Network, a fund started in Berlin in 1978 to support "alternative development." Members paid 14 Deutschmarks (about $5.60) per month, which resulted in funding of nearly 50,000 DM per month that was distributed by a board of directors to various projects. The alternative movement was roundly attacked during its early years by the radical left as being "individualistic utopianism," but as more and more people saw the need for developing real alternatives to what they were protesting against, the combination of political activism and alternative projects became accepted. The alternative movement fostered multiple developments with similar intentions, rejecting forced adherence to any one dogmatic line of thought, a mode of politics they associate with both the Nazis and the Marxist/student protests. They emphasize the connection between inner power, or spiritual strength, and political power. Moreover, they have reclaimed the term *utopia,* as one of their popular sayings demonstrates: "If you don't dare to dream, you have no power to fight."

By 1978 all the elements that formed the Green movement were in place. A small group of liberal and conservative ecologists, the Action Committee of Independent Germans (*Aktionsgemeinschaft unabhängiger Deutscher,* AUD) had been advocating a number of Green positions such as environmental protection and nonalignment for West Germany since 1973, when they had published their first program, based on the American Declaration of Independence. August Haussleiter and other leaders of the AUD contacted Herbert Gruhl, author of *A Planet Is Plundered* and then a Christian Democrat parliamentarian in the Bundestag, urging him to leave the CDU and join them. Instead Gruhl decided to form his own group, Green Action Future. It was he who created the slogan "We are neither left nor right; we are in front." During 1978 local groups of ecologists in the states of Lower Saxony, North Rhine-Westphalia, and Schleswig-Holstein ran Green electoral lists for the legislatures, but did not win the five percent of the vote necessary for representation.

A decision was made by Gruhl and the AUD people to form a Green association in order to run candidates for election to the European Parliament, the Common Market's political organization, in June 1979 and thereby acquire enough money to build a Green party. (West German law awards political parties—and political associations in local or European Parliament elections— 3.5 DM [$1.40] for every vote received.) They contacted two members of the executive committee of the BBU, the umbrella organization of anti-nuclear-power and other ecological groups:

Petra Kelly and Roland Vogt. Many members of the BBU vociferously opposed the proposal to enter electoral politics because they feared cooptation and corruption. Rather than responding with a groundswell of enthusiasm among those citizen groups for a new party, the grassroots were more or less dragged into the earliest stage of the Green party by Kelly and Vogt, who were expelled from their positions for six months.

Hearing of plans for a new party, two other groups who had been meeting together to discuss possibilities for alternative politics became interested. One was Action Third Way, followers of Rudolph Steiner's spiritual teachings known as Anthroposophy, the most widely known manifestation of which is the worldwide network of Waldorf schools. Anthroposophists seek "the spiritual in the material," and their interest in Steiner's complex system of organic agriculture inclined them toward the ecology movement when it arose. Action Third Way was composed mainly of those Anthroposophists interested in developing a new social and economic order that would differ from both communism and capitalism. The other group was the Free International University (FIU), consisting of people from the nondogmatic left. The two organizations wrote to Gruhl to express interest in joining the new party, but he rejected the FIU as being too leftist. However, urged on from within their ranks by Rudi Dutschke (the famous Red Rudi, who died in 1980), the well-known artist Josef Beuys, and a Czech exile, Milan Horacek (now a Green parliamentarian in the Bundestag), the FIU cultivated support among the leftist elements in the various Green state electoral lists. Many people in the FIU had been involved in the fruitless meetings during the mid-1970s on the need for another party and were determined that there could be only one successful new party.

At a founding convention near Frankfurt in March 1979 the "Further Political Association (FPA)-The Greens" was established. The groups mentioned above were invited to send a total of 500 delegates. Gruhl limited the leftists to fifteen delegates, one of whom was Lukas Beckmann who later became the general manager of the Green party. The convention approved a platform consisting of two major issues: a nuclear-free Europe (opposition mainly to the European Economic Community's investments in nuclear power plants) and a decentralized "Europe of the regions." The FPA-The Greens ran a volunteer-staffed, low-cost campaign for approximately $120,000. They won an impressive 900,000 votes, which brought them approximately $1.3 million, although their 3.2 percent of the total vote fell short of the 5 percent necessary for representation.

Throughout 1979 the FPA-The Greens gained members from various citizens' movements, not only ecological but also feminist and Third World activists. The dogmatic left (Marxists affiliated with one of the Communist parties) and many people in the looser nondogmatic left had scorned the Green association before the European Parliament election, but after its promising showing they reconsidered. They mostly kept their distance until after the Green congress in Offenbach in November. Over Gruhl's objections the assembly was addressed by both Rudi Dutschke and Rudolf Bahro, who had just been released from an East German prison to which he had been confined for writing a critical book, *The Alternative in Eastern Europe* (Schocken Books, 1981). Around that time many of the K-groups were dissolved, their members going either into the Greens or the Alternative Lists (AL). The Alternative Lists, and also the Multicolored Lists (named for the multiplicity of groups), are usually local Marxist-oriented organizations that agree that environmental activism is necessary but maintain labor issues as their top priority. In certain cities the AL eventually worked with the Greens; however, these alliances experienced schisms during 1983.

The Green party held its constitutional convention in Karlsruhe in January 1980. The delegates numbered 1,004, each representing ten members at the local level. The new party temporarily kept the executive committee from FPA-The Greens, whose speakers were Gruhl, Haussleiter, and Helmut Neddermeyer. The weekend congress was racked by raging disagreements, and it appeared by Sunday afternoon that they would fail to achieve a constitution. Lukas Beckmann recalled for us that many delegates had to leave at 4:45 P.M. in order to catch their train, so he and some others quietly prevailed upon the janitor of the assembly hall to stop the clock several times. "I believe the constitution was approved at about 5:30," he told us with a wry smile in between puffs on his pipe. Beckmann is a tall, handsome blond whose unflappable calmness makes him seem the eye of the Green hurricane in his job as general manager of the national party.

The Green party assembled delegates for the second time in Saarbrücken in March 1980. They elected a new executive committee to staggered two-year terms; the speakers were Haussleiter (later replaced by Dieter Burgmann), Kelly, and Norbert Mann (later replaced by Manon Maren-Grisebach). The major business was to approve the forty-six-page Federal Program, which involved a very heated argument over the abortion issue (see Chapter 5).

Delegates assembled for the third time in Dortmund in June and decided to participate in the Bundestag election in October, but won only 1.5 percent of the national vote. The Greens did win representation, however, on many town councils, following the first such victory in Bremen, in 1979, which received a great deal of attention in the national media. They then won seats in the legislatures of Baden-Württemberg in March 1980, Berlin (where they ran as members of the AL) in May 1981, Lower Saxony in March 1982, and Hesse in September 1982. Even in the very conservative state of Bavaria the Greens achieved a near miss of 4.6 percent in the October 1982 election. (Five percent of the total vote is necessary for representation.) In these campaigns they incorporated comprehensive strategies for peace into their program for an ecological society. Also in 1982, *Grüne Zeiten (Green Times: Politics for a Future Worth Living)* by Wolf-Dieter and Connie Hasenclever, two Greens who had been involved from the beginning of the party, brought the story of the Greens to a wide audience.

November was selected as the time for the Greens' annual delegates' congress; they also call special-issue assemblies. In 1982 their congress was held in Hagen and became known for the *Frauenprotest* (women's protest), in which women who had prepared position papers on the evolving economic program presented them as a separate group because they said they had not been allowed to incorporate them in the various working groups. There was so much disagreement over the economic program that only a two-page declaration was approved. This became the basis for continuing work at the assembly in Sindelfingen in January 1983, where a full thirty-nine-page program was approved—after much struggle. The Hagen congress also voted to replace Petra Kelly and Dieter Burgmann as speakers with Wilhelm Knabe and Rainer Trampert.

After Sindelfingen the Greens turned their attention to the Bundestag election of 6 March 1983. They ran some television spots, printed about a dozen colorful posters, set up information tables in town squares, and addressed local groups. But the most popular part of their campaign was the "Green Caterpillar," a bus that brought well-known German rock and New Wave musicians and singers to benefit concerts, featuring brief speeches by Green candidates and frequent satires of traditional German political rallies wherein the musicians would don loden hats, pick up tubas, and howl the West German national anthem. The campaign cost the Greens approximately $600,000, which was more than covered by the $3.2 million they received for the two million votes they won.

The results of the election stunned millions of West Germans. Not only did the tiny Green party capture 5.6 percent of the vote to win a voice in the Bundestag, but Helmut Kohl and his Christian Democrats won a landslide victory that dethroned the long-reigning Social Democrats in the federal government as well as in many cities that had had an SPD government throughout almost the entire postwar period. The electorate told pollsters that they voted for the conservatives mainly because they thought Kohl's people would be more able than Hans-Jochen Vogel's to remedy the economic crisis. However, the failure of confidence in the Social Democrats was not limited to economics. Throughout the 1960s and 1970s the left had been associated with fresh insights and innovative approaches. With the breakdown of the economic miracle, Schmidt's decision in December 1979 to deploy even more nuclear missiles, the SPD support of centralization in schools and district government, their inability to address the concerns of the citizens' movements, and their growth-at-any-cost policies, it became apparent that the left no longer comprised the cutting edge of intellectual and political life. Many observers feel that role is being earned by the Greens, who demonstrate again and again that the fine clothes draping the emperor (old-paradigm politics) are merely illusions.

Among the more complicated dynamics within the Green party is the role of the left. The majority of Greens who came from a leftist background had been introduced to Marxist thought during their university years and joined nondogmatic-left groups or had independently identified themselves as leftists. As the Marxist influence in the universities waned around 1976, numerous groups within the left intensified self-critical discussions about their world view, their assumptions, and their actions. They came to admit that their politics had ignored many vital and compelling issues raised by the ecology, feminist,* and alternative movements. A crisis developed within the K-groups, that is, Communist groups, concerning their traditional acceptance of power politics: were they correct in perceiving every movement as a movement against the state, in which tight organization was the only concern and content was irrelevant? Moreover, they had to acknowledge that the socialist commandeering of the power structures in Eastern Europe had not transformed society in a positive way.

The process of moving from leftist groups or identities into Green politics was extremely difficult for some people, especially those from the dogmatic K-groups. Lukas Beckmann recalled that many of them joined the Green party, then left, then rejoined, and that some almost had psychological breakdowns because Green political philosophy required them to change their deeply held convictions about the relationship of the individual to the state. By late 1979, however, when the left entered the Greens in substantial numbers, most of them were sincerely seeking a new politics and have since become "transformed," as we were often told. The experience of Marieluise Beck-Oberdorf, one of the three speakers for the Greens in the Bundestag, is typical:

> I grew up in a middle-class household and was educated as a Protestant with corresponding social and ethical principles. In the student movement I came in contact with Marxist ideas, which I found tremendously fascinating at first. Then I left that environment and began to work in the world, and now things look different to me. During the past ten years, I have learned to think. I have a different world view now, and so do many others.

*The West German feminist movement grew out of the student protests of 1968, so until the mid-1970s much of it had a Marxist orientation. We were told by many West German women that the best feminist analysis had come from the United States because it was not limited to parameters of class struggle.

These people work hard in the party and legislative bodies for Green ideals and are completely accepted by the original Greens. It is only some of the former Communists and a few other "mainly Marxist" Greens whom the majority find problematic, as we shall discuss.

The antagonism between the radical left and the rest of the Greens was so intense during the early stages of the party that many Greens laughed when we asked about the current factions: "There *are* no factions now compared to those days!" The left eventually found its place in the party and has made many positive contributions. It is often said that the leftists contributed political strategy to Green content (although some Greens point out that *die Grünen* received 3.2 percent of the national vote in June 1979 without the radical left and only 1.5 percent of the national vote in October 1980 after the left had joined the party). Wilhelm Knabe, a gentlemanly, gray-haired ecologist and one of the three speakers for the national Green party, told us what the "Eco-Greens" had learned from the leftist Greens:

> From a practical point of view, the chief lesson for the ecologists was organizing—how to organize a conference, a demonstration, or a boycott. A great deal was learned in that area. They also emphasized the role of capital in environmental destruction. And from us they learned that external relationships between people and nature have a great effect, that not everything can be explained by internal, societal forces. In addition, I think many people from the K-groups found it a relief—in fact, a pure psychological release—to be able to be *for* something.

Joachim Müller, a Green economist who describes himself as a post-Marxist, also spoke of the contributions of the left, but at the same time pointed out the necessary role of value conservatives: "If you want to build up something new in Germany without the protective function of the value conservatives, discrimination and suppression come very quickly. With the value conservatives included we are protected; they simply can't outlaw poodle owners. Our success lies in this combination, this integration."

We began to perceive friction between the radical-left Greens and the majority of the party as we traveled around West Germany and asked our interviewees whether a particular goal or strategy they had described was embraced by everyone in this heterogeneous party: "Does everyone in the Greens support nonviolence absolutely?" we asked. "Yes . . . except the Marxist-oriented Greens." "Does everyone in the Greens see the need for the new kind of science and technology you have outlined?" "Yes . . . except the Marxist-oriented Greens." "Does everyone in the Greens agree that your economic focus should be small-scale, worker-owned businesses?" "Yes . . . except the Marxist-oriented Greens." Some Greens spoke fondly of the early days "before the left split the party," while others were more adamant. Roland Vogt, a founder of the Greens, suggested a hidden agenda among certain members: "The major problem with the growth the Greens are experiencing is that more and more people are coming into the party who are not really Green, not holistically minded. The core Greens may become a minority! Those people are using the instrument created by others." He cautioned that there is no overt means by which to ascertain who is sincerely Green and who is not, then added with a slight smile, "However, one indication is that they are all chain-smokers."

We kept a look-out for tobacco-stained Machiavellians as we stalked the offices of Greens in the Bundestag and then visited Green headquarters around the country. Finally, we traveled to Hamburg and interviewed the three best-known Hamburg Greens: Thomas Ebermann, Jürgen Reents, and Rainer Trampert. All three were very cordial . . . and, yes, all three chain-smoked throughout the conversations! We encountered one other stereotype there: when we asked them, as we had all the other Greens we had met, how they personally came to Green politics, all three, independently of each other, spoke mainly of the great historical forces of the 1970s—with the exception of Ebermann, who actually said "I" a couple of times, at our urging. (In West Germany, as here, the most vigorous opposition to the feminist slogan "The Personal Is Political" came from New Left men. Generally they felt that personal life is merely something that happens between political meetings; to analyze it was to falter into "individualism.") All three men are tall with blondish hair, Reents and Trampert resembling each other slightly, rather like curly-haired cousins.

The handful of Hamburg Greens (a convenient term for those Greens in Hamburg who are former members of the KB, or Communist Alliance, and who now constitute part of Group Z within the Green party) have maneuvered themselves into influential positions. Trampert, a full-time representative on the workers' council at Texaco, is one of the three speakers of the national party. Reents, a journalist, is a weighty presence in the Greens' Bundestag *Fraktion* (a term referring to the fraction of the total number of seats, that is, the entire unit of legislators representing a party) and serves with Petra Kelly as the Green parliamentarian on the Foreign Relations Committee. Ebermann, a laborer, unofficially leads the Green *Fraktion* in Hamburg's city council/legislature. He is also an eloquent speaker who pushed through the Marxist-oriented section of the national party's economic program at the Sindelfingen assembly in January 1983. On the day after their package had been rejected by the delegates, Ebermann took the microphone and gave an account of his recent visit to the shipyards in Hamburg, saying he could never face those workers again unless the Green party endorsed a thirty-five-hour work week with no reduction in wages for the middle- as well as the low-level incomes. It was an emotional ploy the leftists would have scorned in opponents, but it worked.

When we told the three men that their names came up often in conversations with Greens around West Germany, they responded good-naturedly. The gist of our discussions with them on nonviolence is presented in Chapter 2. We also asked Reents whether they really have relinquished the Marxist goal of ever-increasing industrial production. He explained that they want the Greens to understand that advocating no growth is an inadequate position unless they examine which class benefits from it. We asked him about the standard Marxist vision of giving workers more leisure time so they can create art, which is expressed in the Marxist-oriented section of the party's economic program: "If you're serious about your brief mention of nonsexist division of labor, why don't you propose mechanisms for encouraging workers to put that leisure time into wiping babies' bottoms, taking care of invalid grandparents, and scrubbing toilets?" we asked. He replied, "I would say that this is a fully justified critique of the traditional unionist and Social Democratic position. What is right about the new ecology concept is that it addresses changing not only the material conditions but also the cultural and psychological conditions of society. However, our critique of the narrow ecological tendency is that the material question is being eclipsed."

We asked Trampert about the charge that the Marxist-oriented Greens are limited to an economics of "workerism," believing the only way to transform society is through the trade unions. "Some Greens say unions are part of the industrial bloc," he responded, "and hence adversaries. Others, like us, say that if we want to avoid a permanent societal schism we must find a convergence. This means we also have to enter the unions and work within them." He pointed out that not everyone will be able to work in small-scale businesses and that in some cases large-scale factories are more efficient. He also seemed not to take the Green ideal of worker-owned small businesses seriously, giving an example of a failed pub where friends had expected the owners to sell drinks cheaply. Overall, we learned that the Hamburg Greens serve to prevent the rest of the party from being head-in-the-clouds theorists on certain issues.

They are at odds with the majority of Greens on issues of strategy as well as content, hoping for a nationwide coalition of Green-AL (Green and Alternative Lists) alliances at the local level. When Ebermann revealed that dream in an interview in the magazine *Moderne Zeiten (Modern Times)*, many Greens considered it more of a nightmare. The Alternative Lists are composed mainly of former Communists and nondogmatic leftists. They are particularly strong in Hamburg, where the Greens operate in a GAL alliance, and in Berlin, where the Greens worked entirely within the AL until a split occurred in the summer of 1983. In Bremen, Marxist-oriented members of the Greens split away to form the Bremen Industrial Workers' Alternative List (BAL) for the city election in September 1983, but received only 1.4 percent of the vote, the Greens winning 5.4 percent (and an unaffiliated conservative Green group winning 2.4 percent). The GAL alliance in Hamburg experienced strong disagreement over whether to support the BAL, whom the Hamburg Greens opposed because of its affiliation with the old-style, Moscow-oriented German Communist party. The electoral success of the Bremen Greens without their radical-left members delighted many Greens; however, there is no talk today of expelling the Marxist-oriented Greens nationally as there was in 1981 when they were permitted to stay only after a Green tribunal heard evidence against them and ruled in their favor.

In addition to their love of radical-left alliances, another aspect of the Hamburg Greens' political behavior that exasperates many other Greens is their adherence to cadre politics; that is, operating in a tight group that makes no attempt to assimilate into the larger Green structure in the way the other groups have largely done. We frequently heard complaints that the radical-left Greens dominate most discussions on economics and that their separatist behavior is reflected in the Greens' economic program. Asked why it is such a discontinuous composition, with a preamble followed by a section of Marxist-oriented "workerism" proposals, followed in turn by more Green economic proposals, sometimes addressing the very same topics again, the response was usually a sigh over "the mosaic that is our economic program." When Ebermann expressed the mild disdain that Hamburg Greens feel toward the rest of the economic program with the comment that "parts of it are silly and extreme," we laughed and explained that many Greens consider the Marxist-oriented section to be "silly and extreme." He shrugged and replied, "It doesn't matter. That is a different position, and the party needs a broad spectrum."

It is the Marxist-oriented Greens' tradition of and fondness for "conflict politics" within that spectrum that is objectionable to other Greens. The Marxist-oriented faction does not indicate any desire to change this orientation in the future, as Ebermann explained to us:

> I hope that the entire left and the Greens will learn to relate positively to the idea of a faction. It need not mean a struggle for power. It can also mean differing experiments, in theory and practice, while accepting plurality—and also learning how to better articulate necessary arguments.
>
> There will always be a contradiction between ecology and economics because people will always argue about what should be invested in the future. Such a field of tension also has to continue to exist within the Green party. Differing factions will continue to argue.

In general the radical-left Greens do not exude respect for their fellow Greens as political opponents. However, the thorn in the side of Group Z is a visionary Green theorist who evolved into post-Marxist politics all the way from the inner circles of the East German Communist Party: Rudolf Bahro. On the thirtieth anniversary of the German Democratic Republic, 6 October 1979, 20,000 criminals were released from prison under a general amnesty. Bahro was included because of public outcry from the West at his sentencing for writing *The Alternative in Eastern Europe.* Some people had discerned "a hidden Green" in his book, and when he moved to West Germany he was warmly welcomed by the nondogmatic leftists who were part of FPA-The Greens. Only a few weeks later he was a keynote speaker at the Green association's assembly at Offenbach, where he surprised the radical-left Greens by stating, "In our own civilization Christ was incontestably the first teacher of our ultimate goal, the first teacher of the general emancipation of humanity." He has continued to surprise and confound the Marxist-oriented Greens—and to inspire the majority of the party—with statements such as: "The Greens are to Marx and Marxism what Einstein was to Newton and Newtonian physics—in short, a qualitative transformation of a worthwhile system whose time, however, is up." Bahro's appeal causes obsessive concern among the Hamburg Greens, as Ebermann's interview in *Moderne Zeiten* revealed. They are baffled that even "the completely cool analyst Wilfred Kretschmann," as Ebermann called him, the only one of the "ecological reformists" they admire, could applaud Bahro's "massive attack against the so-called sacred cows of the left" at the Hannover assembly in June 1983. They insist that Bahro is politically unintelligible when he speaks of withdrawing all energy, including psychic energy, from the old structures. The other Greens, however, have no problems comprehending the message.

Bahro himself is amused by the Hamburg Greens' fretting over which Greens may have become his "disciples" and whether "Kretschmann's troops" will use Bahro's ideas to mount an offensive against them. He has purposely not organized any cadre around himself and considers his role to be that of "a visionary and prophetic Green." Of the tensions within the Greens he told us: "Although no one any longer contends that Marx was correct in a general sense, a big problem within the Greens is that we are still operating with the remains of Marxism, legitimizing things in terms of the old tradition."

Bahro is a charming combination of insight, originality, and innocence, seeming rather like a middle-aged, bespectacled schoolboy with soft-spoken, almost impish ways about him. We were surprised, however, to see his mild-mannered demeanor give way to a style of public speaking that can become quite animated and intense. Bahro has framed influential post-Marxist arguments—which are different from antagonistic *anti*-Marxist positions, he emphasizes—in a number of areas, although some are judged too impractical even by his admirers. Several of his lectures have been collected in a book titled *Socialism and Survival* (London: Heretic Books, 1982). In his first American lecture tour, in September 1983, Bahro attracted leftist audiences who often went home with puzzled or angry expressions. A journalist in *The Guardian* reported on several lectures and concluded that the choice is "socialism or Bahro."

Perhaps the role of the left within the Green party can be described most accurately with the joke we heard frequently: "Two Greens, two opinions." However, the left evokes three general categories of responses. The Marxist-oriented Greens maintain that they are contributing pragmatic economics and attention to workers in very un-Green industrial cities. Even though they are at odds with the majority of Greens on several issues, the Group-Z Greens emphatically feel that they are core members of the party, and they are accepted as such. Ebermann told us "I think those who define themselves as 'the real Greens' make a mistake and are dishonest. The Greens are that spectrum that has come together, and no one can say he is the authentic Green."

A second view, held by some portions of the party, is that the Marxist-oriented Greens hinder the evolution of Green politics, as Roland Vogt explained: "The materialist-leftist approach is destructive within the Greens. Whenever the visionary or spiritual people make a proposal, the Marxist-oriented Greens neutralize it as effectively as acid." Because of the Marxist-oriented Greens, Gruhl left the party in late 1980, as did many members in the state of Schleswig-Holstein (where a takeover by former-Communist Greens was bitterly resented) and in the city-state of Bremen. Gruhl's attempt to form a coalition among those former Greens failed, and he then founded a small organization, the Ecological Democratic Party. (However, tensions between the Marxist-oriented Greens and the rest of the party are much less now than in the early days, as Vogt and others agree.)

A third view is represented by August Haussleiter, who often plays the role of mediator within the party:

> My former colleagues in the Christian Social Union [the Bavarian counterpart of the conservative Christian Democrat Union] often say to me, "We have underestimated the Greens. Green thinking is as sharp as a knife, and we never expected that." This results from our having conflicts between the left and the rest of the party and going through the conflict. The arguments with them, in short, are good training, and they force us to think about certain issues.

As we traveled the Green network around West Germany, we became fascinated with the endless diversity of the citizens involved. "What is the glue that holds the Green party together?" we asked again and again. The most disarming reply came from Helmut Lippelt, a historian and Green state legislator in Lower Saxony: "Success!" He then became more serious and reflected, as the others had, on the primary unifying focus: "We are fighting for survival." Green politics have appealed to so many West Germans because theirs is a densely populated, heavily industrialized nation where the limits to growth are visible at every turn, where the madness of nuclear deterrence has made them prime candidates for thermonuclear holocaust, and where the level of affluence allows "big picture" reflection. They are fighting to save the natural world and humankind, not through force but by awakening the consciousness that a new orientation for society is imperative. When accused by old-paradigm politicians of being dreamers, the Greens respond: "Who is realistic about the future and who is naïve?"

Chapter 2

Principles of a New Politics

Green politics grew out of deeply felt principles long before
there was any thought of forming a party. Among the broad
spectrum of citizens who rallied to stop the spread of nuclear
reactors, the pollution of rivers, and the death of the forests
during the mid-1970s arose an understanding that we are part
of nature, not above it, and that all our massive structures of
commerce—and life itself—ultimately depend on wise, respect-
ful interaction with our biosphere. Any government or economic system that ignores that principle is ultimately leading
humankind into suicide. The more that people perceived the
interconnections among principles of ecological wisdom, a truly
secure peace, an economy with a future, and a participatory
democracy with power channeled directly from the grassroots
level, the more they noticed the absence of such ideals among
the existing political parties.

The Greens begin their Federal Program by explaining why
a new politics is necessary:

The Establishment parties in Bonn behave as if an infinite increase in industrial production were possible on the finite planet Earth. According to their own statements, they are leading us to a hopeless choice between the nuclear state or nuclear war, between Harrisburg or Hiroshima. The worldwide ecological crisis worsens from day to day: natural resources become more scarce; chemical waste dumps are subjects of scandal after scandal; whole species of animals are exterminated; entire varieties of plants become extinct; rivers and oceans change slowly into sewers; and humans verge on spiritual and intellectual decay in the midst of a mature, industrial, consumer society. It is a dismal inheritance we are imposing on future generations. . . .

We represent a total concept, as opposed to the one-dimensional, still-more-production brand of politics. Our policies are guided by long-term visions for the future and are founded on four basic principles: ecology, social responsibility, grassroots democracy, and nonviolence.

The first of the "four pillars," ecology, has several meanings in Green politics. All of them can be understood within the context of "deep ecology," a concept that has also informed American ecophilosophy and activism in recent years. Far more than protecting or repairing the status quo, which is generally the goal of environmentalism, deep ecology encompasses the study of nature's subtle web of interrelated processes and the application of that study to our interactions with nature and among ourselves. The teachings of deep ecology include implications for our politics, our economy, our social structures, our educational system, our healthcare, our cultural expressions, and our spirituality.

Green politics, then, is inherently holistic in theory and practice. It is based on ecological, or "network," thinking, a term used frequently by the Greens. Ecological thinking also includes the realization that the seemingly rigid structures we perceive in our environment are actually manifestations of underlying processes, of nature's continual dynamic flux. Interrelatedness and ongoing process are the lessons the Greens take from and apply to the ecosystems surrounding us. They support "soft" energy production (such as solar power) that works with the cycles of the sun, the water, and the wind, and the flow of the rivers. They call for the development of appropriate technology that reflects our interdependence with the Earth. They advocate regenerative agriculture that replenishes the soil and incorporates natural means of pest control. Above all, the Greens demand a halt to our ravaging of natural "resources" and our poisoning of the biosphere through the dumping of toxic wastes, the accumulation of so-called acceptable levels of radiation exposure, and the pollution of the air.

The broader applications of ecological thinking lead to "social ecology," the perception of societal structures and human interactions as an intricate web of dynamic systems that are simultaneously interrelated parts and complete in themselves. Although Western culture has been dominated for several hundred years by a conceptualization of our bodies, the body politic, and the natural world as hierarchically arranged aggregates of discrete components, that world view is giving way to the systems view, which is supported by the most advanced discoveries of modern science and which is deeply ecological. In its early stages, during the 1940s, systems theory was closely linked with the study of control and regulatory mechanisms of complex machines and electronic systems. During the past decade, however, the focus has shifted to the study of living systems: living organisms, social systems, and ecosystems. The emergent systems view of life was developed by a number of scientists from various disciplines: Ilya Prigogine, Erich Jantsch, Gregory Bateson, Humberto Maturana, and Manfred Eigen, to name but a few.

The systems view involves looking at the world in terms of relationships and integration. Systems are integrated wholes whose properties cannot be reduced to those of smaller units. Whereas for two thousand years most of Western science has concentrated on reducing the world to its basic building blocks, the systems approach emphasizes principles of organization. Examples of living systems abound in nature. Every organism—from the smallest bacterium through the wide range of plants and animals to humans—is an integrated whole and thus a living system. Cells are living systems, and so are the various tissues and organs of the body. The same characteristics of wholeness are exhibited by social systems—such as a family or a community—and by ecosystems that consist of a variety of organisms and inanimate matter in mutual interaction. The specific struc-

tures of all these systems arise from the interactions and inter-
dependencies of their parts. Systemic properties are destroyed
when a system is dissected, either physically or theoretically, into
isolated elements. Although we can discern individual parts in
any system, the nature of the whole is always different from the
mere sum of its parts.

The principles of systems theory were expressed in numerous conversations we had with the Greens and in much of their
printed material, yet they use terms other than "systems thinking" to express these concepts. We asked Manon Maren-
Grisebach, a philosophy professor and one of the three speakers
of the Green party from 1981 through 1983, about this paradox.
Maren-Grisebach, a very self-assured blonde woman with a
quick intellect and warm humor, has written a book on Green
political theory, *Philosophie der Grünen (Philosophy of the Greens,*
Olzog Verlag, 1982). In it she asserts that ecology is the secure
and scientifically sound foundation for the entire Green philosophy. She explained their preference for the terms "network science" and "network thinking" rather than "systems thinking":

> We who have grown up with the history of philosophy [which is
> more influential in European thought than American] have a cer-
> tain aversion to the connotations of "system thinking" because
> often in the course of the history of ideas "system" stood for some-
> thing that was closed, that was a self-contained doctrine and thus
> was quite different from a living object. The great philosophers up
> to and including Hegel were expected to produce a philosophical
> system, which meant something finished, something closed. Only
> since the nineteenth century have we begun to connect "system"
> with living phenomena. Of course, it must be added that living
> systems are technically open and are capable of evolutionary proc-
> ess.

We asked her about the political implications of multileveled
order in nature, an order of systems within systems, integrating
nonorganic materials as well into living systems:

> Integrated doesn't mean primary or secondary. Green politics
> must expose the tendencies to set up hierarchies. Some of us see
> social or ecological or economic issues as primary. Then arguments
> follow. I always try to intercede immediately and say, "Why don't
> you let yourselves be guided by the meaning of ecology, that every-

thing is interwoven, that there is no such thing as a first or a second?"

The emphasis on relations and interconnections—in Gregory Bateson's words, "the pattern which connects the crab to the lobster and the orchid to the primrose and all four of them to me"—is the foundation of Green thought and being, whether it is called grassroots democracy or something else. This consciousness is simply there in the Greens.

That emphasis on relationships and interconnections is the basis of the Greens' ecological work that focuses specifically on environmental protection. Their programs in this area call for humans to find our place in the ecosystems, as their Federal Program states:

> We define ecological politics as those measures that understand human beings and our environment as being part of nature. Human life, too, is embedded in the life cycles of the ecosystems; we interfere with our actions and this, in turn, acts back on us. We must not destroy the stability of the ecosystems. In particular, ecological politics presents an all-encompassing rejection of an economy of exploitation and plundering of natural resources and raw materials, as well as the destructive intervention into the cycles of nature's household.

The Greens' proposals for addressing many of West Germany's ecological crises are believed to have brought them most of their votes in the federal election of March 1983. Their major focus during that campaign was immediate action to lessen and then halt the formation of acid rain, which has caused the rapidly escalating "death of the forests" in nearly all parts of West Germany but especially in the Black Forest and near the Czech and East German borders. Since the problem of acid rain transcends borders (both German republics, France, Belgium, The Netherlands, Czechoslovakia, and Poland are major exporters, mainly to Scandinavia and Austria), the Greens call for international cooperative actions. In May 1983, the Green parliamentarian Wolfgang Ehmke presented a four-stage proposal in the Bundestag for the reduction of sulfur dioxide emissions. The gradual plan, which would reduce all levels by the year 2000 to 1.9 percent of what they were in 1983, was not approved. However, the Kohl government finally agreed to require lead-free gasoline in West Germany as of 1985. Many Green groups at the local level monitor the emission levels of factories to see whether they are complying with federal law, and some Greens have successfully initiated local ordinances in this area. For example, a Green proposal in the city council of Nuremberg resulted in that city's becoming the first in West Germany to restrict the emission levels for its municipal power plant. Not only were nitrogen oxide and sulfur dioxide emissions almost eliminated, but a procedure was installed whereby sulfur dioxide is processed into nontoxic gypsum and sold to the housing industry.

The Green parliamentarians, particularly the attorney Otto Schily, also formally questioned the legality of military deposits of chemical weapons at sites throughout the country. Around the time the Greens were raising this issue in the Bundestag, a scandal broke concerning the disappearance of dozens of barrels of dioxin, which is extremely toxic. It was the Greens who quickly demanded a federal investigation and measures to control the transport of such dangerous substances.

The Greens also called for protection of farmers. Antje Vollmer, a Green parliamentarian who holds a doctorate in theology as well as agriculture, reminded the Bundestag that "Farmers are the primary environmentalists." She proposed a revision of federal policy that would support small farmers and organic agriculture, reversing the trend toward automated, industrialized farms that produce food of low nutritional value, destroy the ecosystems, and pollute the air and water with noxious chemicals.

At all levels of the party, the Greens address a multitude of ecological issues, such as the effects of the considerable traffic problems in West Germany. They also encourage ecological planning for towns and individual residences. At the federal level, the party awarded partial funding to a model ecological village (Ökodorf) now in the planning stage. (Several existing "eco-houses and -villages" in West Germany were modeled after the Integral Urban House in Berkeley.) In its ecological work, the Green party works with alternative institutes such as the Öko-Institut in Freiburg and others that comprise the Association of Ecological Research Institutes (AGÖF).

Although the Greens agree that the Federal Environmental Agency, in Berlin, should be strengthened, they are split over the idea of creating a Ministry for the Environment. Some Greens maintain that such a top-level government agency is necessary to develop effective positive programs as well as halting the damage. Other Greens are horrified at the thought of swelling the federal bureaucracy in the name of Green solutions.

The second of the four pillars, "social responsibility," is understood by most Greens to mean social justice and an assurance that the poor and the working class will not get hurt by programs to restructure the economy and our consumer society ecologically. Social responsibility began in Germany with the Bismarck government, although the concepts were paternalistic. After World War I there was a great deal of fear that the Russian revolution might spread, so the Social Democrats pushed through social legislation to avoid a more radical solution to the postwar problems. The concept of a social contract between the communities, the unions, and industry was developed. Of course, that alliance was insufficient to stop the rise of Hitler's National Socialist Party, which co-opted many of the social themes. In contemporary West Germany the concept of "social" (*sozial*) is behind the practice of companies offering workers benefits or arrangements that do not exist in the United States. It also accounts for a law that all stores and businesses, except restaurants, must close at six o'clock every weekday evening, at two o'clock on Saturday, and all day Sunday so that workers can be at home with their families.

The radical-left Greens, however, read *sozial* as a codeword for socialism, that is, democratic Marxism. Since that political model is specifically not what the visionary, liberal, and conservative Greens have in mind, a battle developed at the preliminary convention in Offenbach in November 1979 over establishing the basic principles. The majority of the assembly wanted the new party to stand for possibilities other than either socialism or the capitalist status quo. The radical-left contingent, on the other hand, insisted on not only including socialism but also on excluding nonviolence as a guiding principle, for reasons we discuss later in this chapter. Various groups shouted their proposals on issues and principles, and it seemed increasingly certain as the frustrating convention dragged on that a party would not be formed.

The breakthrough was achieved by August Haussleiter, who was then seventy-four years old. He recalled for us that someone from Berlin, whose name he never knew, appeared behind him and gave him the final push necessary to shape the chaos into the four pillars of the Green Party:

> I myself had been almost desperate with the situation because there were 3,000 people screaming their own positions in the convention hall. This person kept saying, "Don't give up. Don't give up. They're getting tired." Although agreement seemed impossible, I took a piece of paper and wrote four [in German] words on it: ecology, social responsibility, grassroots democracy, and nonviolence. Then I called together Gruhl [a leader of the conservatives] and Reents [a leader of the radical left] in the room where the journalists were and said, "Sign." We then went back into the convention hall and announced, "We have a program!"

So one of the four pillars, like so much else in the Green Party, has a paradoxical character: it means something different in different parts of the party. Yet the Greens have worked together to propose more legislation to protect the social and civil rights of women and minorities, such as the four million foreign "guest workers" in West Germany, than either of the major parties has ever done. All factions of the party concur that social (which in Germany always includes economic) and ecological issues are inherently linked, as they state in their Federal Program: "The ecological and social spheres belong inseparably together: the economy of nature is linked to the economy of humans for better or worse."

The third pillar, grassroots democracy, was inspired by the West German citizens' movements throughout the 1970s, which in turn were influenced by the civil rights, ecology, consumer, and other movements in the United States. The West German system of government, like our own, is a representative democracy, which means that the people elect representatives to run the party and the government. Direct, or participatory, democracy locates a greater amount of power and control with the local groups, the grassroots *(die Basis)*. This orientation informs the structure of the Green party and is expressed in their Federal Program:

> Grassroots-democratic politics means an increased realization of decentralized, direct democracy. We start from the belief that the decisions at the grassroots level must, in principle, be given priority. We grant far-reaching powers of autonomy and self-administration to decentralized, manageable grassroots units. . . .
>
> We have decided to create a new type of party structure, one founded on the inseparable concepts of grassroots democracy and decentralization. We believe that a party lacking this type of structure would be ill-suited to support convincingly an ecological policy in the framework of parliamentary democracy.

An organization structured with participatory democracy sets its basic policy according to the voting at large assemblies. It allows individuals access to all party officials, and it eschews hierarchical structure. Instead of allowing power to be concentrated in a few people who remain at the top of a hierarchy for years, such groups generally elect steering committees, usually with staggered terms of about two years. As we discuss in Appendix A, Green party programs may be compiled and edited by small working groups, but the content is determined directly by proposals and revisions from the grassroots.

One of the central functions of the Green party is to be the voice of the citizens' movements in the town councils, county assemblies, state legislatures, and national parliaments *and* to relay privileged information from those bodies to the grassroots movements. Although the Greens do not allow dual membership with other parties, most Green party members are also actively involved with one or more of the citizens' movements, that is, the peace, ecology, feminist, or anti-nuclear-power movements.

We were told that if we wanted to see a dynamic Green at work on all those issues and more, we should not miss meeting Emilie Meyer, a Green member of the city council in Freiburg. Freiburg is a charming medieval town near the Black Forest, with mosaic sidewalks, a Gothic church, and an inner city without cars. Meyer is a short, earthy farmer's daughter—and a grandmother—whose intelligence and warm, energetic style reminded us of Grace Paley in the American peace movement. The day we arrived in Freiburg Meyer had just taken part in a peace action that was filmed for a television documentary. The protesters brought attention to the government's preparation for a catastrophe of massive proportions, such as a nuclear war would cause: in a mountainside nearby, the government had constructed a repository of microfilm records of "cultural treasures," for example, the plans of the Cologne cathedral. In the demonstration, ninety women and ten men wore pins with the official symbol for such treasures. They marched with funeral songs and drumming, carrying plaster-cast "death masks" of themselves on black cloth, which they requested be put into the repository saying, "We, too, should be saved. We are cultural treasures." (When the documentary film was televised, West German citizens were outraged not only that the government was planning for a nuclear holocaust but also that it had stupidly selected mountains of government records to save and very little culture. "Not a single line from Goethe, Schiller, or Hölderlin!" a woman in Munich told us indignantly.)

The Greens are clearly lucky to have Meyer, who was the highest vote-winner among their four members of the city council, because she attracts voters among both the conservative farmers and the radical Green university students and faculty in Freiburg. She candidly explained to us that grassroots democracy puts a burden on conscientious elected officials because the citizens' movements expect a great deal of service from the council members but do not always do sufficient work themselves. "Often they have opinions," she told us, "but are not well informed. The *Basis* does not work as hard as is necessary for me to be effective for them on the city council." Still, Meyer makes all her "free" time available to the citizens' groups. Her husband, Gert, is retired and misses her in the evenings but is very proud of her political leadership.

Thomas Schaller, a city planner who is a Green member of the city council in Stuttgart, also spoke of the practical difficulties one encounters as a conduit between the citizens' movements and the legislative bodies: "Each week council members receive a large packet of papers about issues to be decided at the coming meeting, but the citizens' movements usually cannot decide on issues that quickly, sometimes because of poor organization." He feels that working within institutions but wanting to change them is "like walking on a knife." Schaller spends a good deal of his time offering practical assistance to local citizens' groups. He helps them frame arguments, organize the community, set achievable goals in small steps, find an attorney, connect with the local press, and realize they are as important as the other people in the news. He stresses that the Greens are fighting to secure policy-making power rather than just consulting roles for the citizens' groups.

The Greens, in serving as the political voice of the citizens' movements, know that many activists will never join the Green party, or any other, because a particularly strong antipathy toward political parties exists in West Germany. Older people feel the Nazi party tricked them in their youth with a hidden agenda, while young people point to the failure of the "march through the institutions" in the early 1970s. In addition, the West German electoral system, which we discuss in Chapter 6, allows the parties to appoint half the legislators in the Bundestag and the state legislatures to the long electoral lists rather than through popular vote. Hence, obedience to a party can keep one in a high-paying parliamentary job for years with little direct responsibility to the electorate. The voter turnout is very high in West German elections—typically 89 percent of eligible voters, compared to the 52 percent typical of recent national elections in the United States—but pollsters have discovered that most West German citizens vote only because it is a duty in a democracy, not because they feel their vote has any effect on the politicians or the government.

The Green definition of their *Basis*, or grassroots constituency, includes nonmembers who work with and support the party. Some local chapters allow nonmembers to vote at party meetings, and in Hesse even the Green state legislators have included nonmembers. The Green party is said to operate with one leg inside the legislative bodies and one inside the citizens' movements, which Roland Vogt calls the "emergency brakes" of a runaway industrial society. The party's close ties to the citizens' movements are demonstrated in many ways, of which the most impressive may be that the Green party channels a good deal of its money directly to activists' projects through its foundation, *Öko-Fond.*

Öko-Fond is administered entirely at the state level, although funds are derived from national membership dues and from a portion (usually about half) of the monthly salary of the parliamentarians in the Bundestag as well as from those of state legislators. The first *Öko-Fond* was established in Lower Saxony in 1980. In 1983 it received about 200,000 DM ($80,000) from the "extra" half of the Bundestag salaries and 20,000 DM ($8,000) from the "surplus" in the salaries of their Green state legislators. Typical of the 140 projects *Öko-Fond* has supported so far are publicity costs for several protest actions; chemical tests of emission levels; wheelchair access to the office of a peace group; apprenticeships in carpentry, masonry, and roofing for unemployed young people; the deficit from a conference on the problems faced by Gypsies; a film about peace; court costs and legal fees for many groups' lawsuits; an energy-generating windmill; a prison newspaper; a monthly alternative newspaper; a book on the destruction of a moor through the practices of agribusiness; and collectively owned businesses such as an alternative bookshop, a theater group, and a natural foods store. *Öko-Fond* in other states has also funded peace camps and shelters for battered women.

Most state branches of *Öko-Fond* are administered by a board of five people, at least two of whom—and more often three—are activists from the citizens' movements who are not members of the Green party. In Lower Saxony they meet for a full day once a month to decide on new funding and discuss ongoing projects, each of which is monitored in between the meetings by a contact person on the board. To any projects that will earn income *Öko-Fond* will usually give an interest-free loan to be paid back in one to three years. This is called a "subsidy" or "allowance" to avoid violating laws concerning political parties. Nearly all grants and loans are under 10,000 DM ($4,000), and most are from 1,000 ($400) to 3,000 DM ($1,200). Sylvia Müller of the *Öko-Fond* board in Lower Saxony told us of a recurring problem: many projects, especially the larger ones, default on the loans.

One of the most problematic aspects of grassroots democracy for the Greens has been their introduction of the rotation principle. In order to diffuse the concentration of power, the Greens adopted from the citizens' movements the practice of rotating officials after a certain period, usually two years. Rotation has become the expected practice both at the state and the federal level of the party. It is not practiced in city councils, where the Greens feel the chances for accumulating and abusing power are minimal.

What the early enthusiasts of rotation did not foresee was that applying it to electoral politics would be quite a bit more complicated than to steering committees within the citizens' movements. In West Germany's electoral system, as we discuss in Chapter 6, each party runs a list of candidates for the number of seats they anticipate winning in a legislative body. Seats are awarded according to the overall percentage of the vote for the party. The Greens run at least twice as many names as the number of seats they expect to receive so that they have a crew of successors ready to rotate in. For example, there are currently twenty-eight members of the Green *Fraktion* in the Bundestag—actually twenty-seven Greens plus one man from the Alternative List in Berlin. Their twenty-eight successors are called *Nachrücker.* Because there is no provision for such positions in German law, the Green party hires the successors as legislative assistants. Some people feared that there might be a legal challenge to rotation since the top vote-winners on the electoral list are supposed to hold office for four years, but the legislators from the Alternative List in Berlin rotated in May 1983 without incident.

The rotation principle was the subject of spirited debate nearly everywhere we went in West Germany. The arguments in favor of it run as follows. Because a person's thinking is affected by the way she or he lives, eight, or even four, years in the Bundestag—or a state legislature—machine would be very destructive. The Greens do not want their legislators to become insular like the Establishment politicians, who are said to forget what they said three days earlier. Long terms would concentrate information and power, hence are in opposition to grassroots ideals. The Hitler era demonstrated the danger of empowering charismatic leaders. The Greens should pursue the ideal of a network of people without functionaries who are all involved in governing their society.

Against rotation, we heard the following arguments. The Greens present new and often radical ideas, which the public is more likely to accept from legislators who have become familiar and have established some personal credibility over time. For the Greens to accomplish their political purposes, they must know just how far the opposition politicians can be pushed before they shut down, and this comes only with experience. It takes almost a full year for a new legislator to learn the ropes, and the party's efficiency suffers if this beginner phase must be repeated every other year. Rotation causes the Greens to lose expertise, seniority, and influence—as well as some of their most accomplished public speakers. The *Nachrücker* have become a new layer of bureaucracy; many have difficulty finding a useful function in their semiofficial role and so become depressed or unnecessarily competitive with the parliamentarians they are meant to assist.

A compromise was suggested by August Haussleiter and passed by the national assembly of the party at Sindelfingen in January 1983: each state party may decide whether any of its parliamentarians in the Bundestag is exceptional in some way and should have his or her rotation voted on, being permitted to remain if at least 70 percent of a state assembly approves. Roland Vogt, a sage observer of the dynamics within the Bundestag *Fraktion,* predicted what will transpire in March 1985, halfway through this first term: "Some people will be glad to leave the pressure and go home, some people will rotate on principle, some people will be dragged out kicking and screaming, and some people will simply not rotate."

Most of the Greens we spoke with in various states said they would be happy with a rule limiting legislators to one four-year term, rather than one-half of a term, and predicted that such a compromise will come to pass. The problem of electing and gainfully employing the *Nachrücker* would be eliminated, but the problem of continuity would still go unaddressed, we pointed out. Every four years an entirely new slate of legislators would start from scratch because the terms are not staggered, as they are in the American system. No one we spoke with had a remedy for that difficulty.

The fourth pillar, nonviolence, means to the Greens the cessation of both personal violence and "structural violence," that is, violence and oppression imposed by the state and by institutions. For these reasons the Greens support the concept of self-determination for individuals and groups. They also advocate peace education in the schools, which would teach nonviolent means of conflict resolution and show children that the cult of the soldier is a cultural, not natural, condition. As we discuss in Chapter 5, the Greens also call for an end to the violence and oppression toward women, children, and minority groups so common in patriarchal societies. They want to develop a nonexploitative economic system in which employee-owned and -controlled businesses replace huge operations dictated by the state or corporate interests. They want to transform our violent relationship with nature into one of balance and respect. Petra Kelly expresses the centrality of this principle when she says, "Nonviolence is the essential ingredient in an ecological society."

Although most of the Greens emphatically embrace the principle of nonviolence, they also realize that its application is often problematic. Roland Vogt pointed out one of the areas of conflicting values:

> What we have not yet accomplished is to say how we show ourselves to be nonviolent at the moment when we participate in governmental functions, because the state is itself an institution of violence. For example, how will a Green city council act against people who don't pay their rent, although they really could because they receive welfare or because they earn enough. The normal course is warning, warning, eviction notice, and then eviction by force and by police. We haven't solved this. That is, there are still no thought-out concepts of how one can reconcile the demands of social responsibility with the demands of nonviolence.

The Greens extend their principle of nonviolence to their active resistance against the most massive and potentially deadly manifestation of structural violence: the nuclear arms race promoted by the military-industrial complex and the government. In their national headquarters in Bonn the Greens have a poster of Gandhi's adage "There is no way to peace; peace is the way" and one of Thoreau from *The Thoreau Quarterly,* published by the University of Minnesota. In their Peace Manifesto the Greens explain their tactics by citing Thoreau:

> Those who embrace nonviolent civil disobedience, committing breaches of law on the grounds of conscience, are prepared to suffer violence or punishment themselves rather than inflict violence or injustice on others or share responsibility for such acts by remaining passive. "If, however, the law is so promulgated that it of necessity makes you an agent of injustice against another, then I say to you: Break the law."

Perhaps the Greens' most impressive spokesperson for nonviolent resistance to militarism in the nuclear age is Gert Bastian, a former general in the West German army. Bastian is a handsome and charming, silver-haired man of sixty who resigned his commission one month after the "double-track decision" of December 1979 to negotiate in Geneva but deploy the Pershing II and cruise missiles if those negotiations failed. He concluded:

> The ethical justification for a military force—that those people are protecting and defending what they love—is lost in the nuclear age because nothing can be protected in a nuclear war. In fact, military service in such circumstances becomes undignified and is a threat to everyone. Abandoning the military, then, becomes a decision of reason and is the only morally justifiable course.

Since leaving the army and joining the Green party—and later being elected to the Bundestag as a Green parliamentarian—Bastian has received a large number of angry, sometimes life-threatening letters from German men. We suggested that his action threatened the connection between manhood and actual or potential violence on which many men's identity rests (or totters). He agreed that this is often the case, but told us of the network of like-minded military men, mostly retired NATO generals, that has developed since his entering the Greens. In September 1983, when he spoke at the National War College in Washington, D.C., he held up a poster that showed the signatures of fifteen generals opposing deployment of the new missiles in Europe, and the audience of 280 generals and colonels applauded. The college witnessed a reversal of traditional roles that day, as a woman, Petra Kelly, presented the military and political positions and a man, Bastian, related his personal story. Bastian told of having been used in his youth by the Nazi government, who convinced young men to join the army because Germany had been attacked by aggressive nations. Later, when he learned that Germany in every case had been the aggressor, he was shaken by the betrayal. Because young people can be so easily misled and used, Bastian maintains, it is the duty of older people with their wiser perspective to expose the systems of violence, oppression, and mass murder. His message and Kelly's were received with genuine appreciation and questions about the moral force of Green politics that far exceeded the depth of previous questions from State Department personnel.

Bastian is one of the chief architects of the Greens' program for a secure alternative to militarism, and he has taken part in the front lines of numerous peace demonstrations. He and the majority of Greens strongly endorse—and live—the concept of active, nonviolent resistance. However, the Marxist-oriented members of the party have never been fully supportive of that principle. They view it merely as a "moralistic" tactic that should be abandoned in favor of escalating resistance if it does not prove sufficiently effective. Petra Kelly's account of the leftists' attitude on this issue was similar to what we had heard from many other Greens:

> They do not understand that nonviolent action is an extremely subversive force. They think it's harmless, is a form of obedience, and changes nothing, that it's like begging from the state. "It's just a tactic, a tool," they say. To them everything is to be used. But there are some things you should never misuse—or even use. They are simply integral. Nonviolence cannot be compromised.

We asked Jurgen Reents, a member of the Bundestag from Hamburg, where he is also a member of Group Z within the Greens, whether the radical left might not have a romantic attachment to the vision of armed struggle in the streets since they are steeped in the Marxist prediction that that is how change will occur. He smiled and replied, "I don't believe this problem can be approached with such a psychological explanation, that we are romantic enthusiasts of street fighting. On the same level, I could talk about the romanticism of nonviolent transformation of society."

Reents is a tall, attractive man with an intensity and air of personal power that has served him well in politics. His responses on the subject of nonviolence, as well as many other topics, are representative of the radical-left Greens with whom we spoke. For instance, we asked him about the strategy the peace movement should use if it wishes to remain a broad-based, popular force. Other Greens had pointed out the irony involved when the radical left, who pride themselves on being "objective," fail to perceive objectively that there is a narrow path the peace movement must walk between active nonviolent resistance and violent action, which would alienate a large portion of the movement plus its nonactive supporters in the general public. Reents responded:

> I do not believe that we can win the struggle against deployment by militant resistance. I agree that it can be prevented only politically, as you say, by mobilizing broader and broader parts of the population, which will increase the political costs of deployment to such an extent that it finally becomes impossible. My critique of those who have turned nonviolence into an absolute, inviolable ideology is that it leads to martyrdom, which makes me fear that one will remain morally clean in the end but politically without success.
>
> I, too, participate in sit-ins. We sit down and we are carried away by the police. But someday the situation will arise where we will have to demonstrate that we refuse to be carried away. The question is: when will we have that political force? At present we don't, but this cannot be turned into an argument for absolute nonviolence.

Any movement that had gained enough "political force" to win widespread public support for violent resistance against the police would also by then have won enough seats in the legislative bodies to be achieving its goals nonviolently. Moreover, we objected, violent resistance at any time in the foreseeable future would cause hundreds of thousands of citizens to drop out of the peace movement. "For me," Reents replied, "this is a matter of changing consciousness. The majority of the population and the majority of the peace movement are currently adherents of absolute nonviolence. But to say 'I won't resist the police; I am just a martyr' is not the expression of supreme political consciousness."

He further argued that many successful, violent revolutions

followed a period of nonviolent actions, which had failed. However, the historical survey by the American defense analyst Gene Sharp, *The Politics of Nonviolent Action* (Porter Sargent, 1973), demonstrates that numerous nonviolent struggles were completely successful without escalating to violence. Moreover, we were reminded of the recently coined slogan in certain new-politics groups in the United States: "What you get is how you do it." *Process,* that is, is directly related to the end result. "Out of violent action almost never comes a nonviolent society. We can practically guarantee that violence will breed more of itself," we observed to Reents. "I cannot deny that critique," Reents conceded. "What you say is right, and it is an argument of great moral integrity. But I do not believe that it can be used to support social resistance when it reaches its limits and the question arises: shall we give up? When they won't let us blockade the gates any longer, what shall we do then?" This is precisely the dilemma that plagued the West German peace movement throughout 1983, although many of the advocates of nonviolent resistance argued that such a course cannot be dismissed as "merely moralistic" since it is also absolutely rational (that is, history shows that violence breeds violence—structural as well as personal—so we must find another way to effect change, especially in the nuclear age). For most members of the Greens the choice was clear, as Petra Kelly often expresses with a citation from Martin Luther King: "We no longer have a choice between violence and nonviolence. The choice is either nonviolence or nonexistence."

Some Greens feel that the principle of decentralization should have been a fifth pillar, as it is essential to Green politics. All Green proposals are built on the conviction that people must have more direct control over the complex interplay of social, ecological, economic, and political forces. They maintain that overbureaucratization and the hierarchical structure of government thwart the initiative of citizens. Moreover, the Greens state that the impenetrability behind which various economic and political interests hide has become a danger to democracy. They oppose the strong tendencies in industrialized nations toward authoritarian measures, such as surveillance and censorship of books. To facilitate greater participation by citizens, the Greens advocate decentralizing and simplifying administrative units with a greater share of government revenues going to states, regions, counties, towns, and neighborhoods. The Greens, then, are the vanguard in West Germany of the movement to reclaim power from the centralized state. This same impulse is finding expression in the United States.

The Greens advocate not only smaller units of domestic government but also smaller countries, which they refer to as regions. They believe the nation-state is inherently dangerous because the enormous centralization of power is inevitably used for economic competition, large-scale exploitation, and massive wars. Many Greens mentioned Max Weber's observation that the state is the seat of legitimized violence. They argue that smaller units of population would result in a safer world on all counts, and they suggest that cultural and ecological boundaries could determine the regions. There are many such regions in Europe, usually determined by a shared dialect. They often cross national borders, such as Friesland (West Germany and The Netherlands), Flanders (Belgium and France), Alsace-Lorraine (West Germany and France), and Dreyeckland (West Germany, France, and Switzerland).*

The increase in regional consciousness in Dreyeckland is an example of the entwining of the issues and actions that inform Green politics. In the early 1970s the people of the region—who speak Allemannisch as well as German or French—discovered that the national governments had devised a plan to make the entire Rhine Valley an industrialized zone from Basel to Rotterdam. In 1972 the Allemannen from the German side of the Rhine crossed the river to occupy the site of a car battery plant that would have produced lead wastes—and was funded with German capital. The following year the Allemannen from France and Switzerland crossed the river to join the long occupation of the two sites, first Breisach and then Wyhl, proposed for a nuclear reactor in the Black Forest area. The Friendship House built by the protesters at Wyhl hosted programs on numerous political issues and highlighted their interconnections

*A map titled "Devolving Europe: Nations Re-Emerging from States" has been published by CoEvolution Quarterly (see Appendix C).

for activists who came from all parts of Germany. The local people strengthened their transnational bonds and established an underground radio station, Radio Dreyeckland, which now broadcasts twice a week—in Allemannisch, of course. They also print posters for antimissile demonstrations and other actions in Allemannisch, and they speak once again of their long history of resisting government oppression by the princes. Every year on Pentecost Sunday the people of Dreyeckland hold a bicycle race that crosses the bridges linking the Swiss, French, and German sections of their region; at the climax of the race they throw the flags of all three nations into the Rhine.

The opposition that the Allemannen feel toward intrusive, damaging projects masterminded by politicians and financiers in distant capitals is representative of localist sentiments all over the world. Although the Allemannen themselves do not speak of secession, many other regional peoples do demand independence. In fact, the central government of nearly every major nation today is battling the open rebellion, or simmering discontent, of at least one regional group. The Greens advocate a nonaligned "Europe of the regions" and hope that the model would eventually be adopted by the entire northern hemisphere as well as the Third World. They admire the federal system of the United States, although they strongly oppose a "United Europe" that would become a third military power and would continue the forced exploitation of the Third World. They favor cooperative economic exchanges and only minimum coordination, such as would be necessary for transportation systems. The eco-decentralist model in Green politics for all economic, social, and political structures is that they be *überschaubar,* that is, overseeable or manageable units. Appropriate scale is the central issue.

Since the Greens oppose all exploitation, they are keenly aware of the exploitation of women in patriarchal society. Their official programs are unequivocally nonsexist, and the party is committed to the goal of a postpatriarchal future. The leading roles of Green women in election campaigns and in legislative bodies at all levels signal a radical departure from customary electoral politics in West Germany and are a key aspect of the Greens' public image. For example, the first news photograph of the Greens in the Bundestag featured the two women among their three speakers, Marieluise Beck-Oberdorf and Petra Kelly, the former of whom delivered their opening statement in parliament.

The Green party strongly supports women's rights in numerous areas. However, in the analyses of other major issues in their Federal Program, such as militarism, economics, education, and healthcare, the feminist perspective is absent or nearly so. We asked Green men all over West Germany why the "holistic" analyses of the Greens were often missing this part. Almost invariably they answered, "Oh, yes, we're extending the guideline of having fifty percent men and fifty percent women on all elected committees and electoral lists into a rule!" The first few times we heard this response, we laughed, and later merely sighed, after which we politely explained that their answer had little to do with our question. While quotas are clearly needed in that situation, as in other patriarchal societies, such a mechanical solution is mistaken by many men as an adequate response to sexism within the Green party.

Although the average proportion of women on elected committees is one-third, the national steering committee in 1983 had only two female members among its forty. Even as the fifty-fifty rule is being adopted more widely, the Greens sometimes are unable to find enough women willing to be candidates for committees and electoral offices. We asked the men why, and the reply was nearly universal: "The women are busy with their families." "Come now, isn't there another reason?" we inquired. They answered slowly, "Yes, they say it's something about the style of politics we use, that it's too aggressive and competitive."

We asked women the same questions, and the level of agreement among them was as high as among the men but the consensus was quite different. Although women comprise one-third of the membership in the Greens, their numbers are declining in some areas. Many women in the citizens' movements, where female activists usually play a strong role, refuse to join the Green party at all. They told us that men often vote for women merely as quota fillers rather than considering and valuing particular qualifications. In order to be respected and be awarded political jobs by the male majority, we were told, women must "work in the way of men," that is, make aggressive arguments and allow no emotions or feelings into discussions. Most women are not interested in learning how to operate in such a style, which they consider crude and out of keeping with Green ideals. They told us that some men, too, are dissatisfied with the patriarchal style of politics but put up with it "because of their greater need for a public identity." Many thoughtful men told us they know there is something wrong with trying to make new politics by using the old style, but could not suggest any changes or concluded that the standard, "efficient" ways are necessary since the Green party is small and faces such huge tasks.

At several local and state offices we visited during the summer of 1983, we were told that sexism in the style and content of Green politics was to be the topic of the first meeting in the fall. Women and men are working together to address this problem in some local chapters, less so at the state level, and very little at the federal level. We asked several female parliamentarians in the Bundestag *Fraktion* whether the Green principle of "the emancipation of both sexes" was practiced. Petra Kelly explained:

> Inside our parliamentary group women have to fight very hard, even more than before we entered the Bundestag, to get our views collectively known. The men now tend to consider abortion and other social issues less political and therefore less important than others. We women sometimes have to argue very aggressively to make sure that the questions are treated as part of the larger question.
>
> When a strong male figure operates in our group, he can make people think along his lines and then they fall into traps. A few of our women have fallen into those traps, but I would say there are five or six [of the ten] who are not susceptible. They stay cool and spontaneous and won't let themselves be corrupted.

Gabi Potthast is a parliamentarian whose office contains political novels by Marge Piercy and a citation from Virginia Woolf: "As a woman I have no country. . . . As a woman my country is the whole world." She has long sandy hair, a quick sense of humor, and a very clear sense of sexual politics:

> The patriarchal structures here and the hectic schedules mean that all interpersonal contacts are superficial and everyone functions on the outer level. The men like that because it's safe. Only the

women are conflicted, and each woman must try to figure out how conflicted each of the others is. Because of that, you often find that women and men in patriarchal institutions understand each other better than do women and women.

Another female parliamentarian, Waltraud Schoppe, whose address on abortion rights and marital rape caused pandemonium in the Bundestag and attracted national attention (see Chapter 5), concurred that the patriarchal style of politics is often obnoxious and boring, but called on the Green women to begin criticizing the content as well:

> Most of the men in our *Fraktion* make the mistake of feeling they must compete with the men in the other parties. By fighting back they bring attention to themselves as competitors. But when these men—not our own men in the *Fraktion*—make a speech that is so clearly wrong, I and other Green women simply do not listen. Only the men feel they must indulge in competition.

The Greens, like all of us, are still conditioned by patriarchal socialization. The struggle to move beyond that mode of being is usually slow and difficult, yet essential. Marieluise Beck-Oberdorf spoke of the need for compassion toward men as well as women:

> There is simply a cultural lag. We simply carry our history around with us, and to act as if it weren't so is doing violence. It is also difficult to judge how strong chauvinism is among men. Even "soft" men [she used the English word] are certainly chauvinistic. But they no longer dare to articulate it, because in our circles you would fall flat on your face as a man if you spoke like a chauvinist. Now, there are really men who want to find a new approach to things. But in spite of this, I think that it simply pains them when they see a woman standing there up front.

Even with all the problems, the Greens propose much more feminist legislation and have a much higher proportion of women in leading positions than any other party in West Germany. Most of the Green women, and many of the men, see issues of women's rights as part of a larger context of postpatriarchal values that are essential to the goal of a nonexploitative society. This sense of "big-picture feminism" is slowly gaining more ground among the Greens but is not widely understood outside the Green party and the feminist movement. As Petra

Kelly related: "I am shocked when people say to me, 'Feminism has nothing to do with ecology. What are you talking about?' To me feminism is ecology and ecology is feminism. It's a holistic way of looking at things."

The Greens include in their analysis of our interrelated crises the "spiritual decay" and "spiritual impoverishment" of our industrial societies, and they call for the inclusion of "spiritual subjects" in the education of our children. We were especially interested in the spiritual aspects of Green politics because both of us have spent many years of our personal and professional lives exploring the connections between ecology, politics, and spirituality. We feel that deep ecology is spiritual in its very essence. It is a world view that is supported by modern science but is rooted in a perception of reality that goes beyond the scientific framework to a subtle awareness of the oneness of all life, the interdependence of its multiple manifestations, and its cycles of change and transformation. When the concept of the human spirit is understood in this sense, as the mode of consciousness in which the individual feels connected to the cosmos as a whole, the full meaning of deep ecology is indeed spiritual.

Many, if not most, of the Greens we met consider themselves Christians but are not often involved with institutionalized religion. When we asked Greens at all levels of the party and in most parts of the country whether there is a spiritual dimension to Green politics, most emphatically answered "Yes" although almost no one could discuss the concept except in vague terms. The main reason spirituality remains largely unarticulated in the Green party is that Hitler manipulated the pre-Christian Teutonic myths, or sacred stories, to serve the propaganda machine of his National Socialist party. Hence, as Petra Kelly remarked, the overt linking of spiritual values and politics is nearly forbidden: "A problem in the *Realpolitik* of West Germany is that any time you mention spirituality people accuse you of talking about something perverted—because it *was* perverted by the Nazis." In addition to the Nazi legacy, there is the Marxist insistence among most of the radical-left Greens that the spiritual dimension of life does not even exist so naturally it is not permitted to be discussed in connection with political goals.

Many of the early members of the Greens recalled that the

spiritual impulse was stronger in the days before the movement became a party, partly because moving into party politics within the post-Nazi context made them cautious about expressing spiritual principles and partly because the influx of radical-left members after the impressive showing in the European Parliament campaign in June 1979 squelched expressions of spirituality. However, during the early period of the Green movement the Anthroposophists, followers of Rudolf Steiner's spiritual and ecological teachings, played an important role, as we discussed in Chapter 1. They are still a strong force in the Green politics of Baden-Württemberg: Dr. Gisela von Kügelgen, a wise and charming white-haired woman who is well known in the Anthroposophist community, was the top vote-winner for the Greens in the Stuttgart city council election of June 1980.

In addition, *To Have or to Be?* by Erich Fromm (Bantam Books, 1981) was mentioned frequently as having influenced the spiritual development of many pre-Green ecological activists after its hardcover publication in 1976. Fromm delineated two modes of existence: having (acquiring, controlling) and being (experiencing, sharing) and argued that it was an economic necessity of humankind to shift from the former to the latter orientation. The final chapter, "Features of a New Society," is a remarkable previewing of Green politics. Fromm, by the way, believed that the United States, which was his home most of the time after fleeing Nazi Germany until his death in 1980, was the country closest to a breakthrough into a new consciousness: "It's just that the wealth is greater here, and therefore the consciousness that there must be more to life than buying and owning is also most powerful here."

One obvious expression of spirituality in Green politics is the holistic sense of our embeddedness in nature and the interconnected character of all phenomena, which is parallel to the principles of the Native American, pre-Christian European (that is, Pagan), Taoist, and Buddhist traditions. A poster the Greens used in the state of Hesse showed vibrant green tendrils overgrowing a bleak field of "developed" tree stumps, conveying the life force of cyclic regeneration and renewal. Precisely that, not any artificial and hierarchical structures of control, is sacred in life. A pre-Christian German would surely have concluded that such a poster is spiritual art, although the Greens emphasize that their symbols and posters are merely selected casually from various artists since the Nazis manipulated such political devices so successfully that symbols are regarded suspiciously in West German politics.

Petra Kelly stresses that true acceptance and understanding of Green politics requires inner change and growth:

> The spiritual content of Green politics—which unfortunately is not expressed, and is almost opposed, in the party structure—means understanding how everything is connected and understanding your relationship with planet Earth in daily life. We've become so divorced from our ties with the Earth that most people don't even understand what the Greens are fighting for. With the holistic sense of spirituality, one's personal life is truly political and one's political life is truly personal. Anyone who does not comprehend within him- or herself this essential unity cannot achieve political change on a deep level and cannot strive for the true ideals of the Greens.

This consciousness of deep ecology and its exemplary expression in Native American spirituality was mentioned by Kelly and many other Greens. When Waltraud Schoppe observed that developing such an understanding must be much easier in the United States since we are fortunate to have the living traditions of the Native Americans here, we explained sadly that their wisdom is not valued, except in small circles, and that it is a rare federal judge who even comprehends the meaning of their claims to the small parcels of land onto which they have been pushed: "The Earth is our church."

Lukas Beckmann is another Green who believes in the spiritual core of their politics, but from his overseer position as general manager of the national party he knows this view is not unanimously held: "If people do not understand that ecological politics involves a changing of themselves, that problem will become a major danger for the Greens in the next few years. For me, I would say the Greens are a spiritual movement, but our members who still think in the old ways cannot feel that way." That radical-left faction is the audience Rudolf Bahro has addressed numerous times on the political need for spiritual transformation. In general, they feel he is going too far or just plain crazy. The following is a passage from an article Bahro wrote for *Rot und Grün (Red and Green)*, a leftist publication:

> I am interested in the forces for cultural revolution that lie, in no small way, in Christ, Buddha, and Lao Tzu. Forces that have made history. We need the gnostic tradition—as one aspect, not to fill the whole of life. I have long been drawn to such thinkers as Joachim di Fiore, Meister Eckhart, Spinoza and Pascal on account of the affinity of their mysticism to real freedom, which remains incomplete as long as it does not also include freedom of the spirit. I recently read that someone discovered a mystical experience of the young Marx, which would then be analogous to Luther's experience in the tower. I can well see this as possible. Taken realistically, mysticism, at least clear-headed mysticism, means a profound mobilization of emancipatory forces in the human psyche, a phenomenon that has nothing otherworldly about it, and should be made accessible to everyone, for example by a practice of meditation.

Finally, many Greens cited spiritual feelings that arise in the context of peace work. Gert Bastian told us, "I feel it in myself and in men my age. It is a new spirit, a very strong power which grows in their own hearts and their own heads." We asked him how the "new spirit" was awakened in him and in others:

> By the doing of peace actions. By being side-by-side with others in the same situation—men, women, friends and not friends, strangers—who sit or stand or walk by your side, all moving together with the same life-protecting values and convictions. This creates a force, a peaceful power that is a spiritual power.

All seven of the principles we have presented—ecology, social responsibility, grassroots democracy, nonviolence, decentralization, postpatriarchal perspectives, and spirituality—are intertwined, although we have separated them for the purpose of discussion. They are further linked by the principle that all things—abstract and concrete, personal and political, or economic, or social—are *in process*. The Greens are quick to declare that theirs is a politics of transition. They strive to be not the end but the means, which, like the visionary goal of an ecological society, is continually evolving.

Chapter 3

The Politics of Peace

We live with fifty thousand nuclear warheads secretly circulating in our skies and our seas and hidden in subterranean silos. They are continually being "improved" with more and more computerized automatic controls so that a chain reaction of nearly uninterruptable events could result at any moment from a mechanical failure. Each technological breakthrough, each escalation in aggressive "security" makes the opponent insecure, defensive, frightened—and hence more dangerous. The conclusion that humankind may be living on borrowed time haunts everyone who has seriously and honestly considered the nuclear situation.

It is tempting to refuse to think about the escalating tensions caused by adversary foreign policies, the proportions of the possible holocaust, the very odds against survival. We try to assure ourselves that the storage places for our missiles—which are secret only to the American public, not to Soviet intelligence—are not in *our* backyards. This is a large country, after all. Perhaps some of us are not targets.

Such comforting, if desperate, rationalizations are unavailable to the West Germans. They live in a land that is roughly the size of Oregon, with sixty million inhabitants instead of 2.5 million and with 5,000 nuclear weapons. In addition, there are armed forces from the United States, England, France, The Netherlands, Belgium, Denmark, and Canada. Soviet medium-range missiles are targeted on West Germany, as are those of the French. The American nuclear weapons in the NATO arsenal include rockets that travel only thirty miles and so will also come down in "the front lines" of that densely populated country. Since the deployment of the American Pershing II missiles, if a serious conflict involving the Soviet Union erupts anywhere in the world, the first thing she must do to protect herself is knock out the Pershings in West Germany because they can reach Russia in six minutes. Moreover, the deployment of the American cruise missiles, which fly so low that they are almost impossible to detect on radar, adds to the anxiety of the Soviet leaders.

The entire peace program of the Greens extends from their experience of living in the prime thermonuclear battlefield. Hence it is not surprising that they reject both the "more is better" response to nuclear arms and the attitude of resignation adopted, for example, by the Harvard Nuclear Study Group in *Living with Nuclear Weapons* (Harvard University Press, 1983), which advises us to regard the arms race as a necessary evil, rather like sin, and to concentrate on modest steps to stabilize deterrence. The Greens' proposals are more closely aligned with Jonathan Schell's call to move beyond the current political view that elevates national sovereignty above human survival and to "reinvent politics." (That the Greens have been expressing such ideas since 1979 may have been a factor in the German translation of Schell's *The Fate of the Earth*, Avon Books, 1982, enjoying several months on the best-seller list in West Germany during 1983.) Green peace policies can also be clustered with the positions presented by Richard Falk in *Indefensible Weapons* (Basic Books, 1982): "It is important for the movement against nuclearism* to grasp that realizing its goals is inseparable from the triumph over time of the holistic orientation."

---

*"Nuclearism" refers to the practices and extension of the government in a nuclear state. The Greens maintain that nuclearism is devouring the very freedoms it is said to protect: they point to the new laws proposed in 1983 designed to keep citizens from assembling to protest deployment of the Pershing II and cruise missiles. Richard Falk explains the dynamic in this way: "Being constantly

The Greens maintain that the either/or situation created by the emergence of the two power blocs after World War II has resulted in a loss of self-determination for the allies of both the Soviet Union and the United States, as well as the remilitarization of West Germany. The tensions between the two superpowers have engulfed not only the nations of Europe but also the entire world and even the "territory" of outer space.

Of particular concern to the Greens in the immediate situation is the lack of historical perspective on Russian and German interactions that they perceive in the foreign policy of the Reagan Administration. The Soviet Union naturally feels the same sort of anxiety from the missiles in West Germany as the United States did when Soviet missiles were in Cuba, but the roots of Russian distrust of an armed Germany go back hundreds of years. We discussed this dynamic with August Hausslei-ter, a founder of the Greens who, at age seventy-eight, is the editor of their weekly newspaper, *Die Grünen.* His far-reaching knowledge and ready humor explained to us why he has long functioned as a mediator among various factions within the Greens.

He told us that while many people believe the Germans to be naturally aggressive, the Russians have especially good reason to think so. Germany pushed far into Russia during World War I and then made an unjust peace with her; during World War II the Germans again drove deep into Russia, killing 18 million people. We suggested that the German concept of *Lebensraum,* their self-proclaimed natural right to more living space, was amplified by the Nazis but has been present in German political thought for centuries, as is well known among Eastern Europeans. He agreed and gave us a startling example of how deep that thinking goes among some of the Germans:

In 1947 I was the second highest ranking person in the Christian Social Union [the Bavarian counterpart of the conservative party,

---

ready to commit the nation to a devastating war of annihilation in a matter of minutes on the basis of possibly incorrect computer-processed information or pathological traits among leaders creates a variety of structural necessities that contradict the spirit and substance of democratic governance: secrecy, lack of accountability, permanent emergency, concentration of authority, peacetime militarism, extensive apparatus of state intelligence and police."

the Christian Democratic Union]. Konrad Adenauer and I and some others were invited by the American military to inspect some installations near Wiesbaden. At the dinner they served a very good wine which at that time was difficult to get, and Chancellor Adenauer drank rather freely. Afterward he said to me, "Now we have the strongest ally in the world. We can give some land west of the Rhine to the French and then take vast land to the east." I was so shocked that I told him, "Stop planning the next war or I'm going to get out of this car!" Later, in my capacity as a professional journalist, I reported this incident in my newspaper, *The Independents*. Professor Noack, who was present at the conversation with Adenauer in the car, also reported it in a newspaper called *World Without War.* The important thing to remember is that this attitude of Adenauer's—that the Germans should make a contract with the West and then push east—was the basis of his foreign policy and his enthusiasm for remilitarization. Kohl today proclaims he is "the political grandson of Adenauer." Therefore, one must understand that when Kohl goes to Moscow, with Reagan's support, and says to the Russians, "We want peace but we want Germany to be reunited" that is almost like a declaration of war to them.

The Greens are probably the only party in West Germany that does not favor a reunified German state. They believe the modern nation-state is inherently dangerous, particularly now that security is construed within the framework of nuclearism. As Petra Kelly expressed it, "Nation-states are very egotistical, chauvinistic, and competitive." An additional reason to seek an alternative to reunification was related to us by Gert Bastian, who, with Kelly, is the foremost architect of the Greens' anti-militarism proposals and spokesman for withdrawal from NATO. Unlike the postwar generation of young Germans, who seem surprisingly oblivious of the hard feelings toward Germany that linger in many people's minds because of World War II, Bastian knows that "the wounds are still real." He continued, "German national unity brought unhappiness and was not a success for Germany or Central Europe or the world at large. It is better that the German-speaking people organize themselves into several small states. I believe this is a necessary concession to the other European countries and the world." Bastian's own argument for regionalism is only one component of the official Green position. It will probably never attract a broad following in West Germany, as there are numerous indications, principally demographic, that the era of guilt and remorse over the Nazi horrors appears to be drawing to a close. Politicians in both major parties speak more and more frequently of reunification, although East Germany is officially opposed to joining the downward spiral of "late capitalism."

The Greens agree that the border should be dissolved but for a far different end than that of their political colleagues: they wish to see the population organized according to regions (see Chapter 2). A means of self-defense for the regions—and also for the existing nation-states during a transition period—has been proposed by Bastian in his book *Frieden schaffen! (Create Peace: Thoughts on the Politics of Security,* Kindler Verlag, 1983). The series of actions he recommends are endorsed by the Greens and are being developed further by many peace researchers in West Germany.* First, he would have West Germany ban nuclear weapons and reduce the level of troops there. Next, it would withdraw from NATO and establish itself as a nonaligned country in what he hopes would become a bloc-free Europe. It would defend its borders with a relatively small number of active troops backed up by a large reserve army, a contemporary practice that has proved to be efficient in other neutral European countries. At first, West Germany would comprise a zone in which only defensive weapons were allowed; eventually this would become a weapons-free zone protected by social defense.

In developing the concept of social defense, Bastian, Kelly, and numerous other strategists in the German peace movement were influenced by the examples of Gandhi, Thoreau, and Martin Luther King, as well as by the contemporary works of Theodor Ebert and Gene Sharp. Sharp's work includes his

---

*The major institute for peace research, the German Society for Peace and Conflict Research, had its funding cut off after 1982 by the Kohl government. Both money and a great deal of information flowed through that organization; there were nearly forty peace research institutes in West Germany during the 1970s, but most have disappeared now. Still, demand is growing among the public for peace education to counteract the militaristic guest lectures that young army officers now give in the high schools. Also, numerous peace workshops are thriving, teaching the connection between inner growth and outer action and bringing together the coalition of outer-directed, ecological/left/technological people with the inner-directed, spiritually oriented people.

three-volume historical study, *The Politics of Nonviolent Action: Power and Struggle, The Methods of Nonviolent Action,* and *The Dynamics of Nonviolent Action.* Social defense protects a population from foreign or internal attacks through active, nonviolent resistance and noncooperation. It includes large-scale symbolic actions, economic boycotts by consumers and producers, social and political boycotts of institutions, strikes, overloading of facilities and administrative systems, stalling and obstructing, deliberate inefficiency, ostracism of persons, and numerous forms of noncompliance in all sectors of a society. Bastian points out that traditional defense strategy prevents an adversary from committing armed aggression by demanding a high price of entry at the border, that is, battle losses, whereas social defense sets an unacceptably high price on staying, that is, occupation. The Germans have a successful example of social defense in their own history: the *Ruhrkampf,* or civilian defiance of the French and Belgian troops in the Ruhr region in 1923.

Compared to the militaristic mode of defense, Bastian emphasizes, social defense demands more courage, more strength of character, and more willingness to place the individual self after the interests of the whole. He admits that such commitment could not be expected from the population today with its "egotistical and self-centered ways of thinking," but he believes the necessary degree of awareness and readiness could be developed.

It was apparent to us that the Greens' concept of social defense would depend on well-organized, tightly bonded affinity groups in every neighborhood who are prepared to conduct nonviolent civil disobedience on short notice. "Exactly right," Petra Kelly responded. "Every neighborhood will have to know how to conduct resistance and become subversive, but the peace movement in the United States is far ahead of us in nonviolence training and the development of affinity groups." So frustrated with that lag in the German peace movement is Kelly that she willfully violates a Green party rule by giving a portion of her salary directly to nonviolence training rather than putting it into a common pot "because the pot isn't doing anything except gathering interest!"

Along with bloc-free regionalism and the eventual development of weapons-free zones, the Greens' peace policy calls for global coordination in two areas: peace and the ecological balance of the planet. To address these two tasks, the Greens' Federal Program calls for a restructured United Nations, one with minimal centralization that would respect the right of self-determination of all peoples. Its work would include worldwide disarmament treaties; control of the weapons trade; protection of human rights, with special attention to the rights of minorities, women, and children; control over pollution of the world's oceans; and the introduction of renewable-resource technology, as well as birth control assistance, to the developing nations. In addition, the Greens call for an international tribunal that would subpoena the politicians, technologists, and military strategists who plan, build, operate, or support weapons systems or technologies leading to mass destruction and genocide. We asked whether the Greens can see any alternative to such an "enforcer" body in their vision of a peaceful future. At this time they cannot.

Partnership with the peoples of the Third World is an integral part of the Greens' peace policy. In the United States, the crushing problems of developing nations have been ignored by nearly everyone except the radical left, who continually attempt to draw attention to the suffering and its causes. In West Germany, in contrast, there is a broad-based Third World movement that includes church groups, student groups, and community groups, as well as the left. Almost every city has a Third World store, which sells coffee and other products from cooperatives, that is, worker-owned businesses in the developing nations.

Because of this movement, the Greens have a great deal of popular support for their Third World policy, as expressed in the peace section of their Federal Program:

> There can be no realistic hope for a stable world peace as long as there is no hope for the world's poor and as long as the merciless fight for raw materials and markets continues. What the industrialized nations choose to call "growth" is in reality merely a shoving contest of the strong against the weak, ending inevitably in the defeat of both. The rule of the world market by the conglomerates leads to an ever increasing impoverishment of the Third World

and must finally end in the collapse of our present economic system. . . . Using insidious methods of economic blackmail, sometimes in open cooperation with the most inhumane regimes of the Third World, the industrialized nations of the West perpetuate their age-old colonialism: West Germany against the peoples of South Africa; the U.S., above all, in Latin America; and France by its direct military presence in its former African colonies. . . . The peace movement must show its solidarity with the liberation movements in countries of the Third World in their attempts to free themselves from their dependency on the superpowers and to find their own, independent ways.

The Greens urge West Germany and the other industrialized nations to increase foreign aid to developing nations—with no economic strings attached—to .7 percent of the GNP, which is the United Nations recommendation. We asked Walter Schwenninger, a Green parliamentarian in the Bundestag who has long been active in the Third World movement, about the problem of getting the money past the rich people in the capital cities to the people who would actually use it for small-scale, community-controlled projects. He told us that the Greens work with independent aid agencies, such as Bread for the World, and that they would like to develop more direct channels. They currently give medical aid and educational materials directly to Nicaragua, preferring to support nonviolent liberation movements, according to Schwenninger, but helping all the ones they can. He believes there will be elections there soon.*

Schwenninger was leaving for Paraguay shortly after we

---

*The Greens adamantly oppose American intervention in Nicaragua. They emphasize that though Nicaragua now has only one party, the Sandinistas, there is a great deal of grassroots decision making. Block groups (often consisting mostly of women since they head nearly half of the households) meet weekly and send representatives to the weekly meeting of neighborhood coordinators, which sends representatives to a zonal committee, which sends representatives to a regional committee. A national steering committee both initiates and receives programs and policies.

On 10 December 1983 the Hamburg and West Berlin state party branches issued a joint appeal for Green state legislators and federal parliamentarians to go to Nicaragua in shifts. According to Thomas Ebermann, who spoke for many Greens fearing a U.S. invasion of Nicaragua, "The Americans should be forced to face the fact that if they attack Nicaragua, they will be killing members of parliament of an allied NATO country."

spoke with him. The other specialist for Third World affairs in the *Fraktion*, Gabi Gottwald, was visiting Nicaragua that summer. Schwenninger himself has traveled to many developing nations during the past decade inspecting not only government programs but also independent grassroots movements, such as Sarvodaya in Sri Lanka, of which he spoke admiringly. Sarvodaya operates projects in community development, appropriate technology, and education in 4,000 villages using a framework of Buddhist ethics and Gandhian principles of small-scale self-sufficiency.

We asked Schwenninger if he considers the United Nations effective in moving toward the sort of world order the Greens envision:

> The United Nations Development Fund and similar agencies can do a great deal for the Third World by showing the right way in which foreign aid should be given. Also, the U.N.'s World Health Organization plays an important role by, for instance, declaring that the Nestlé corporation cannot continue its false advertising for selling formula to mothers in the Third World. However, if you look at the structure of the United Nations, you see that the Third World countries don't really have a chance against the power of the industrialized nations. The United Nations mirrors the political situation.

The Greens are quite proud of their Third World policy with its central focus on the right to complete self-determination. Yet they do not seem concerned that this principle potentially conflicts with other Green ideals. For instance, women worldwide perform two-thirds of the work hours, receive one-tenth of the income, and own less than one-hundredth of the property (see "Progress for Half the World's People: The United Nations Decade for Women" in *Issues of the Eighties*, published by the U.N. Association of the United States, October 1980). Most rural women in the Third World are regarded as beasts of burden, while most of their urban sisters suffer under customs and laws institutionalizing male dominance—patterns that were introduced, in many cases, during the colonial era. If self-determination in Third World countries includes continuing patriarchal oppression, then the Green principles of nonexploitation, nonviolence, and social responsibility will be violated.

This extremely complex issue is one the Greens will have to address.

The major role played by the Greens in the larger West German peace movement is informed by their long-range peace program, described above. Foremost, the Greens unconditionally oppose the deployment of the Pershing II and cruise missiles and urge West Germany to withdraw from the NATO bloc. We noticed that missing from their program is the chief priority of the American peace movement: reduction of the dangerous tensions between Moscow and Washington. The peace movement in the United States is brimming with such schemes as exchange programs and the strengthening of communication channels beyond the "hot line." When we asked Petra Kelly about the Greens' immediate perspective on Soviet-American relations, she told us it was "problematic because of internal factional squabbling." She emphasized that the Greens' position is to reduce the tensions inherent in the competitive bloc system by calling for the dissolution of both NATO and the Warsaw Pact. However, she went on, the few formerly Communist members of the Greens disagree that the problem is the "two-headed dragon," or the system itself:

> I have always stood up at Green party assemblies and declared that those Greens who came from the Communist groups should not be thrown out of our party because I thought they had really changed. But now I see that they have not changed. They often deny that there is any such thing as nuclearism and imperialism on *both* sides. They say, "Petra, all we need to think about is arms, American capital, industry, and multinationals." When I reply that there is a form of capitalism on both sides, state capitalism on one side and private capitalism on the other (which is the position held by almost all of the Greens), they say, "No, the Communists are just reacting and balancing the situation." There is a real bias in those groups, and I say that if that sort of thinking comes a bit more into the foreground of the Green party, we are finished because the integrity of the Green position of nonalignment will be destroyed by insisting in this very primitive way that everything is simply a matter of capitalist imperialism.

We told Kelly that we understood why opposing deployment of the new missles is the top priority for the West German peace movement but that there were doubts in the American peace movement about the Greens' call for unilateral disarmament. She replied:

> As long as we keep Poseidon, Polaris, Trident, and the rest, we cannot tell the Russians to simply take away all their medium-range weapons; we must start first, as we have far more in terms of quality. The Russian SS-20s, SS-4s, and SS-5s must be reduced alongside the category of Poseidon, Polaris, and the French and British forward-based systems, but we must begin the first phase, without conditions attached. What's incredible is the horrible lying lately about the thousand missiles the United States has pulled out of the European NATO forces. In fact, they have replaced two old missiles with a new, more powerful one. That is not disarmament; it is rearmament and hypocrisy. What we demand, first and foremost, is the removal of the Pershing II cruise missiles from Europe. They are first-strike weapons, which change the so-called balance qualitatively and strategically.

Educating the public about such facts comprises a large portion of the Greens' peace work. Elected officials and party activists at all levels often address groups and rallies. One of the dynamics they try to get people to recognize is the connection between militarism and ecological damage. Most obvious is that military maneuvers directly endanger the environment. In addition, the plutonium produced by nuclear power plants in a modern industrial state is deadly toxic waste and the essential material for nuclear bombs. Military planes consume an enormous amount of fuel in their routine exercises, and arms factories devour natural resources. In fact, the resource- and energy-intensive modes of production employed in nearly all industries necessitate continuing armed coercion and competition to secure raw materials. West Germany is the fifth-largest producer of weapons, so a sizable segment of the economy depends on the flourishing of that industry. This is true to an even greater extent in the United States, where a bloated defense budget is one of the major causes of inflation and cutbacks in social programs.

The linking of peace with ecology within Green politics was largely the accomplishment of Roland Vogt and Petra Kelly, who focused attention on the concept of *Ökopax*, an ecological peace as the foundation of a new society. Vogt and Kelly met at the

1975 Easter rally at Wyhl, site of a proposed nuclear power plant near the Black Forest, and three years later became key figures in the founding of the Greens. He is a large, handsome man of calm demeanor who is deeply involved with the peace movement and with the networking of European Green movements. He always wears a metal peace symbol that was made by one of his three children. Vogt explained that the holistic structure of Green politics developed in stages:

> The original focus was ecology, then we joined peace, and then we realized neither had a chance without restructuring the economy. Once we realized that Green thinking can inform every area of politics and life and that our central issue is survival, I created the term "vitalism" as a contra-term to "exterminism."*

The connection between a lasting peace and a radical restructuring of the economy and societal habits is also stressed by Rudolf Bahro. He stunned left-oriented American peace activists during his lecture tour in 1983 by telling them, "The slogan 'Jobs and Peace' is a lie. We cannot get rid of the tanks unless we are ready to get rid of the cars." Banning cars is an extreme position, even as a metaphor, and is not shared by all Greens, but Bahro wants people to understand that what he calls our "death-dealing habits" are not limited to military practices but are inherent in our complicity with "the Great Machine":

> Our material system cannot work without arms. Hence our entire industrial, materialist culture is leading us to the nuclear holocaust. We must react not against one superpower or the other but against the *system* they have created. We must live differently in order to survive! Conversion through a world-wide counter-movement is necessary, and it will not come about through anti-neurosis [a term used by Bahro to refer to the process of merely

---

*"Exterminism" was coined by E. P. Thompson, one of the leading theorists of the European peace movement, to refer to the fact that the arms race is no longer a rational contest between the superpowers, but owes its existence in large part to the functioning of huge, self-aggrandizing, and out-of-control bureaucracies (military, governmental, and corporate) in both countries. We would add that since all the countries involved are patriarchies, recognition of the connections between militarism, war, and patriarchal ways of thinking is also illuminating (see "Naming of the Cultural Forces that Push Us Toward War" by Charlene Spretnak, *Journal of Humanistic Psychology,* Summer 1983).

striking out with "anti movements" against the neurosis of the current system]. There must be an affirmative spiritual basis.

Like increasing numbers of activists in the American peace movement, most Greens have come to realize that there is a spiritual, moral, and ethical dimension at the core of the peace issue and that only a shift at this deep level can really effect change—change away from the pervasive individual, group, and national selfishness that arises in the spiritual vacuum of modernist culture. The Greens have emerged as the major voice, along with the churches, for the moral and ethical force of *nonviolent* active resistance within the West German peace movement. In addition, their Peace Manifesto explains why they reject the cultivation of enemy figures as objects to hate:

> The inflating of enemy figures has always been used in preparations for involvement in war. Everything bad in the world, in our community, and in ourselves is laid at the enemy's door. It is projected onto him until the human face of the opponent becomes that of a grotesque caricature, a monster, an untamable beast, and finally of nothing, a void, so that the threshold of inhibition for the annihilation of the enemy is easily overcome. . . .
>
> If anything is going to change in this mechanism, we have to stop thinking and feeling in terms of enemy figures. We must learn at last to distinguish in our thoughts, feelings, and speech between person and role, between regime and population. "Enemies" are people with weaknesses and faults, with friendliness and strengths like ours. They are fathers and mothers, daughters and sons, members of clubs, students, workers, who are glad and sad, who quarrel and make up, who can be incited and who can put up resistance, who obey and doubt, and who, like us, want to live in peace. . . .
>
> Therefore, the credibility of our work for peace, for the formation of new relations with the states of the Warsaw Pact and the Third World, depends on the verbal, physical, and psychological way in which we treat our political opponents, those in government, and the agents of state violence. Whoever is unable to see his or her opponent as a human being cannot expect his or her concerns to be recognized, let alone to be accepted. Nonviolent resistance and destructive hate are incompatible.

Throughout the summer of 1983, the West German government reiterated its support of the NATO deployment of the

Euromissiles that fall and proposed a number of laws designed to frighten people from joining the peace actions. For example, one law declared that if only one person in a crowd is violent, the entire crowd can be arrested. There was widespread belief that the police were employing *agents provocateurs* because violence at demonstrations in the preceding months had broken out mostly in large, open areas where armed police troops were waiting. Caught between the nearly suicidal acceptance of the new missiles and the potential violence of the German police, the peace movement became confused and disheartened. "Perhaps a think tank organized in time—even though it would have been a rather centralized solution—could have developed a better strategy for the peace movement, some sort of Manhattan Project of disarmament," Roland Vogt observed with resignation.

In the face of such uncertainty 30,000 people assembled at Krefeld on 25 June 1983, the occasion of Vice-President Bush's speech commemorating the emigration three hundred years earlier of Quakers from that city to America in search of religious freedom. (The irony that the celebrated emigrants were pacifists was not lost on the peace movement.) Before Bush's address, twenty to thirty "punk-type" young people pelted the well-armed police with rocks, eliciting a predictably violent response in which one hundred more demonstrators joined. Calm was restored, except for a few rocks thrown at Bush's limousine. Throughout the entire disturbance, the vast majority of the crowd was peaceful.

A split developed within the Greens about how to respond to the violent peace activists at Krefeld. Kelly, Bastian, Vogt, and all the other Greens who firmly advocate a nonviolent strategy—and they are certainly the majority of the party—had maintained for months that violent protesters did not belong in the larger movement the Greens were building. The radical left inside and outside the party, on the other hand, had been pressing to end the dominance of the "ideology" of nonviolence and continually called for greater militancy in the peace movement. On 13 July, Jürgen Reents and other Hamburg Greens issued an open letter in the *Tageszeitung,* the daily national alternative newspaper, criticizing in particular the positions of Bastian and Kelly, who had participated in the Krefeld demonstration, and stressing that as the violent activists have the same goals as the rest of the movement, they should be understood and accepted. That statement, together with a similar one signed by other Greens as well, and many other statements, were published in a forty-eight-page booklet, *Krefeld Dokumentation*. It reached the bookstores in early August and featured numerous photographs of police brutality.

We asked Kelly for her response to the Hamburg statement:

> They are correct to say that we should try to understand why those people have become violent, to identify the root of their aggression. We know that the violence of the state and the politicians is much greater. Yet I cannot say that the violent people are part of the Green movement. I would like to include them once they see that violence is no solution, but right now their aims are diametrically opposed to an ecological society. Both our methods and our goals must be nonviolent; if any step toward the goal becomes corrupt, everything will become corrupt. That is the power of the so-called truth. It must be the right way because it means never causing hurt or damage to anyone.

By the end of the summer, it had been discovered that an *agent provocateur* (a federal intelligence agent from West Berlin) was among the small group who initiated the violence at Krefeld. Still, doubt was growing throughout the peace movement—and not only within the radical-left groups—about a strictly nonviolent strategy for the "hot autumn." Certain Greens in the Bundestag *Fraktion* warned against splitting the peace movement by alienating the violent people and insisted, somewhat obliquely, that the lines of communication had to be kept open. A majority agreed that the policy of contacting the police before a nonviolent action had the effect of turning the demonstration site into a "playpen." They recommended "spontaneous" actions instead. Meanwhile, certain reactionary newspapers were claiming that the peace movement was training paramilitary gangs who would soon be terrorizing citizens.

The specter of violence was not the only problem that fall. "Our form of mass demonstrations, just having speakers line up, is still too traditional," Kelly told us. "I noticed at Krefeld that no one listens anymore and the whole crowd becomes apathetic." She was extremely interested in our description of the Women's Pentagon Actions in November 1980 and 1981, which moved innovatively beyond the patriarchal format in which an audience sits passively for hours while addressed by the pinnacle of a hierarchy. The Action was participatory, cathartic, and inspiring, drawing on ritual content in four phases: mourning, rage, defiance, empowerment. During the defiance phase, the women used the ancient metaphor of women as weavers—weavers of cloth, of culture, of one generation to the next—and wove closed the doors of the Pentagon with large webs.*

Kelly recognized that several of those elements had been used subsequently by the women at Greenham Common in England. She compared the ritual content to the Berrigans' using bread and blood and water. "It's very spiritual, but we haven't accomplished that yet in our big demonstrations. We could go far beyond just making a sit-in somewhere; we could go far, far beyond."

The Greens worked closely with the coordinators of various peace actions that fall. In the months preceding the tense season of confrontation, Green activists conducted a number of public actions designed to educate people about the dangers of the new missiles and to establish stronger contacts with the peace movement in other countries. The American campaign for a bilateral freeze of development and production of nuclear arms was important for the Greens because it showed the West Germans that being against the nuclear arms race does not mean being anti-American. The Greens also referred to the U.S. Catholic bishops' statement against the arms race and publicized a translated edition of speeches and letters by Archbishop Hunthausen of Seattle (Catholic Academy of Austria, 1983).

The first educational event, the "Tribunal against First-Strike and Mass-Destruction Weapons in the East and West," was a conference held in Nuremberg on 18–20 February. A jury of seven people from West Germany, the United States, the Soviet Union, Japan, Austria, and The Netherlands heard testimony first against the nuclear powers and then against the West Ger-

---

*The Women's Pentagon Action and similar ones are described more fully in "Spiritual Dimensions of Feminist Anti-Nuclear Activism" by Gina Foglia and Dorit Wolffberg (*The Politics of Women's Spirituality,* ed. Charlene Spretnak, Anchor/Doubleday, 1982). Also see *Reweaving the Web of Life: Feminism and Nonviolence,* ed. Pam McAllister (New Society Press, 1982).

man government. American participants included Philip Agee, Philip Berrigan, Rosalie Bertell, Barry Commoner, Daniel Ellsberg, Richard Falk, Jack Geiger, Robert Livingstone, George Wald, and Howard Zinn. The Tribunal, which was initiated by Petra Kelly, distributed a ninety-five-page booklet of position papers and documentation, including alarming excerpts from *Conventional-Nuclear Operations* (Reference Book 100-30, Volume One) by the U.S. Army Command and General Staff.

In May the Greens participated in a peace conference in West Berlin. After an all-night planning session, six of them— Gert Bastian, Lukas Beckmann, Milan Horacek, Petra Kelly, Gabi Potthast, and Roland Vogt—crossed the border dividing that city and staged a peace demonstration in Alexanderplatz, a large square in East Berlin. They used the slogan of the autonomous peace movement in East Germany, "Swords into Ploughshares," and issued a declaration urging the governments of both German states to work for peace instead of increasing armaments.

Although the Alexanderplatz demonstration, calling on *both* East and West to end the arms race, brought the Greens unusually favorable press coverage in the West, the radical left within the party denounced the action. The three leading Hamburg Greens—Thomas Ebermann, Jürgen Reents, and Rainer Trampert—issued a statement opposing the bilateral action because it cast a socialist state in the role of enemy and shifted the blame from the United States, who has led in the escalations ever since the arms race began in order, they insisted, to further its capitalist, imperialist goals. This position was supported by Otto Schily and Marieluise Beck-Oberdorf, who, with Kelly, are the speakers of the Green *Fraktion* in the Bundestag. The opposition died down, however, when the president of East Germany, Erich Honecker, wrote to Kelly, agreeing with the Greens' proposal for a nuclear-free zone in Central Europe. Honecker's letter also pointed out that the Warsaw Pact had issued a declaration the previous January agreeing to the principles of mutual renunciation of military force and disarmament measures based on parity and equal security.

In July the Greens sent two delegations abroad to strengthen contacts with the international peace movement. Two parliamentarians, Gabi Potthast and Waltraud Schoppe, and several other Green women traveled to England for the International Women's Blockade at Greenham Common on 4–8 July. At about the same time, a group of eight Greens went to Washington, D.C. They included six parliamentarians—Gert Bastian, Marieluise Beck-Oberdorf, Petra Kelly, Otto Schily, Walter Schwenninger, and Roland Vogt—plus the press secretary for the *Fraktion*, Heinz Suhr, and one of the three speakers of the national Green party then, Manon Maren-Grisebach. At a press conference in Bonn the day before their departure, the Greens announced their intention to make a similar trip to Moscow. This they did in October, stopping in East Germany on their way home to meet with government officials.

The trip to Washington had been proposed by Kelly and, after weeks of arguments, was finally approved by the *Fraktion* and the party. It was also Kelly who organized most of their meetings and itinerary. First they met with representatives of the peace, women's, ecology, and Third World movements in New York and Washington. The Greens urged the American activists to conduct demonstrations in October in solidarity with the German ones or even to come to West Germany and participate directly. (Several American rallies were indeed held that fall, but they were smaller than the German peace movement had hoped.) The Greens also held a small demonstration in front of the White House and issued a peace declaration jointly with American peace groups. This declaration stated that any use or threat of use, including the planning and construction, of atomic, biological, or chemical weapons is criminal because it is contrary to international law and morality. Use of these weapons disregards protection of the civilian population and the proportionality of means. The declaration urged the American people to persuade Congress to vote for a one-year delay of the deployment of the Pershing II and cruise missiles in Europe in order for the peace process to continue. It also appealed to the people of the Warsaw Pact countries to continue to build grassroots peace movements.

The other function of the trip was to meet with officials from the State Department, politicians, defense analysts, and members of various think tanks. President Reagan declined to receive the Greens, but they had a round-table discussion with Thomas Niles, Undersecretary of State, and other officials. At their meetings and at a press conference, the Greens presented a paper, "Questions to the U.S. Government," which posed twenty-seven questions on general issues of defense and on the Pershing II and cruise missiles specifically. On 10 July, Petra Kelly appeared on NBC's "Meet the Press," delivering what even her most critical colleagues conceded was a brilliant presentation of the Green positions in response to some challenging, nearly hostile questions. After the telecast, Robert Novak, the journalist who had been Kelly's most aggressive questioner, told her that he wished she were on his side.

Back in Bonn a few days later, the Greens held a press conference and reported that their conversations with U.S. officials and defense analysts had largely validated Green positions. An analyst from the Brookings Institution explained to them that the U.S. president has a duty to the American people to restrict conflicts—to Europe, for instance. It was also admitted that the Pershing II missiles have no military, strategic, or technological connection to the Soviet SS-20s; they can be understood only within the general defense strategy of the United States. Several Greens spoke of being horrified by the intensity of the anti-Soviet paranoia in the State Department. However, they praised the knowledge and wisdom of Paul Warnke, who was the chief U.S. negotiator at the SALT II talks.

Bastian said that the deployment of the Pershings reflected the view that if war looks inevitable NATO should make a surprise first strike. Moreover, the Greens learned that the United States never expected the Soviet Union to accept the zero-option proposal and that American officials know that the Salt II agreement did not favor the Soviets, as is often claimed by Washington, because the British and French missiles were not included in the count. (The SALT II treaty is observed, for the most part, by both sides even though it was never ratified by the United States.) Finally, Bastian held up a copy of *Future Fire: Weapons for the Apocalypse* (Warner Books, 1983) by Ann Marie Cunningham and Mariana Fitzpatrick. He had brought it back as an example of the many American books proving that the United States is not behind in the arms race, that we have always led in the escalations, and that there are many slanted ways of counting the missiles. (We later sent him a copy of *First Strike! The Pentagon's Strategy for Waging Nuclear War,* South End Press, 1983, by Robert Aldridge, an aeronautical engineer who formerly supervised weapons projects at Lockheed.)

Walter Schwenninger went along on the Washington trip principally to discuss with State Department officials the problems in the Third World. He related to us a three-hour discussion that was largely fruitless. Each side cited proof of human rights violations in various countries, dismissing the others' examples because of the particular form of government involved. Schwenninger's evidence that the United States is destabilizing Central America was denied by the officials.

The Greens' trip to Washington resulted in several constructive accomplishments. However, it was marred by problems within the delegation that typify many of the difficulties plaguing the party as a whole, as we discuss in our evaluation (Chapter 7).

The Greens began their participation in the "hot autumn" of protests in 1983 with the blockades on 1–3 September at Mutlangen and Bitburg, in which Daniel Ellsberg and Philip Berrigan participated at the Greens' invitation. Although the Bundestag *Fraktion* had pledged, almost unanimously, the day before the actions to take part, very few actually showed up. The West German police were nonviolent at Mutlangen but not at Bitburg, where they used dogs, water cannons, and other strong-arm tactics. For the most part, however, the police demonstrated sympathy for the antimissile cause throughout the fall actions, especially after they encountered parliamentarians, doctors, judges, and bishops championing it. In an article titled "What's Wrong with the Cops?" in *Der Spiegel,* the secretary of the police union in Mainz revealed, "It would crack you up if you knew how many take off their uniform on Saturday and stand on the other side on Sunday. Some have asked for a leave in order to be able to demonstrate."

The Greens worked closely with the peace movement's national coordination bureau that planned the week of demonstrations from 15–22 October, culminating in rallies in various cities and in the human chain stretching almost sixty-five miles from the U.S. Army's VII Corps headquarters in Stuttgart to an American artillery unit at Neu-Ulm. The major rally was held in Bonn, where the crowd heard speeches by various peace workers and politicians. Arlo Guthrie sang "We Shall Overcome" and "Blowin' in the Wind," and Willy Brandt made a controversial appearance to declare that his Social Democratic Party did, after all, oppose the new missiles. As he spoke, Lukas Beckmann and other tall Greens held up a sign that read "Our Missile Inheritance—SPD." Another demonstrator held a sign toward Brandt that read "You hypocrite!" Petra Kelly, speaking on behalf of the Greens, chided Brant for finally saying "no" with too many "buts" on the issue of deployment: "It is absurd when Brandt says no to the missiles but yes to NATO." Such an absolutist position, however, ignored the fact that the majority of West Germans agreed with Brandt: they did not want the new missiles but they were not ready to leave NATO.

The Greens' hostility toward the Social Democrats annoyed many factions within the West German peace movement who felt it was merely petty and a sign that the Greens were possessive of the antimissile issue as "their" cause. The Greens, on the other hand, pointed out that they had many reasons to resent the SPD's behavior concerning the Euromissiles. In December 1979 the Social Democratic government, under Helmut Schmidt, agreed to the NATO double-track decision. Schmidt was, in fact, a prime initiator of this decision, and his party refused to yield to the broad-based demands of the peace movement even during the federal election in March 1983 when Schmidt's successor, Hans-Jochen Vogel, waffled (using what the Greens called a *jein* position, that is, a combination of the German *ja* and *nein*). Later that spring and summer, the SPD in the Bundestag refused to support the Greens in their public opposition to the missiles and in their call for a "consultative referendum" on the scheduled deployment. They also declined to back the Greens' attempt to move the parliamentary debate on acceptance of the missiles to early autumn, leaving it at 21–22 November on the Bundestag calendar. The Greens became exasperated not only with the SPD but also with the majority of the peace movement for embracing the SPD's minimal opposition, that is, their rejecting the Euromissiles while accepting NATO.

Four days before the Bundestag debate and vote on deployment, a German television company arranged a showing for the parliamentarians of the American film *The Day After*, which depicts the effects of a nuclear war that is triggered by military actions in Germany. Although the event was well publicized, only four parliamentarians attended: Bastian, Kelly, one person from the CDU, and one from the SPD. The very weekend before the Bundestag debate, the SPD held a party congress in Cologne which they had already postponed twice. There they officially switched their position and came out in opposition to the imminent deployment of the Pershing II and cruise missiles. During the same weekend, the Greens sponsored an assembly of representatives from the entire West German peace movement in Bad-Godesberg-Bonn. Shortly before the televised two-day debate in the Bundestag, a poll found 78 percent of the West German public opposed to deployment. The Bundestag session was highly emotional with strong anger expressed toward the Greens. In the end, most of the SPD voted with the Greens against deployment, which made the vote a relatively close 286 to 226, but Kohl's center-right coalition triumphed. Deployment began the following day.

At the invitation of Soviet leaders, the Greens sent a delegation to Moscow on 29–30 October. The group consisted of Gert Bastian, Marieluise Beck-Oberdorf, Milan Horacek, Petra Kelly, Manon Maren-Grisebach, Jürgen Reents, and Otto Schily. They met first with thirty women from the official Soviet peace movement, who spoke of how they lived, how they had suffered from the war, and that their only goal was peace. "But what began so warmly," according to Maren-Grisebach, "and with the smile that unites all women in the world then changed into officialdom and propaganda speeches." The Greens found the committee for environmental protection quite hospitable and their speeches interesting, but asked, "Where are the deeds?" Maren-Grisebach concluded, "In a country where the glory of technology and the glitter of economic growth still radiate so seductively, radical environmental protection does not have much of a chance even with the best of intentions." Russian university students found the Greens' message puzzling: They are against status quo capitalism, but also speak against communism? They condemn the American first-strike weapons, but don't want us to deploy our defensive weapons? They say they are not against technology, but want us to give up nuclear power? Finally, they are for nonviolence, but want to "attack" the power structures? Strange birds, these Greens. . . .

The focus of discussions with Soviet officials, including a member of the Politburo, were the Greens' peace proposals. They called for an end to the policy of deterrence and for unilateral disarmament in East and West. The Greens implored the Soviets not to rearm, assuring them that their refusal to do so would be a strong signal and would increase the security of both Russia and Europe. Maren-Grisebach reported on the response:

> With those demands we got nowhere. We heard exactly the same arguments as in Washington: "We are forced to take countermeasures. We are threatened by nuclear blackmail. What about the Americans? Can you guarantee that they won't take advantage of us? We are surrounded by enemies. No, no, your proposals are illusory. Unilateral disarmament would be an enormous risk." We felt we were listening to a fight between kids, each one pointing to the other and crying "He started it!"

The Greens were allowed to conduct a brief demonstration in Red Square. They carried banners, which Petra Kelly had prepared in Bonn, proclaiming in Russian "Respect for Human Rights." Kelly herself wore a sweatshirt painted with Cyrillic letters that proclaimed "Dissolve NATO and Warsaw Pact!"

Two weeks later the Greens adopted a peace resolution, "The Way to Peace," as the main business of their annual congress in Duisburg. They urged the peace movement not to limit itself to the antirearmament cause, but to develop its own peace politics. The Greens rejected the possibility of returning to a "German power state" or creating a "European superstate," and renewed their call for cooperation among the decentralized, autonomous movements in Central Europe. They set as their immediate task the building of a network of contacts among grassroots movements in both blocs.

Since the Greens maintain their concept of social defense in the face of the deployment of the new missiles, advocate a "Europe of the regions" when the reality is a deeply rooted bloc system, and uphold a weapons-free world when we have come to live with deadly brinkmanship, we wondered whether they consider their peace proposals a matter of "Demand the impossible; obtain the possible." "Yes, it's part of a strategy," Gert Bastian agreed. "We know very well that the sort of thinking necessary for our solutions hardly exists now among the population, yet it is necessary to begin to change the consciousness."

What would it take, though, to dissolve the two power blocs peacefully? Beyond the call to demilitarize West Germany, the Greens have not developed step-by-step scenarios that might assuage the skepticism and fear most people feel about any radical shift in world order. Moreover, we doubted that either superpower would willingly give up its economic satellites. Bastian pointed out that a few of Russia's, such as Poland and Romania, require more money than they produce. He believes that if the military threat to the Soviet Union were greatly reduced and a world order created in which the Soviets did not have to fear an enemy superpower controlling all the global resources, the U.S.S.R. would release its grip on Eastern Europe.

Rudolf Bahro, who studied the governmental and economic systems of the Warsaw Pact countries in depth for his critical book *The Alternative in Eastern Europe,* agrees with Bastian that the rationale for the occupation by Soviet troops is military rather than economic.

> The more enlightened people within the power elite in Moscow know there is no possibility of seeing the military forces in Western Europe reduced without some complementary "gift" in the East. They understand the interdependence between Eastern and Western Europe. Abolishing the military threat would change the internal politics of Eastern Europe. If the Soviet Union receives the conditions for a "Finlandization"* of Eastern Europe, it will happen. There could be no more subversive action than the withdrawal of the American army from Western Europe.

*"Finlandization" refers to an accommodation with the Soviet Union whereby political independence and autonomy in domestic affairs are exchanged in return for avoiding foreign policies unfriendly toward the Soviet Union. Such a situation in Eastern Europe would not be an entirely "bloc-free" arrangement, but would constitute a major step toward that goal.

What would it take for the American, European, and Japanese multinational corporations to loosen their grip on satellite regions as well? Different economic structures at home in which enterprises were nonmonopolistic, appropriately scaled, and self-organized, comprising an ecologically aware society that applied its scientific prowess to the challenge of appropriate technology and the minimal use of resources? Widespread consciousness-raising among the public about the plight of the Third World? A postpatriarchal generation of men who were no longer willing to "prove their manhood" in "patriotic" foreign wars?

Would it require, then, Green ideas to guide us out of the global crisis? They would have to be developed with courage and creativity, with caring and trust. The old system is about to devour itself and us with it. So if we retreat from building a way out, overwhelming as that task may seem, we should not fool ourselves about the choice we are making. It may almost be time for the end of time, as August Haussleiter reminded us: "As a young boy, I saw the First World War coming, and, of course, I watched the Second World War come. I know what the first signs look like. We're seeing them now."

Chapter 4

Restructuring
the Economy

Although nuclear war is without any doubt the greatest threat to humanity today, it is the economic crisis that worries people most in their daily lives. We can suppress our fear of nuclear weapons, at least from time to time, but the steadily rising costs of living, the scarcity of jobs, and the threat of bankruptcy are pressing features of the economic reality that affect most of us in one way or another. Hence the popularity of governments depends crucially on the successes and failures of their economic programs. Following the elections of Reagan, Thatcher, and Kohl, pollsters discovered that in each of their victories, the promise of economic recovery had been the primary factor.* Since then all three have claimed popular mandates for all kinds of radical programs, such as escalating the nuclear madness and Reagan's increasing the defense budget by 100 percent from the 1979 level to that of 1984.

While all these politicians did receive mandates to solve the

*New York Times, 16 November 1980, 8 March 1983, and 11 June 1983.

economic crisis, they have been unable to do so except for some fluctuating improvements in a few areas. The reason they and other political leaders—whether right, left, or center—cannot find appropriate solutions is that they and their economic experts subscribe to narrow perceptions of the problems. As we pointed out in the Preface, these problems are systemic in nature, that is, closely interconnected and interdependent. The current fragmented approaches merely shift around the critical economic and social factors in a complex web of relations, creating vicious circles of inflation, high interest rates, government budget deficits, and unemployment.

Present-day economists, whether neoclassical, Marxist, Keynesian, or of the many post-Keynesian schools (monetarist, supply-side, and others), generally lack an ecological perspective. Instead of recognizing the economy as one aspect of a whole ecological and social fabric, they tend to isolate it and to describe it in terms of highly unrealistic theoretical models. Most economists define their basic concepts—efficiency, productivity, GNP, and so forth—in a narrow way, without considering the social and ecological context. In particular, they disregard the social and environmental costs generated by all economic activity. Consequently, the current economic concepts are inadequate to map economic phenomena in a fundamentally interdependent and limited world. As the *Washington Post* rather cynically put it in an article on 20 May 1979: "Ambitious economists elaborate elegant mathematical solutions to theoretical problems with little if any relevance to public issues."

The situation is further aggravated because most economists, in a misguided striving for scientific rigor, refuse to acknowledge the values on which their models are based. Instead, they tacitly accept as givens the particular values that dominate their cultures and are embodied in their social institutions. These values have led to an overemphasis on hard technology, wasteful consumption, and rapid exploitation of natural resources, all motivated by a persistent obsession with undifferentiated growth. A continually growing economy is seen as essential by virtually all economists and politicians, although it should be abundantly clear by now that unlimited expansion in a finite environment can only lead to disaster.

Belief in the necessity of continuing growth is a blatant illustration of the fallacy of linear thinking: the erroneous belief that if something is good for an individual or group, then more of the same will necessarily be better. The prevailing creed in government and business is still that the common good is best served when all people and institutions maximize their own material wealth—"What's good for General Motors is good for the United States." The whole is identified with the sum of its parts. The fact that it can be either more or less than this sum, depending on the positive or negative interference among the parts, is ignored. The consequences of this reductionist fallacy are now becoming painfully visible, as economic forces collide with each other with increasing frequency, tear the social fabric, destroy the natural environment, and generate international political tensions.

The global obsession with growth has resulted in a remarkable similarity between capitalist and communist economies. The two dominant representatives of these so-called opposing value systems, the United States and the Soviet Union, are in reality not all that different. Both are dedicated to industrial growth and hard technology, with increasingly centralized and bureaucratic control, whether by the state or by so-called private multinational corporations.

Paradoxically, most economists, in spite of their insistence on growth, are unable to adopt a dynamic view. They see the economy as frozen arbitrarily in its current institutional structure, instead of as a system that changes and evolves along with the natural and social environments in which it is embedded. Today's economic theories also accept, without questioning, past configurations of power and unequal distributions of wealth, both within national economies and between the Third World and industrialized countries. An alliance of corporate and other rigid, hierarchical institutions—the Fortune 500, the big unions, the medical industry—dominates the global and national arenas, their economic and political power permeating virtually every facet of public life. Many of these giants are now structurally obsolete institutions that generate polluting and socially disruptive technologies. They lock up capital, energy, and resources and are unable to adapt to the changing needs of our time. The

American automobile industry and the West German and Belgian steel industries exhibit striking examples of such "dinosaur" corporations in states of profound structural crisis, even though many of their leaders still insist that the problems are merely cyclical.

The systems approach to economics will make it possible to bring some order into the present conceptual chaos by allowing economists to put their models into an ecological context. According to this view, the economy is a living system composed of human beings and social organizations in continual interaction with one another and with the surrounding ecosystems on which our lives depend. Like an individual organism, an ecosystem is a complex web of relationships in which animals, plants, microorganisms, and inanimate substances are all interlinked and interdependent, a network of processes involving the exchange of matter and energy in continual cycles. Because linear cause-and-effect relationships exist very rarely in ecosystems, linear models are not very useful to describe the embedded social and economic systems.

Recognizing the nonlinearity of living systems is the very essence of ecological awareness and immediately suggests two important rules for the management of social and economic systems. First, there is an optimal size for every structure, organization, and institution. Deviations from this size that result from maximizing any single variable—profit, efficiency, or GNP, for example—will inevitably destroy the larger system. Second, the more an economy continually recycles its natural resources, the more it will be in harmony with the surrounding environment.

The first rule shows that the question of scale will play a central role in the reorganization of our economic and social structures. The criterion governing all considerations of scale derives from the comparison with human dimension. As E. F. Schumacher put it in his book *Small Is Beautiful,* we need "a technology with a human face." Decentralization—in government, business, and in most of our social institutions—will be essential to restore ecological balance, and we will have to realize that this will also require a redistribution of wealth, especially between industrialized countries and the Third World. Global ecological balance is simply impossible when 5 percent of the world's population consumes one-third of its energy.

In the systems approach to economics, the basic concepts and variables of economic theories will have to be related to those used to describe living systems. Energy, so essential to all industrial processes, then becomes one of the most important variables for measuring economic activities. Energy modeling, pioneered by the engineer and environmentalist Howard Odum in *Environment, Power and Society* (Wiley Interscience, 1971), is now pursued in many countries by progressive scientists from various disciplines. In spite of many unresolved problems and differences in methods, the mapping of flows of energy is coming to be viewed as a more reliable method for macroeconomic analyses than conventional monetary approaches.

Measurement of the efficiency of production processes in terms of net energy, which is now being widely accepted, suggests that entropy—a quantity related to the dissipation of energy—is another important variable for the analysis of economic phenomena. Jeremy Rifkin argues persuasively in his book *Entropy* (Bantam Books, 1981) that energy dissipation, as described by the second law of thermodynamics, is relevant not only to the performance of steam engines but also to the functioning of an economy. As the thermodynamic efficiency of engines is limited by friction and other forms of energy dissipation, so production processes in industrial societies will inevitably generate social frictions and will dissipate some of the economy's energy and resources into unproductive activities. Like efficiency, the concepts of productivity, profit, and GNP will have to be redefined within a broad ecological context and related to the two basic variables of energy and entropy.

At present it is far from clear how such a restructuring of economic theory will be achieved, as only very tentative steps in this direction have been taken. It is evident, though, that the task of properly mapping the economy will transcend the boundaries of present-day economics. The restructuring cannot be left to economists alone but will require a multidisciplinary approach, using insights from ecology, sociology, political science, anthropology, psychology, and other disciplines. Such a comprehensive approach to economic analyses is already visible in a number of recent books by noneconomists on subjects that formerly belonged exclusively to the domain of economics. Innovative contributions of this kind include those of Richard Barnet (political scientist), Barry Commoner (biologist), Jay Forrester (systems analyst), Hazel Henderson (futurist), Frances Moore Lappé (sociologist), Amory Lovins (physicist), Howard Odum (engineer), and Theodore Roszak (historian), to name just a few.

Even this brief assessment of our economic crisis makes it obvious that there are no easy solutions. To formulate a new economic theory based on ecological principles and to restructure the economy accordingly are enormous tasks which the Greens, in their relative infancy as a political party, have only begun to address. In preparation for the March 1983 federal election, the Greens held an assembly in Sindelfingen in January to complete work on a statement of their economic program, *Meaningful Work—Living in Solidarity.* They begin that document by emphasizing that it is preliminary work that presents for public discussion and further development the most immediate, urgently needed measures.

Awareness of the ecological context of all economic problems is fundamental to Green political philosophy. It is expressed not only in their economic statement but also in their Federal Program:

> The economic and financial policies of the Establishment parties are concerned neither with ecological aspects nor with the long-term interests of the people. Their main concern is to promote destructive economic growth. . . .
> A complete restructuring of our nearsighted economic thinking is necessary. We consider it an error to believe that our current wasteful economy is furthering happiness and life fulfillment. Just the opposite occurs: people are becoming more harried and less free. Only to the extent that we free ourselves from overrating the material standard of living, that we again make self-realization possible and realize once more the limits of our own natures, will our creative powers be able to free themselves to form life anew on an ecological basis.

The Greens, of course, are not the first to voice such a critique. But they are the first political party to provide an outline for restructuring the economy according to ecological and human criteria. The Federal Program continues:

> We are for an economic system oriented toward the vital requirements of people and of future generations, toward the preservation of nature and the judicious handling of natural resources. We have in mind a society in which interpersonal relationships and the relationships between humans and nature become ever more the subject of conscious consideration, a society where attention to nature's life cycles, the development and use of technology, and the relationship between production and consumption become the business of all those concerned. An economy founded on ecological principles does not mean renouncing the quality of life; it means people supporting those products that fulfill their needs and are compatible with the natural environment.

To approach these goals, the Greens propose a series of specific measures, which are set out in their Economic Program. We discussed this program in some detail with Joachim Müller, a Green economist who is a *Nachrücker* in the Bundestag *Fraktion*. Joachim Müller—"Jo" to his friends—at first glance could very well be a young executive from Standard Oil or a computer scientist from MIT. He dresses neatly, has short hair, carries a briefcase. He is a manager type, concentrated and efficient, but with the friendliness and openness of all the Greens we encountered. Our discussion with him was always very focused and he made his points emphatically, but he also showed a great sense of humor. For example, in discussing economic growth he said categorically: "Look, in the near future there isn't going to be any growth anyway!" Then he added with a mischievous smile, "The demand for zero growth has been fulfilled by capitalism without any struggle." He seemed particularly to enjoy mixing Marxist and "bourgeois" language, having come from a Marxist background but having clearly transcended the framework of Marxist analysis.

Müller explained to us that the Economic Program must be read politically, as a document of compromise among diverse currents within the Green movement. He emphasized, however, that it does have a unified thesis. "The way in which technology is applied threatens both jobs and the environment. This fundamental thesis runs through the program more or less coherently." We asked whether it was just technology that posed a threat, or was it the entire attitude underlying it. "Technology and what you would call mechanistic thinking, that is, thinking only in quantified values while ignoring qualitative effects," he explained.

The long-term goal of Green economics is under lively discussion within the party. What is sometimes called the Bahro-Trampert debate is a representation of the conflicting priorities of the visionary/holistic Greens and the Marxist-oriented Greens. Rainer Trampert and most of his radical-left colleagues are structurally conservative in that they believe a steady-state, no-growth economy can be achieved simply by scaling back the current levels of production. They do not support—at least not with any enthusiasm—the structural shift called for by most Greens to small-scale, overseeable units of commerce and industry. Rudolf Bahro, in stark contrast, calls for a radical shift in our patterns of production, consumption, and living so that we will return to a "preindustrial" society comprised largely of self-sufficient villages of about 3,000 people. Most Greens, although they admire Bahro's thinking in other areas, find this proposal entirely impractical, just as they find Trampert's proindustrial stance unsatisfactory. They bemoan the fact that a truly Green, creative, and pragmatic model beyond both Trampert's and Bahro's has not yet been developed by the party.

To organize their economic policies the Greens have used, once again, the three principles: "ecology," "social responsibility," and "grassroots democracy." The fourth principle, "nonviolence," is implicit in the entire program; an economy that is ecologically balanced and socially just will naturally be nonviolent.

The ecological measures proposed by the Greens flow from their rejection of purely quantitative growth—especially growth that entails environmental destruction. The fallacy of unlimited quantitative growth is eloquently exposed in their Economic Program:

> In 1950, 1 percent growth meant increased goods with a value of 1.9 billion DM. Today 1 percent growth brings with it additional products with a value of 9 billion DM. To cure unemployment by means of growth—a method rejected by the Greens—would require a growth rate of 6 percent per year. This would mean that in ten years we would have to produce and consume twice as much

per year as we do now. Twice as many cars, refrigerators, televisions, machines, concrete, nuclear power plants, tanks, cheeseburgers, psychiatric megaclinics, artificial fertilizers, etc. It requires only common sense to see that it is neither possible nor admissible to take this course.

The Greens demand the dismantling of life-threatening industries, above all of the nuclear and weapons industries, and the reorientation of production toward ecologically benign and socially necessary products. One of their slogans is "No investments without a future!" They propose a number of specific ecological investments in the areas of energy production, recycling, water management, agriculture, housing, and traffic. Economic decentralization, utilization of existing local resources, and judicious use and recycling of raw materials are the outstanding characteristics of these ecological investments. In addition, the Greens strongly support numerous emerging alternative projects, typically collectively owned and operated, in which many new social and economic patterns are developed and tested.

One of the main social concerns of the Economic Program in the area of social responsibility is the current high rate of unemployment. A socially responsible economy, for the Greens, is a full-employment economy, and they propose to move in this direction by redistributing the available work through a shortening of work time and simultaneous rehiring of unemployed workers. Another significant feature of Green economic policy is its revaluation of North-South relations. The Greens demand an orientation toward a self-reliant internal economy, rather than exploitation of the Third World, and they declare their solidarity with Third World countries in their efforts to lessen their dependence on the northern hemisphere.

A grassroots democratic economy, finally, according to the Greens, is one that allows for self-managed, cooperative enterprises, in which those involved in the production process are able to decide themselves *what* is produced, as well as *how* and *where* it is produced.

The ecological economy envisaged by the Greens is not guided by economic growth leading to exploitation of nature, but rather by a sense of partnership between humans and nature. The rejection of purely quantitative growth is central to the Green economic critique:

> We are fundamentally against all quantitative growth, especially when it is fueled by craving for profits. However, we are in favor of qualitative growth when it proves feasible, using the same or a smaller amount of energy and raw materials.

The shift from quantity to quality proposed by the Greens would halt the current destruction of the environment and enhance the quality of human life, both individual and societal. Jo Müller strongly emphasized this point:

> The Greens' criticism of growth is simply based on the fact that until now additional growth has always brought with it environmental destruction. This connection is simply true, and this is our starting point. We don't say every form of growth has to be rejected. We reject it only as long as this functional connection continues to exist.

The concrete demands following from this critique are, for the immediate future, the dismantling of life-threatening industries and, for the medium- and long-term future, a fundamental reorientation of production toward ecologically benign and socially necessary products. Müller explained the new criteria:

> The strategy would be no longer to judge what is produced just by its quantitative effects, but qualitatively as well. From this follows something like ecological investments in the future. Wherever you have investment programs, their first priority must be undoing damage to nature. For example, the problem of acid rain makes it clear that we simply can't afford to produce power plants without filters anymore. And we maintain that such programs would also create jobs in this crisis. . . . We are therefore trying to develop an approach in which ecology, economy, and social concerns are united.

The Greens' critique of *what* is produced includes their rejection of armaments, wasteful packaging, dangerous chemicals, and frivolous household gadgets. One of the most effective ways of reducing and, eventually, eliminating the "need" for production of these dangerous and wasteful products would be through restrictions on advertising, and this is indeed what the Greens propose. In today's economies, in Europe as in the United States, advertising is a crucial element in the ability of big companies to "manage," that is, create, the demand in the marketplace. For the system to work, not only must consumers keep increasing their spending, they must do so *predictably*. As a consequence of this practice, the frustration created and sustained by massive doses of advertising, on top of existing social inequities, contributes to ever increasing crime, violence, and other social pathologies. The disastrous effects of advertising are especially noticeable on television. In the book *Four Arguments for the Elimination of Television* (Morrow, 1978), Jerry Mander explains how advertising on the American television networks influences the content and form of all programs, including the "news shows," and manipulates the tremendous suggestive power of this medium—switched on for more than seven hours a day by the average American family—to shape people's imagery, distort their sense of reality, and determine their views, tastes, and behavior. The exclusive aim of this dangerous practice is to lure the audience into buying products advertised before, after, and during each program.

Although the advertising on European television is not so excessive, the trend toward American practices is increasing. Radio and television in West Germany are partially supported by taxes, and advertising is limited to certain blocks of time. However, attempts are now being made by powerful German corporations to introduce American-style television—low-quality programs packed with commercials—through cable TV. The Greens demand that radio and television should be entirely free of advertising. In addition, they demand that all advertising of dangerous and unhealthy products, including cigarettes, sweets, liquor, pesticides, and chemical fertilizers, be prohibited.

The Green critique of *how* things are produced, as we discuss below in more detail, addresses the problems of monotonous work, undignified working conditions, and the discrimination against women. Moreover, the Greens advocate decentralizing production to bring it closer to local and regional markets, thus reducing traffic and saving energy. The necessity of such measures is also becoming apparent in the United States, where distances are huge compared to those in West Germany and where more and more large enterprises suffer from excessive centralization. The heat wasted by big American power plants in the processes of generation and transmission to the points of use would be more than enough to heat every house in the United States. Similarly, the rising costs of transporting goods across the country are rapidly making it possible for regional and local enterprises to compete with national companies.

The Green economic program contains, among many others, the following concrete proposals for ecologically meaningful investments. *Energy production:* Conservation measures should be designed and encouraged; "soft" production modes of energy should be developed; energy regulations, which now permit the establishment of monopolies, have to be modified. *Recycling:* Production generating waste that is not safely disposable must be outlawed; new recycling techniques have to be developed. *Water management:* Biological water treatment processes should be expanded; closed water systems for industrial production and cooling should be mandatory; the self-purification capacities of rivers must be supported by ecological means. *Agriculture:* Ecological agriculture should be promoted and developed on decentralized self-reliant farms; rural areas must be revitalized and regional administrative structures improved. *Housing:* A radical reorientation of housing policies and restructuring of financial instruments to support housing construction will be necessary; the decisions about financing have to be transferred from the federal to the community level; land prices have to be controlled and financing has to be uncoupled from the real estate market by direct use of public money. *Traffic:* Public transportation is to be increased together with a substantial reduction of fares; car traffic has to be restricted while pedestrian and bicycle traffic is encouraged and facilitated; all further construction of freeways and airports must stop.

The Greens' deep ecological awareness is evident from their detailed and often very beautiful formulations of these proposals. For example, the section dealing with water demands a reorientation of policies "doing justice to the importance of water as the carrier of life" and opens with the following statement:

> Water is the most complex and, besides air, the most important substance of life on earth. Its quality is the environmental indicator par excellence. . . . Water is not consumed but borrowed—and borrowed things should be returned in their original condition.

The restructuring of the economy along the lines proposed by the Greens will offer tremendous opportunities for human creativity, entrepreneurship, and initiative. There will be plenty of growth in the new economy, but all growth will be qualified; it will proceed in the direction of small-scale, community-based enterprises and of new forms of technology that incorporate ecological principles and are consistent with a new system of values.

Although the demand for the necessary shift from hard to soft, that is, environmentally benign, technologies runs through the entire Economic Program, the Greens have not yet been able to clarify their basic position vis-à-vis technology. One school of thought is quite hostile to new technologies and demands slowing down or even blocking new developments. Another favors new technologies and sees problems merely in their application; some Greens would even support fully automated factories as long as the machines are taxed and new forms of meaningful work are developed. A third school, perhaps the most thoughtful, questions the values underlying various kinds of technology. Müller, who belongs to that third school of thought, asserts, "The way in which we develop technology today is not only a question of application; what we need is a radical restructuring and rethinking of the broad way in which we practice science and produce technology." Within the broad range of positions, a cautious and critical attitude toward technology is common to all the Greens we spoke to, and this is also expressed in their Federal Program:

> Before new technologies are introduced an evaluation period should be instituted during which these technologies are tested for their compability with the environment, economical energy consumption, and contribution to humane working conditions. To this end, a cost-effect analysis for the entire society, listing all cost factors, should be carried out.

The major problem in reorienting production is that it will necessitate a far-reaching restructuring of employment patterns. The Greens are aware that this will involve not only a redistribution of work tasks but also a thorough redefinition of work itself. They address these problems in connection with the social aspects of their economic program. At this stage they realize that they are unable to address all the consequences and repercussions of reorienting production and employment in the ways they feel are necessary. However, they point out that there are now many enterprises in West Germany that serve as social and economic "laboratories" to test new ideas as they are grown from the grassroots. Support of these alternative enterprises and projects is a central demand of the Green Economic Program:

> Small as the contributions of self-organized projects to the entire economy may be, they have great significance as a field of important social and political experiments. . . . For these reasons the Greens support the development of alternative projects.

Since the mid-1970s, a growing number of alternative projects have sprung up in West Germany. Today over ten thousand of these projects are in existence, involving approximately a hundred thousand people. Alternative projects are typically carried out by small, self-organized, and self-determining groups of five to ten members, predominantly teen-agers and young adults. The projects may be craft or repair shops; restaurants or cafés; newspapers, theaters, or other forms of media; or social services such as childcare or therapeutic groups. They may form around citizens' initiatives dealing with environmental or social issues. In West Berlin 25 percent of these alternative projects provide the only source of income for the people involved, while 40 percent are spare-time projects carried out without pay, and the rest have mixed structures.

According to the Greens, alternative projects represent grassroots responses to the alienation of work in large industries and large offices, to the evident uselessness and senselessness of large portions of industrial production, and to the quantitative and qualitative lack of care in social institutions like kindergartens or daycare centers. A special kind of alternative project has developed in the self-help initiatives of unemployed people, which the Greens strongly support through their demands for free use of appropriate localities, free public transport, and equal rights in unions for the unemployed.

The experiments carried out in alternative projects involve

many new social and economic patterns that are likely to be extremely important in the proposed reorientation of the economy—new forms of cooperative property and of work motivated by real needs rather than profits, new forms of autonomy for women, new economic activities rooted in neighborhoods and city districts and evolving through networking, the many soft technologies now being developed, as well as new forms of social organization involving the integration of people of different generations, races, handicaps, and talents. The Greens encourage all social and economic experiments along these lines. They reject the current financial discrimination against alternative projects and demand state-financed, self-administered funds to assist the projects, raising these funds by decreasing the subsidies for large industrial corporations.

Jo Müller pointed out to us that all the alternative projects taken together—the *alternative Szene,* as it is known in Germany—represent the beginning of an important new economic sector.

> This new sector is necessary because the traditional sectors are no longer in a position to create jobs. . . . In a few cities we already have many, many people with jobs that they themselves determine, in most cases at a sacrifice of income. People are evidently ready to accept this if they can determine their own work.

Alternative economies of this kind—also known as "informal," "dual," or "convivial" economies—are now springing up in many countries around the world. One of their interesting aspects is the fact that such informal, cooperative, and nonmonetarized sectors are predominant in most of the world's economies and that the institutionalized and monetarized sectors grew out of them and rest upon them, rather than the reverse. It is clearly necessary for any modern society to have both formal and informal sectors in its economy, but our overemphasis on money—dollars, marks, yen, or rubles—to measure economic efficiency has created huge imbalances and is now threatening to destroy the informal sectors. The Greens' strong support of alternative projects is therefore important not only because these projects represent ideal opportunities for social and economic experimentation but also because they help to balance the economy.

The outstanding social concern in most industrialized countries today is the high rate of unemployment. In West Germany the unemployment rate was very low for many years but has recently risen dramatically and is now practically as high as in the United States (9.6 percent in February 1983). Consequently, unemployment is perceived by most Germans as the primary economic problem. The Greens state very forcefully in their Economic Program that the social economy they envisage will be a full-employment economy:

> In a social economy there will be no unemployment. Instead, there will be a just distribution of socially necessary work. . . . Unemployment is a condition forced upon the affected; it can arise only when some have the power to exclude others from work and, by doing so, to also punish them by loss of income.

The Greens recognize that there are no easy solutions to the problem of unemployment. Our economies are characterized by excessive dependence on energy and natural resources and by excessive investment in capital rather than labor, which makes them highly inflationary and also generates high unemployment. To remedy this situation, a thorough reorientation of our patterns of production and consumption will be necessary, emphasizing small-scale, decentralized, and labor-intensive technologies based on self-reliant cooperative, and ecologically harmonious life-styles. Several recent studies have shown conclusively that such a reorientation of the economy is the most effective strategy for creating secure jobs (see, for example, *Fear at Work* by Richard Kazis and Richard L. Grossmann, Pilgrim Press, 1982), and this view is also expressed in the Green Economic Program: "Measures against unemployment must also introduce, or at least support, at the same time a restructuring of the economy according to ecological, social, and democratic standards."

While the Greens view the restructuring of the economy as a long-term goal, they propose as their principal short-term strategy in fighting unemployment an immediate redistribution of work through shortening work time and rehiring unemployed workers. Specifically, they agree with the proposal within the West German labor movement to shorten the work week from the current forty hours to thirty-five hours as a first step, to be followed by further steps beyond the thirty-five-hour week if necessary. Shortening the work time in this way is seen by the Greens as the most effective and most reasonable measure to increase employment. As Jo Müller put it, "There is no sense in shortening the work week to zero for the 2.5 million registered unemployed while others continue to work. Equitable distribution of jobs is simply a reasonable demand."

Our first question to Müller was: What happens to the wages when the work week is shortened? He told us that there was a difference of opinions on this question among the Greens. The Economic Program states that the work week is to be shortened without reduction in pay for low- and middle-income employees, but exactly what is meant by "middle income" remains to be defined. The Greens are well aware of the possible abuses of this proposal. For example, they emphasize that the shortening of work time should not be accomplished by intensification of the work load, and would have to be accompanied by a redistribution of the work load at home (housework and childcare) between women and men. They also demand that women should be given preference in the rehiring until equal employment patterns are reached and that foreigners living in Germany should have the same rights as German workers.

The Green employment program raises many questions that have not yet been answered. Will men get more involved in housework and childcare as the Greens suggest? What about people who prefer to make extra money moonlighting rather than spend their new free time on "self-determined leisure activities," as suggested in the Green program? Should the unions, or anyone else, have the power to prevent people from working overtime? Reflection on these and other questions makes it clear that the Green employment program can be successful only if it goes hand in hand with profound changes in our attitudes toward work and leisure, changes that cannot be imposed but have to happen gradually at the grassroots level. Ultimately, the Green proposals depend on a thorough redefinition of the nature of work, including bartered labor and community self-help, a goal that is also stated explicitly in the Economic Program:

> In terms of today's economy, work is recognized only as the means for earning income. Rather than a means for personal self-development, work . . . serves primarily to secure one's livelihood.

All the bleak and oppressive aspects of the work process are accepted for the sake of wages. The Greens want to contribute to deemphasizing paid labor in order to reclaim work as free, self-determining activity and as a possibility for self-development.

In addition to enriching the nature of work, the Greens want to reduce the psychological stress caused by separating various spheres of human existence in industrial societies, as Rudolf Bahro has argued passionately:

> Today the question is not just one of emancipation in economics, but a perspective at least of emancipation from economics, of rising above the realm of necessity, as Marx considered it.
>
> What is needed is to completely reprogram the whole of economic life, the entire relationship of production and need as well as the regulation of the economic process. Without this there can be no human emancipation—an emancipation that involves the individual, otherwise it's not emancipation at all. The psychological dimension of the problem of individuality in super-complex industrial society must be made completely clear. The different spheres of life—work, education, housing, recreation—are so separated from one another, almost all activities are so depersonalized and even private ties stripped of so many necessities, that the alienation of one person from another threatens to become the general fate. The misfortune of loneliness, of total loss of communication beneath the gigantic surface of abstract, spiritually indifferent functional activities, bites ever deeper. We find a loss of emotional connection even in the intimate contacts of the nuclear family, this last residue of the original community. A model of life that leads to such disharmony for individuals may be progressive according to some criterion or other, but it is devoid of any perspective of human emancipation.

The restructuring of the economy envisaged by the Greens involves not only a redefinition of work but also of private property. However, what they have in mind, contrary to rumors spread by the American media, is not at all nationalization of private property but rather a profound reorientation of society that is consistent with their principles of decentralization and grassroots democracy. In fact, the Economic Program contains the following explicit defense of private property:

> A further prerequisite for individual freedom is the private ownership of those goods which serve to shape one's life.

On the other hand, the Economic Program also states:

> It is our presupposition that current conditions of private property and of control over the means of production contribute to the alienation and to the exploitation of humans and nature. Property in the hands of private individuals—as well as in those of the state—must no longer be permitted to result in control over human beings, the destruction of nature, and the direction of the economy, the society, and of politics.

Since the question of private property is a very sensitive issue, in Europe as well as in the United States, we asked Jo Müller to explain exactly what the Green position is.

> Ownership of the means of production is no longer the decisive question. If I take the statistics of the last twenty years, I simply have to realize that income from private capital has clearly decreased in comparison to other forms of income. . . . The problem is not necessarily surplus value or profit, but rather control. But this is a question that can be resolved to a large degree politically.
>
> Okay, let's take an example. The problem we have in many German cities is speculation in housing, which results in houses staying vacant. This is an abuse. We even have laws in the Federal Republic [West Germany] prohibiting this kind of abuse, but they are not enforced. I can easily imagine that we in the Bundestag could tighten up enforcement against such abuses. For me that would be enough to deal with housing speculation. It is a political problem, not necessarily a problem of property.

We asked Müller whether this meant that the Greens did not favor nationalization of private property. He stated emphatically that they did not.

> Expropriation, as Marx demanded it, necessarily implies centralization. But the Green principle is decentrality. For me this is a decisive point, because it is well known that smaller entities are more easily subject to democratic control. This thesis is simply true. . . . This is why we say: no expropriation and central planning, for heaven's sake! Rather, wherever possible, create something like community property. . . .
>
> The decisive entity in our society has to be, from the perspective of our politics, not the federal government but the traditional notion of the community. This could even be the traditional Christian community or, in a different manifestation, the commune. For us it is interesting that where the connection between life and work

is concrete—which is in the community—there and only there do processes of change occur on a long-term basis. This is where consciousness is formed, where learning takes place, where people live together, where conflicts arise; and it is here that human beings are really affected.

Because the Greens are economic iconoclasts, many people confuse their positions with those of the radical left. For example, Helmut Lippelt, a Green state legislator in Lower Saxony, told us that the Green *Fraktion* was visited by radical trade unionists who assumed the Greens would support their leftist solution to the current crisis in the steel industry: nationalize the steel mills, have the government pay all costs, and gear up high levels of production again, which can be sold to the Third World and even sold in Europe after five years of open-ended growth policies. The Greens emphatically declined to participate in such demands on the grounds that they oppose nationalization, overproduction, and exporting industrialism to the Third World.

Perhaps the most difficult part of the reorientation of society envisaged by the Greens will be the redistribution of wealth. Today's world economy is based on past configurations of power, perpetuating class structures and a grossly unequal distribution of wealth within national economies, as well as exploitation of Third World countries by rich, industrialized nations. While these social realities are largely ignored by conventional economists, who tend to avoid moral issues and accept the current distribution of wealth as given and unchangeable, Green economic thought includes both national and global redistribution of wealth as important conditions for achieving a social economy. Thus we read in the Economic Program:

> The restructuring of economic conditions includes a change in the totally unequal and unjust conditions of income and wealth in our society. A social redistribution of generated values and income, however, must also be applied on a global basis and must become one of the standards of conduct in our relationship with the Third World.

While the Greens have specific suggestions concerning the relations between industrialized countries and the Third World, their program is vague about ways to redistribute wealth within the industrialized countries. When we asked Jo Müller for more information he did not have very much to offer either. He mentioned once more the proposed shortening of the work week and rehiring the unemployed, and also the possibility of redistributing wealth through graduated taxation and shifting of federal subsidies. In particular, he mentioned a project of financing alternative enterprises by taxes that was tried out in Berlin and could be developed further. However, Müller also cautioned against the illusion, traditionally nursed by the left, that one would be able to achieve a more just society through tax policies. "Tax structures," he reminded us, "are very difficult to get under control. . . . We shouldn't have any illusions about this." The Greens, then, feel strongly that redistributing the wealth is a moral imperative, but they still lack creative and practical ideas of how to go about it.

Their Third World policies are much more specific. The Greens' Economic Program contains a short but clear analysis of current North-South relations. They point out that in the current system of so-called international division of labor the industry and agriculture of Third World countries are controlled by foreign aid and by credits from international banks so that their production is primarily oriented toward the needs of the industrial countries. They are forced to sell their goods cheaply and to buy expensive industrial products in return, which leads to massive indebtedness. To pay their debts, Third World countries have to increase their exports, which is possible only by paying starvation wages. At the same time, their purchasing power keeps decreasing. Thus massive poverty becomes the foundation of an economy totally oriented toward foreign countries.

The Greens maintain that honorable trade relationships based on partnership with the Third World are impossible under the present political circumstances. They support all efforts leading to a lessening of the Third World's dependence on the world market, and some Greens even favor the decoupling from the northern hemisphere that is now being discussed by several Third World leaders. An impressive characteristic of Green Third World policy is the recognition that such a policy has to start at home. Müller was quite clear on this point:

> We simply have to see that the wealth of industrialized countries, also the wealth of the individual, is clearly based also on the exploitation of the Third World. We first have to get used to this idea. . . .

There is no question about it. If we really want something like solidarity with the Third World—and I consider that a pressing and necessary matter—if we are really serious about it, . . . it surely means restrictions here as well. Anyone who doesn't see this is lying to himself about his solidarity with the Third World.

Accordingly, the Economic Program states:

> The political measures that can support . . . the Third World concern first of all the economic structure in the Federal Republic of Germany itself. The economic decentralization promoted by the Greens, based on utilization of existing local resources, and the economical use and recycling of raw materials reduce the necessity to import from the Third World. . . . Our orientation toward the internal economy is the basis for trade relations in solidarity with the economically weak countries of the Third World.

As far as the development of Third World countries is concerned, the Greens demand to stop all export of nuclear technology to these countries. They support the development of appropriate, labor-intensive technologies, fundamental land reform, and a shift from industrialization and export orientation toward increasing self-reliance. They also propose to establish a realistic, future-oriented price structure of natural resources that will give Third World countries the means for their own development, instead of forcing them to sell off their resources cheaply merely to ensure their short-term survival. Finally, the Greens support South-South relationships, affirming that "the people of the Third World themselves will find the solution to their problems."

The Green Economic Program contains not only specific proposals for ecological, social, and economic measures, but also suggestions for financing these measures. The Greens maintain that all federal, state, and local budgets have some room for maneuvering and that the financial means to support Green proposals do actually exist. The question of orienting the budgets accordingly is essentially political. Specifically, the Greens propose a reduction of defense spending; the immediate halt of other anti-ecological and uneconomical megaprojects (for example, nuclear power, further freeway construction, and the much-debated Main-Danube canal); a drastic reduction in expenditure for state pomp; a reduction of "trickle-down" subsidies; and the elimination of subsidies for energy-intensive enterprises.

The Green proposals for new tax policies are based on two guiding principles. First, the funding for social and ecological programs must be obtained from those wealthy individuals and corporations responsible for current harmful policies. Second, the purpose of Green financial policy is to avoid putting an additional tax burden on the economy and the population. The Greens maintain that the existing framework of taxation, if applied properly, is sufficient to generate the necessary means. The specific demands listed in the Economic Program include elimination of tax loopholes and of benefits and privileges counteracting progressive income tax schedules; a marked tax increase in the highest bracket; and elimination of joint tax returns for couples, which favor the rich and discriminate against women. In the long run, the Greens advocate a tax structure that should be socially just, clear, and understandable, oriented toward ecological criteria, democratic, and decentralized.

The last two characteristics—democracy and decentralization—are important aspects of the entire Green economic program. The envisaged economy will be not only ecological and socially responsible; it will also be grassroots-democratic. The Green principle of grassroots democracy has several meanings in the economic context. First, it means that those involved in production should decide themselves *what* is produced as well as *how* and *where* it will be produced. In other words, the Greens advocate self-managed, cooperative enterprises. We asked Jo Müller what model for self-management they had in mind.

Our model of self-management is above all compatible with the existing system. This is decisive. Let me give you an example. I am consulting with a company in Bremen, a tool factory, which is supposed to close. The board of employees expresses the desire to continue production because if it isn't continued they will all be out in the street. Now the workers there have said that they don't want to produce weapons but, rather, ecologically safe products, and they have proposed a few such products—heat pumps, biogas stations, etc.—all of which can be produced there. So we say, "This has to happen now." The orthodox leftists say, "For heaven's sake, you are worrying about the problems of management, of the capitalists." We say, "It is important to do something here and now, to help people now: First, to give them a chance to keep their jobs; second, to give them a chance to organize their work themselves; third—and this is the decisive, new aspect—to discuss *what* is produced." This is new. This is the qualitative aspect. This is a real advance.

Beyond self-managed enterprises of this kind, the Greens also apply the principle of grassroots democracy to their entire economic program. They emphasize that the new economic order they propose must develop from below, that they do not want to impose any solutions to the current problems but are merely making suggestions to be further elaborated and improved upon through ongoing work at the grassroots, as the Economic Program states:

> We are aware that the changes advocated by us cannot be reached by means of the parliamentary system alone. A fundamental transformation must occur in all areas of society. This can be achieved only by means of a movement from below, from those affected who recognize the necessity to take further developments into their own hands. We are not claiming to have found the solution to the problem nor to have a program that can be immediately implemented. We are of the opinion that this program must be modified and improved as the Greens and the extraparliamentary movements develop.

In another section of the Economic Program the Greens explicitly state that the new economic structures will have to emerge from the existing capitalist structures. They reject the Marxist notion of the "revolutionary vanguard" who plan the economy for the rest of us:

> It is clear to us Greens that the ecological and social conditions we seek must be developed out of the structures of the present capitalist industrial system. . . . Our principle of nonviolence means that all notions of dictating to the majority of people what is good for them are foreign to us. We trust that the wish to live and work in a different way will take hold of a great majority of people.

For all their trust in the grassroots movements, the Greens are nevertheless aware that their suggestions for restructuring the economy will run into the powerful opposition from all those who profit from the existing conditions. Therefore, they conclude the Economic Program with a section titled "Strategy for

Political Implementation." They expect that corporations and banks, as well as special interest groups and their representatives in parliament and in the political parties, will do everything they can to prevent a form of politics that might curtail their power and their profit. The Greens point out that this can already be seen in the strong anti-Green propaganda in the media. For example, the June 1983 issue of *Fortune* contained a thirteen-page advertising supplement from West German bankers and industrialists that, among other things, assured American investors that the Greens were merely gnats in the summer camp of open-ended growth: "Industrialists tend to dismiss the Greens as a misguided nuisance rather than a serious political threat to orderly government. But they are one of the main reasons," they conceded, "why some of the major construction activity has come to a halt." In addition, the Greens expose the repeated attempts of industry to play off employees and unions against environmentalists, which has been amply documented in the United States by Kazis and Grossman in *Fear at Work.*

The Greens plan to counteract the divide-and-conquer strategy of the ruling establishment by developing a grassroots network of individuals and organizations in which all those affected by the present destructive system support one another in solidarity in their multiple forms of resistance. They emphasize in the Economic Program that this network can succeed only by changing public consciousness: "The societal and economic changes can only be accomplished democratically and with the support of the majority of the population."

The forms of resistance encouraged by the Greens and listed at the end of the Economic Program include nonviolent actions developed by citizens' groups, intensive information and consciousness raising, the boycott of harmful products, the development of alternative projects and self-help organizations, resistance on the job and through the unions, and, finally, the parliamentary work of the Green party supplementing and supporting the other forms of resistance. Resistance alone, however, will not be sufficient. The Greens emphasize throughout their Economic Program that any resistance has to be motivated and accompanied by profound inner change, leading people to harmonize their individual aspirations and social needs with the new ecological consciousness.

Chapter 5

Green Perspectives on Social Issues

The Greens' vision of how we shall live in an ecological, nonexploitative society is no better developed than their economic vision for the future. Attention to both areas has been eclipsed during the party's first few years by the focus on environmental and peace issues. We wondered how the Greens' insistence on "self-determination and the free development of every human being," as their Federal Program declares, will be reconciled with the ecological law of interdependence and mutuality. How will we agree upon and implement the shared values that must underlie a new social orientation? What would human interactions—in everyday city life, for instance—be like in a Green society? How would our sense of self and family, friends and coworkers, community and global citizenship be different from that of our present consciousness? The Greens do not yet have answers to such fundamental questions. Neither are they attempting to construct a grand scheme of social ecology. Instead, they try—perhaps by default as well as design—to develop Green responses to a number of specific issues. We found that their most innovative work on social issues concerns women's rights, social control of technology, education, and healthcare. In addition, we present some of their proposals for minorities' rights and for cultural and media issues.

Building a peaceful, nonexploitative society requires progression beyond patriarchal values. In West Germany, as elsewhere, the largest group of exploited persons are women. Hence the title of the committee within the Green *Fraktion* for social issues is "Women and Society." The programs of the Green party at all levels address the structural and attitudinal walls women encounter in education, wage-earning, and politics. However, the major focus at the national level has been Paragraph 218 of West German federal law, which declares abortion illegal in the first three months unless the pregnant woman can get permission from three doctors on the basis of her health or eugenic problems, her economic situation, or proven rape, and illegal in all cases after three months. The current law is a compromise solution passed by the Social Democratic government in 1976. Prior to that, under the Christian Democrats, abortion was a criminal offense under almost any circumstances.

There is by no means a consensus within the Green party on abortion. As their Federal Program states, this issue brings into conflict two of their basic ideals: the vigorous support of self-determination and the commitment to protect all forms of life. Petra Kelly recalled for us that arguments over abortion "nearly blew the party apart" at the national assembly in Saarbrücken in 1980. The feminists argued that a woman must have control over her own body, while the conservative Green women—whom Kelly speaks of respectfully as "very good people, very moral and ethical"—argued that to approve of abortion is impossible because it kills in the same way that radiation and toxic chemicals kill.

> I and others tried to mediate between the two positions, but the majority opinion is that abortion cannot be ruled out as long as there are no ecological contraceptives, for men as well as women; as long as we have this incredibly hideous law, Paragraph 218, which says a woman is a murderer if she has an abortion yet does not include under the law the man who made the baby with her;

and, finally, as long as there is so little respect for life that fifteen million people a year—mostly children—are allowed to starve to death. The Greens maintain that because abortion is a dangerous procedure it must be done with the best medical care, with the best advisory services, and full coverage by government-sponsored medical insurance. Abortion, of course, is a class issue.

The official position of the Green party is that abortion should be made safe as well as legal and that research in safe, organic forms of contraception for both sexes should be adequately funded. (Many activists in the women's movement, by the way, are annoyed with the Green feminists for raising ecological issues concerning abortion rather than declaring an unqualified yes.) This issue caused the first split vote in the Bundestag among the Green *Fraktion*. Kelly explained the internal dynamics:

> We had a big discussion, and I presented the position that we must get rid of this law because it is unjust to women as it considers them murderers and leaves men out entirely. There should never be a situation where a board of men—some doctors and judges—tells a woman what she must do. That's impossible. It's completely patriarchal. Of the ten women in the *Fraktion,* eight of us voted for my position, but the majority of the men agreed with the Catholic nurse that much of the law should remain. Most of the women argued that the law must be repealed because it is being used by the Christian Democrats to cut off money from hospitals and family planning centers. The position we finally arrived at is that we reject Paragraph 218, we call for ecological and safe forms of birth control, and we call on men to take responsibility for contraception.

That position was presented in the Bundestag on 5 May 1983 in a ten-minute speech by Waltraud Schoppe, a high school teacher who has become a voice for women's rights in several areas. She is a serious yet friendly woman with long red hair and one who knows firsthand the struggles many women face, as she raised her two teen-aged sons alone for ten years. Schoppe's speech caused pandemonium in the Bundestag and was excerpted in many newspapers in West Germany. The Green men, who are not beyond sexist attitudes and behavior at times, were shocked as the laughter, thigh-slapping, jeering, and insults— most of which were not recorded by the Bundestag stenographers—intensified among their male colleagues in the other parties.

The following passages are excerpted from Waltraud Schoppe's speech, which was critiqued and approved by the entire Green *Fraktion* beforehand:

Ladies and gentlemen, dear friends.

The discussion of Paragraph 218 has begun once again. This paragraph, allowing women the termination of pregnancy under certain conditions, has not been able to lessen the suffering such a termination brings with it. This paragraph has humiliated women facing a crisis and has abandoned them to the arbitrary mercy of male experts. Especially women from lower economic strata, those who, for example, already have three children and cannot afford a fourth and who would be thrown into even greater financial difficulties by a pregnancy and the birth of a child, still find it possible, because of the financial assistance, to have an abortion. Women in better economic circumstances, of course, or those women who happened to be involved with a man who did not mind paying quite a bit for certain things, have always undertaken terminations of pregnancy with sufficient medical attention.

But if, as is now being discussed, the costs shall no longer be assumed by the government in cases of economic hardship this would mean an enormous negative extension of Paragraph 218 and the codification of social injustice.

(Applause among the Greens and representatives of the SPD)

One must assume that the criminalization of abortion on the basis of economic hardship will be the next step, followed possibly by a policy of making abortions illegal altogether.

An abortion is a time of trial for a woman and not a form of birth control.

(Applause among the Greens. Dr. Däubler-Gmelin, SPD [a woman]: "True, true!")

Nevertheless, there are situations in which the woman sees abortion as the only way out. With the decrease in social services, these emergency situations will occur more often. It serves no purpose to promote a grandiose program for the protection of unborn life when there is insufficient care for those already born. One protects the unborn best by protecting those now living.

(Applause among the Greens and certain representatives of the SPD)

We are living in a society where uniformity is the norm—uniform dress, living quarters, opinions, and also uniform morality. This uniformity is carried even into bed, where, just before falling asleep, people conduct a uniform exercise, with the man most commonly executing a careless penetration . . .

(Shouts from the CDU/CSU: "What is that supposed to be?")

. . . careless, for the majority of men do not use any contraceptive devices.

(Shouts from the CDU/CSU: "How do you know?")

Men are as responsible for pregnancy as women, but they evade their responsibility. The law punishes only women for abortion. It is only after the fact that men intervene again as the defenders of our morals, drafting criminal legislation, thundering against abortion from the pulpit as high dignitaries of the Church, and helping women or humiliating them, according to their convictions, as doctors.

(Applause among the Greens and individuals of the SPD)

A majority of the Greens, including myself, demand the elimination without replacement of Paragraph 218 and thus place ourselves behind the demands of the women's movement.

(Applause among the Greens)

When a woman has an unwanted pregnancy she must be allowed to decide herself whether or not she wants a child. The termination of pregnancy, being a question of moral attitude and personal circumstances, must not be the object of legal persecution.

(Applause among the Greens. Gerster, CDU/CSU: "What's your stand on euthanasia?")

Even with the legalization of abortion there remains an ethical conflict and a moral question that must be borne.

Our thoroughly patriarchal society is in a crisis. In times of crisis patriarchy abandons its pose of benevolence and points the oppressed back to their places. . . . Jobs are scarce, and during times of unemployment marriage is the only guarantee of economic and social security for women. Women thus exchange their autonomy for dependence on a man to whose wishes and interests they must subordinate themselves. This is what Mr. Kohl means—he is not here today—when he praises the family. Back into the family circle: That is the patriarchal-reactionary attempt to solve the unemployment problem.

We are not here to denounce those who, with great effort, attempt to find a bit of happiness in marriage. However, the prerequisite must be equality between the partners. This means that both should be able to participate in meaningful work, in politics, and in the education of their children.

(Applause among the Greens. Bohl, CDU/CSU: "Everyone can do that as he wants!") [Editors' Note: He used the male pronoun.]

In a society in which people are exploited, in which a politics is practiced that treats war as a calculated risk, in which deterrence means the capability to destroy human beings, violence becomes a means of resolving disputes even in the most intimate of human relationships.

(Shouts from the CDU/CSU: "You need rhetorical disarmament!")

In this society swamped with consumer goods, we demand economic security for all women, independent of the security of marriage. We demand a sufficient pension especially for women, even if they have not had a job because there was no job open to them.

(Applause among the Greens)

We demand punishment for rape within marriage. We call upon you to finally realize that women, too, have the right of self-determination over their bodies and their lives. We call upon you all to eliminate the day-to-day sexist stance here in parliament.

(Applause among the Greens and individuals of the SPD; laughter and shouts from the CDU/CSU and the Free Democratic Party (FDP). Shouts from the CDU/CSU: "The love Parliament! . . ." Further shouts and continuing laughter)

I see that I have hit a nerve. Obviously I have said something right.

(Applause among the Greens and individuals of the SPD; renewed shouts from the CDU/CSU)

By excluding women from the areas of work, politics, and culture, society is robbing itself of a creative impulse. We, Mr. Chancellor, view your politics of renewal with horror. We demand policies enabling women to decide for themselves how their lives shall be run.

(Shouts from the CDU/CSU: "How long are you going to lecture?")

Part of this self-determination is the decision of whether or not a woman wants a child. Instead of putting women under increased pressure with the negative extension of Paragraph 218, one should consider making birth control measures more effective. It would be a real turning point* if someone stood up here, for example, a chancellor, and pointed out to people that there are forms of lovemaking that are pleasurable while completely excluding any possibility of pregnancy.

(Laughter among the CDU/CSU and the FDP)

However, it is true that one can speak only of those things one understands at least a little.

(Applause among the Greens and individuals of the SPD; laughter among the CDU/CSU and the FDP. Shouts from the CDU/CSU)

Obviously there was little or no interest in the Bundestag in the kinds of legislation Schoppe was suggesting. However, her reference to marital rape was the first one in the federal government, and a male Social Democrat subsequently introduced a bill in the Bundesrat, the other federal house of legislators, that would outlaw such violence. Schoppe told us the large number of letters she received after the speech were divided along gender lines: positive from the women, negative from the men. Many of the letters from men were quite vulgar, assuring her, for instance, that she is "the biggest whore in Germany."

The Federal Program of the Greens calls for legislation in numerous areas of women's lives such as education, employment, health, mothers' rights, and violence against women. Gabi Potthast, another member of the Bundestag *Fraktion* who focuses on women's rights, suggested that the central figure of concern in the Greens' social programs should be the single mother because if she and her children can have a decent, fulfilling life then the structures and attitudes that make that possible will also benefit the more privileged and protected women, that is, those in marriages and/or with predominantly career-oriented lives. Potthast made a speech in the Bundestag proposing a permanent committee on women's issues that would

*Schoppe is making a reference to the buzz word "turning point" *(Wende)* used by the Kohl government in connection with the West German economic crisis.

have the power to veto bills discriminatory to women, but the jeering and shouts were so loud and frequent that most of her message went unheard.

Another issue of central concern to the Greens is the role of science and technology in society. The concept of social control of technology is widely supported among them, but our search for Greens who could explain the practical application of that ideal in such a wide and complex field was usually disappointing. The issues that concern them, as well as much of the West German public, are also problems in the United States: the loss of privacy through centralized computer data banks, the effects of automation in the workplace, the abuses that may result from dispersing office workers when computer terminals are installed in their homes, the damaging effects of new chemical compounds marketed by pharmaceutical and pesticide companies, the dangers of nuclear power and toxic wastes, and the potential hazards of releasing genetically engineered organisms into our biosphere.

In the spring of 1983 a citizens' movement arose to stop the proposed national census on the grounds that the information would be centralized in a "Big Brother" computer file—either within the national police data bank in Karlsruhe, which was supposed to be only for criminals, or in a similar system. The Greens brought the citizens' protest into the Bundestag by introducing a bill to halt to the census, and they worked with attorneys who were bringing a suit with the same aim in federal court. As a result the census was suspended by a court decision in late 1983. The Greens also joined the fight against proposed government-issued, computerized identification cards.

Like some lawmakers in the United States, the Greens are extremely wary of the computer files about one's personal life that will accumulate when—it hardly seems a matter of "if" anymore—two-way interactive cable television comes into the home bringing not only selected programs and movies but also certain newspapers (via teletext) and the means for shopping and business transactions—*and* keeps a record of everyone's selections for billing. In 1982 the American Civil Liberties Union, working with the League of California Cities, several city governments, and the cable industry's own organization, the California Cable Television Association, supported a landmark piece of legislation designed to outlaw all invasions of privacy via two-way cable. The bill was introduced in the state assembly by Gwen Moore (D-Los Angeles) and passed in September. It states that a customer's order file may not be released to private or government agencies except under court order, subpoena, or other "legal compulsion," in which case the cable company must notify the subscriber. The Greens, like many Americans, view such safeguards as frail protection once the personal files are established. Their main focus at this time is to require the new cable industry in West Germany to offer one-way cable service in addition to the two-way interactive service the industry is pushing, which would even incorporate one's telephone.

One of the most urgent and complex issues is the control of genetic engineering. The new biotechnologies are backed in Europe by huge pharmaceutical and chemical corporations. Among their aims is the production of high-yield crops grown from seeds that are fertile only once and hence must be repurchased every year. In 1983 the West German government spent more than $40 million on biotechnology research, and corporations spent several hundred million dollars more. Although the field is dominated by American firms, Europeans are entering the race to develop and market products synthesized by "bugs," that is, new biological organisms produced from gene-splicing or fermentation. Thus far such inventions have been confined to the laboratories, either by law or voluntary cooperation from the companies, but the safety is only temporary since the governments and corporations fully intend to market the results of the expensive research. In the United States the first two instances of releasing genetically engineered organisms in the open were approved by the National Institutes of Health in 1982. However, Jeremy Rifkin, author of *Algeny* (Viking Press, 1983), a critique of the coming era of bioengineering, filed suit in the fall of that year in Federal District Court in Washington to block release as a potential hazard.

The Greens, like many Americans, warn against the unforeseeable effects of releasing the altered organisms into the environment, for example, in the food industry, medicine, and other applications, as well as farming. Erika Hickel, a Green parliamentarian and professor of the history of science and the history of pharmacology at the Technical University of Braunschweig, introduced the discussion of genetic engineering in the Bundestag in fall 1983 and called for the formation of a permanent committee on the subject. (Like so many other Green proposals, this one was rejected by the rest of the Bundestag.) She told us of her plans for this area of social control of technology:

> Two steps are needed. The first is an educational program now to change the consciousness of people and make them aware of the issues. Later there should be a democratically controlled committee in every community where genetic engineering is conducted that would be composed of people working within the field who have doubts about the wisdom of pursuing such a path, people in the immediate area who might be affected, and people who have been involved in ecological education and activism. The committees would discuss whether the genetic engineering companies should proceed as they wish, or with some limitations, or not at all in certain areas. Such citizens' groups are being organized now in Braunschweig, Heidelberg, Bielefeld, and Munich. What I will try to do is bring together the critics from the ethical, philosophical, and religious sides who maintain that for ethical reasons we should not do genetic engineering at all, other people who want genetic engineering outlawed only with humans, and others who believe there is some middle path between the two positions. Then we will try to develop a political program and make that a topic of public discussion. We cannot stop it, of course, because of the huge corporate interests, but we can bring it into the public arenas of discussion within the government.

Hickel, who did postdoctoral work at the University of Wisconsin and has lectured at Yale, told us that the German citizens' movements have been very much inspired by the consumer movement in America and by such groups as Ralph Nader's organization. Even so, the successful aspects of the consumer movement are far less ambitious than what the Greens' theoretical statements in the Federal Program would require for social control of the huge "high-tech" industries. When we wondered about the practical possibilities, Hickel responded that the "watchdog" groups must become more political and that a fundamental reassessment of science and technology must occur.

The whole issue of the politics of science and technology is not developed yet in the Greens' program at all. It is missing. We must introduce into the scientific field our ecological thinking and our belief in participatory democracy. That is the key to responsible developments in the future. The problem is that in Germany, as in the United States, we have the attitude that science is value-free, but it was obvious to me as a woman—and also clear to me as a historian of science—that science is not at all value-free. It is a male-oriented endeavor in a system of male-oriented institutions dominated by male attitudes and male values. Only with the rise of the ecology and the Green movements did we begin to realize that society must establish, by democratic means, the values that are to be held in science. Here, as in your country, the large technological corporations do whatever they want because they pretend they are doing value-free work.

The widespread belief throughout the industrialized world that science is intrinsically value-free was, in fact, invalidated by science itself when Heisenberg showed that the patterns scientists observe in nature are intimately connected with the patterns of their minds. Heisenberg's discovery in quantum physics shattered the illusion of a value-free science: the results scientists obtain and the technological applications they investigate will be conditioned by their frame of mind, that is, their concepts, thoughts, and values. Although much of their detailed research will not depend explicitly on their value systems, the larger paradigm within which this research is pursued will never be value-free. Scientists, therefore, are responsible for their research not only intellectually but also morally.

In the discussion of science and values it is especially important to realize how much the scientific enterprise in our culture has been conditioned by the patriarchal value system. Several feminist scholars in the United States have shown that the domination and control of nature, which became the overriding goal of science in the seventeenth century, has gone hand in hand with the domination and control of women, who have been identified with nature throughout the ages. Carolyn Merchant, a historian of science at the University of California, Berkeley, discusses this issue in her book *The Death of Nature* (Harper & Row, 1980):

> In investigating the roots of our current environmental dilemma and its connections to science, technology and the economy, we

must reexamine the formation of a world view and a science which, by reconceptualizing reality as a machine rather than a living organism, sanctioned the dominion of both nature and women. The contributions of such founding "fathers" of modern science as Francis Bacon, William Harvey, René Descartes, Thomas Hobbes and Isaac Newton must be reevaluated.

We suggested to Hickel that the patriarchal values of dominance and control of nature seemed to be paired in science with an arrogance and technological ego that emphasizes "If we can figure out how to do it, let's do it, and someone else can ask questions about it later on." She agreed:

That's the argument scientists have been using for three hundred years, that they are the only ones able to make judgments about what they are doing. That is simply an ideology, in my opinion, which allows them to take privileges in society that no one else has, that is, to work freely without any control or social responsibility— and to accrue high status and salaries for their sometimes unwise and dangerous work. I fully agree with Paul Feyerabend [professor of philosophy at the University of California, Berkeley] that scientists must be challenged in their acting like the priests of our time when they bear responsibility for nothing.

Although the ecological world view promoted by the Greens is clearly supported by modern science, in particular by the emerging systems theory of life discussed in Chapter 2, the scientists developing this theory, who are profoundly holistic thinkers and often deeply spiritual individuals, are still a small minority within the scientific community, as are the ecologists within society. The majority of scientists and scientific institutions cling to the mechanistic and reductionist concepts of Cartesian science and do not realize that such a framework is no longer adequate to solve social, economic, and technological problems in a fundamentally interconnected world. That is why our high technologies are often antiecological, inhumane, and unhealthy. They may involve the latest discoveries in electronics, biochemistry, genetics, and other fields of modern science, but the context in which they are applied is that of the Cartesian conception of reality. They must be replaced, according to the Greens, by new forms of technology that incorporate ecological principles and are consistent with a new system of values.

We wondered about the positive vision that would evolve if Green values were widely adopted. "You mean the utopia?" Hickel asked laughingly. "It's my favorite subject!" She continued:

> The hard technology for which nature is no longer able to compensate on an evolutionary scale should give way to soft technology. And, of course, utopian science must be feminist science! [more laughter] I really believe women have a duty to help in the shift away from the old science because most men are involved in such a deep way in all their thinking, their values, their opportunities, and their social standards—their tight connection with the status quo—that they are unable, really, to make the deep change by themselves that would be necessary. They must learn to view nature not as potential chaos but as a teacher who shows us how to see it and listen to it and learn from it.
>
> Many scientists have entered the Green party, especially university faculty and students, and they understand intellectually that we must move away from regarding nature as an object to be dominated and exploited, but most of the men among them cannot make the connection to see the implications at other levels. They cannot really accept the consequences. Because they cling to patriarchal standards and values, they have much more difficulty than women in making the change.

The Greens hope that ecologically responsible scientists and engineers will take an active role in steering research away from the purely economic interests of corporations—a problem in American technology, as well—toward a science in the service of humanity and nature. They propose commissions composed of scientists and representatives from the public that would gather and present information on the consequences of various research projects. The Greens would also like to see strengthened support for research into ecological processes and relationships, and they support all efforts to maintain, or re-create, free scientific and political inquiry within the universities.

In the area of education the Greens call for programs and attitudes encouraging the full development of each student, which have influenced American education since the late 1960s but are largely absent from German schools. On the other hand, the decline in scholastic skills that plagues the American system today does not exist in West Germany. The focus of the Greens is to broaden and humanize the educational process without sacrificing academic standards. In their Federal Program, they call for improvement in several areas:

> Education today offers the child the following: pressure, for grades, driving competition, rewards for the spineless, anxiety sometimes leading to suicide, overcrowded classrooms and the simultaneous lack of instruction due to teacher unemployment. The present school and university system encouraging the model citizen and the model technocrat must be supplemented increasingly in those areas necessary for development of the total personality. Those include spiritual, intellectual, social, and ethical education, as well as the development of practical, physical, and especially creative faculties that are a basic human need. Also needed is instruction that encourages ecological consciousness, socially responsible and democratic behavior, and tolerance and solidarity toward one's fellow humans, both here and in other countries.

One of the reasons, besides the economic crisis, for the downfall of the Social Democratic government in October 1982 was the growing disillusionment with their centralizing of primary education and civil administration. Young children in West Germany now must travel long distances by school bus to large schools that are considered more modern than were the district schools. The Greens, however, want to build up the local schools and see them governed by the parents, teachers, and students. They feel that smaller schools would enable pupils of different ages to work together so they could become more self-directed and self-confident without authoritarian pressure from above. They also want to protect the private, alternative schools—such as the Waldorf, Glocksee, and Tvind schools—and hope that the educational experiments in those schools will affect the public schools. For example, they favor restructuring the kindergartens to encourage the multifaceted development of personality.

The Greens' Federal Program calls for a holistic orientation in the curriculum: "Education should encourage an interrelated, systemic thought process so that students can comprehend more easily society's interrelatedness and the nature of ecological cycles." They also want schools to train students to see clearly the individual interests that lie at the bottom of all conflicts. They feel that children should be taught to solve disputes peacefully and to formulate their own interests assertively in cooperation with others.

Gert Jannsen, a member of the Bundestag *Fraktion* who specializes in education, explained that the Greens want to see learning, living, and working more integrated through projects that teach a work process and build confidence. As their Federal Program states, they would like "music, theater, painting, work, and play" to be incorporated in German education. Jannsen also told us that most Greens favor teaching computer skills to all children to avoid the development of an elite class who alone acquires this knowledge in childhood.

The Greens also wish to introduce peace education in the schools. The Christian Democrats maintain that peace is best taught by providing information on governments' defense policies, armed forces, and weapons. The Social Democrats favor a somewhat broader position: there is violence among people and among societies so one must know ways to address it. The Greens, however, do not accept the inevitability of violence and wars and want to teach students that there are alternatives: "If we do not explain peace to our children, they will later explain war to others."

The American holistic health movement has spread to West Germany in recent years via a stream of books, lectures, and workshops. Since that movement is a leading force in the development of a new understanding of human nature, the relationships between people, and our embeddedness in the surrounding ecosystems, it is not surprising that the Greens' Federal Program calls for a system of "ecological medicine":

> Ecological medicine is holistic medicine. The sick person must be treated as a being subject to various environmental conditions. His or her self-conscious and self-determining personality must be strengthened and placed at the center of all care. Ecological medicine supports people's bodily defense mechanisms. Treatment should not focus on a single organ, as it often does in the current medical system. The patient must neither serve as a guinea pig for the pharmaceutical industry nor as a factor in the cost-benefit analysis for expensive pieces of equipment. Hence ecological medicine must avoid the overconsumption of drugs, unnecessary surgery, and overly technological mega-clinics. . . .

Small hospitals in closer proximity to people should be established, as well as sufficient outpatient clinics. . . . Treatment in these facilities will have to deal also with the social and psychological aspects of illness and encourage a doctor-patient relationship that is no longer characterized by the ignorance and dependence of the patient. . . . In addition, alternative healthcare projects exploring methods of natural healing and promoting healthy life-styles should be developed.

The Federal Program of the Greens identifies old-paradigm thinking as a major part of the problem with healthcare, not only the invasive allopathic treatments mentioned above but also the unrealistic separation between health problems, environmental conditions, and "our work, our leisure, our life in general." They maintain, "The forces destroying our health and the health of our environment are the same forces driving the present economic system." Hence the Greens call for stronger controls on the use of pesticides, chemicals, and medicines that cause side effects. As we discussed in the previous chapter, they want to outlaw all advertising of tobacco, alcohol, and drugs. Finally, they point out that health will not improve unless stress in the workplace is reduced, especially that caused by technology designed with indifference toward the people tending it.

The social programs of the Greens extend to improving conditions for several specific groups: the elderly, the handicapped, children and adolescents, homosexuals, foreign workers, and Gypsies. The proposals in some of these areas are not yet well developed, but they are united by the core principles of self-determination and civil rights. Among their proposals for the elderly are "the legal, social, and material prerequisites that would make multigenerational communal living possible," better programs for home-visiting nurses and other community-based forms of assistance, and a tax-free guaranteed minimum income. They also advocate communal living with the handicapped, plus better educational and employment opportunities for them and improved access to buildings and mass transit. The Greens maintain that the psychological and physical living space of children and adolescents is increasingly restricted in industrialized societies. They support laws requiring severe punishment for violence against children, and they oppose "repressive laws that thwart the tenderness, warmth, and self-development of adolescents." The Greens reject all social and legal forms of discrimination against homosexuals and call for revision of several paragraphs in West German federal law.

Discrimination against the four million "guest workers" in West Germany—mostly from Turkey, Italy, Yugoslavia, Greece, and Spain—is implicitly condoned by the major parties and by most of the population. Only the Greens demand that the foreign workers, who, after all, made the German economic miracle possible with their supply of unskilled and semiskilled labor, be considered along with their dependents "an important and fully equal part of the population." The Greens oppose the limited duration of work and residency permits for foreigners and the denial of citizenship to them. They believe that foreigners should be allowed to vote at the local level immediately and at the federal level after five years of residency; to call attention to this proposal they symbolically put the name of a "guest worker" at the top of their local electoral list even though he is not permitted to vote, let alone run. (The West German electoral system is explained in Chapter 6.) The Greens often join demonstrations demanding the release of Turkish political prisoners in both West Germany and Turkey, which is controlled by a junta of pro-NATO military men. Finally, the Greens believe that the children of foreigners should be treated neither as outsiders nor Germanized but, rather, should have the right to live as equals according to their own customs.

On the issue of culture, the Greens oppose the development of a "culture industry" because "it breaks the connection between culturally creative people and those to whom the creative expressions are addressed, developing instead pure 'culture consumption,' because it accepts cultural underdevelopment caused by hard working conditions and lack of education, because it keeps a large number of people in a state of passivity, and because it encourages the marketing of culture and the cult of 'stars'." Rather than "professional culture factories," the Greens support the grassroots cultural movement in theater, dance, music, art, and literature. They also want the "classical cultural institutions"—museums, theaters, concert halls, libraries, and movie houses—to concern themselves more than they have with the requirements and daily problems of the population and to feature more traveling exhibits for the suburbs and countryside.

In the area of the media, the Greens oppose the swallowing of small newspapers by more heavily capitalized newspapers and the forced mergers of independent newspapers because of rising costs of printing and of covering events. They state in their Federal Program, "A comprehensive and critical analysis of the news takes place ever less frequently. In order to create once more a true marketplace of ideas, it will be necessary to pass retroactive legislation hindering monopolization and unification of the news industry. State support for struggling newspapers should be increased." The Greens insist that the system of free public radio and television in West Germany be maintained with no exception for the new cable system and with no commercials.

The Green perspective on social issues—the rights of women and minorities, education, the role of science and technology, healthcare, and many others—is guided by the realization that the social, economic, and ecological realms are inextricably interlinked. Although the term *sozial,* which incorporates economic considerations, has different shades of meaning for different schools of thought within the Greens (as we discussed in Chapter 2), they all agree that the expression of ecological *and* social consciousness is the very essence of Green politics. Manon Maren-Grisebach was emphatic on this point:

> For me the social realm is not separate at all. Critics often come and ask me: Where do you stand within the Greens? Are you part of the social or the ecological movement? This question, for me, is totally irrelevant because it is based on a separation of areas that I cannot separate. Ecologically recognized necessities can never be realized if one does not know the relevant social mechanisms. Moreover, I believe that one should not take the term "ecological" in such a narrow sense that it concerns only the exchange of matter and energy with nature. Ecology is also a concept that has to be transferred to social questions, which we have done all along.

Chapter 6

Bringing Grassroots Ideals into Electoral Politics

Participatory democracy is not for the impatient. The development of a party program, which also stands as a campaign platform, involves extensive consultation with the grassroots membership. The Green party in the state of Hesse, for instance, selected a program committee who invited suggestions from all members on the issues of peace; employment and the economy; energy; the environment; city planning, living places, traffic management; democratic rights; culture and education; women; children and young people; elderly people; discrimination against minority groups; and health. They also included an appendix presenting four global alternatives for the future. When the committee members had compiled the ideas from the general membership, they sent the program back to the one hundred local groups in their state, asking for refinements, changes, and further ideas. After the committee had incorporated the changes, a statewide party assembly met for six consecutive weekends to discuss the various points in contention and to agree upon a final draft of the program.

Representative democracy is seemingly more efficient, as party leaders appoint a few people to sit in smoke-filled rooms and compose the campaign platform, which is then approved at a convention after some discussion. What the Greens in Hesse, as elsewhere in West Germany, gained through the participatory process, however, was a 165-page program with which nearly all party members identified since they had worked on its evolution. It was a document for which they could campaign sincerely and enthusiastically, one that addressed all the key issues in their state with the best and most innovative Green thought. Voters knew that the Greens' program had been composed by their neighbors throughout the state rather than by a handful of professional politicians. This is part of the reason the Hesse Greens won an impressive 8 percent of the vote statewide in September 1982, the first time they ran for the legislature. (The Greens won 5.6 percent nationally the following March.)

The Greens also use grassroots, participatory democracy to select their candidates. In the West German electoral system, the ballot has two parts: one is simply the names of the parties running, and the other is a list of individuals' names under each party. The system of proportional representation awards a party the number of seats in a legislative body that corresponds to the proportion of the vote they won as a party. For example, the Hesse Greens' 8 percent of the vote got them nine seats in the state legislature (*Landtag*). Those Greens who became legislators were the first nine names on the party's direct-vote list—unless the citizenry reorganized the list by giving a high number of votes to names further down. This feature of the electoral system, allowing voters to overrule the selection of a party clique, was devised in the years immediately following the Nazi era.

A prospective candidate for the Greens first asks the local group whether he or she may have an endorsement. An endorsed candidate then submits to the state organization a résumé and political statement, which are distributed to all members. Finally, the candidates go before a weekend statewide assembly, explain their political perspectives and what their priorities would be in the legislature, and answer questions from the floor.

There were twenty places on the list for the 1982 election,

since the Hesse Greens anticipated winning no more than ten seats and would need an equal number of successors because of the rotation system. Approximately fifty people ran for the twenty slots in 1982, but not all ran for the top several positions. They were voted on by the six hundred people in attendance at the party assembly, and each position required two or three rounds of voting. To win a particular place, a candidate had to receive 50 percent of the vote. If no one received this, there was a second round of voting with the same rule. If again no one received an absolute majority, a third vote was taken with the place going to the candidate with a simple majority. (By the third vote, many of the original candidates for a particular slot had dropped out.)

The Greens' campaign was conducted mostly at the district level, coordinated by a small statewide office. Their strategy consisted of three parts: distributing their printed material, working with citizens' movements, and producing a few brief ads for television. The central publication among the Hesse Greens' printed material was the program, which was illustrated with numerous photographs of various situations in the state. They also published a short version of the program in pamphlet form with the holistic title *Thinking within Contexts: Acting for a Future Worth Living In.* In it they discussed nature conservation, health, jobs, energy, traffic, centralization, and democracy. They employed a cross-linked presentation to show the interrelated ecological and economic consequences in these areas resulting from large-scale projects in progress: black type for consequences of the partially completed Runway West at the Frankfurt International Airport, and red type for consequences of the proposed nuclear processing plant near Frankenthal. The Hesse Greens also utilized the traditional association of red with the Social Democrats and black with the Christian Democrats. Black type on a red-screened block presented the causes of the problems through old-paradigm thinking and cited the responses of the traditional parties. Green type indicated the Greens' proposals.

In addition, the Greens printed a colorful poster showing the Hesse lion, their state symbol, having stepped down from his ferocious, medieval pose and become a rounded, smiling cat lounging contentedly on the grass before green, rolling hills. The slogan was "Let Hesse Become Green." Another Hesse poster featured a wasteland of sawed-off tree stumps (the result of reckless development policies in old-paradigm thinking) from which strong, bright green tendrils were beginning to grow. The Hesse Greens also used some of the posters printed by the national office, especially the basic one with sunflowers and the "four pillars" of Green politics: ecology, social responsibility, grassroots democracy, and nonviolence.

During the campaign, the Hesse Greens distributed their printed material from information tables, particularly in town squares on market days. In reaching a broad spectrum of voters, the Greens were assisted by support groups from various citizens' movements, for example, the anti-nuclear-power movement, the environmental movement, the network of citizens fighting construction of Runway West, the peace movement, the women's movement, and the Third World movement. We assumed at first that the Greens sent party representatives to speak to those groups and request their help, but we were told that the process was the opposite. In most cases, the citizens' movements approached the Greens to offer campaign assistance because they realized that only the Greens would represent their perspective in the legislature. Hence, even in some districts with no Green party organization, the Greens won more than 10 percent of the vote. In a district near the huge cleared site that later became Runway West, they got 18 percent, and one town gave them 33 percent. (The Greens oppose the additional runway because it will have severe ecological consequences and because it is not even needed since air traffic is expected to *decrease* with the new larger planes. In addition, there is evidence to suggest that its real purpose is military as there is a NATO/American base adjacent to it.)

A media group in Frankfurt volunteered their services to produce several television spots for the Greens' campaign, which were later used by the national party in the Bundestag election in March 1983. Television in West Germany is government-owned so all parties receive equal free air time. Beyond that they may purchase additional time, although the Greens did not do so. One of the Green ads featured a man ringing the doorbell of a row house and then stepping back to lean casually against the five-foot-high nuclear rocket he is bringing. When the householder opens the door, the man says, "Hello! Here's a nuclear warhead to put in your backyard so you can be safe!" The householder expresses astonishment at the suggestion, and the man continues, "Oh, you don't want to live with nuclear weapons? Well, then, the only thing for you to do is declare your yard a nuclear-free zone." Soon neighbors all along the block are hammering signs into their small lawns declaring such a zone.

Another ad began with a camper in a forest taking photographs of the trees, which are nearly bare with only a few brown leaves remaining, as in autumn. He unloads his film and dips it into the nearby river to develop the pictures, which he then admires. Then Professor Hoimar von Ditfurth, a widely respected ecologist and Green supporter who hosts a nationally broadcast television program about issues in science, enters the scene. Von Ditfurth explains to the audience that the forest is not really in its autumnal phase, at which news the photographer looks disappointed and says merely, "Oh." It is an ordinary forest, continues von Ditfurth, that has been affected by acid rain, and the river is just one of the ordinary German rivers, some of which contain so much chemical waste that they are almost like processing fluid. Instead of saying "Vote Green!" this ad and all the others end with an animated version of the poster showing green tendrils growing from the tree stumps and then the party's logo, the plump rounded letters spelling their name:

DIE GRÜNEN

In another televison spot, a family is sitting around their dinner table when the lights go out. They all begin to cry and yell, and one family member whines, "This has happened because the Green party ended nuclear power!" Suddenly the door opens and Professor von Ditfurth enters and turns on the lights. He explains to the audience that there will be no power failures in the future, even without dangerous and expensive nuclear power, if society will seriously develop renewable sources of energy such as wind power, solar power, and cogeneration, along with conservation measures. Contradicting the government's assertion that the failure to build nuclear plants would lead to power shortages by 1980, this ad informs West Germans that even without nuclear sources of energy, their country now has a 40 percent overcapacity in energy production.

A fourth television ad features a baby playing on the grass. He will be a voter in the year 2000. Sequences of him reaching out and exploring his environment are alternated quickly with scenes of militarism, of pollution, and of dead plants.

Not only were the ads produced with volunteer labor but nearly all of the campaigning was carried out by volunteers. Total campaign costs, mostly production and overhead, totaled 200,000 DM (about $80,000). The Hesse Greens subsequently received 800,000 DM (about $320,000) from the government because West German law provides that a political party shall be paid 3.5 DM (about $1.40) for every vote received in a state or federal election. This ability to earn four times more than they spend in elections is typical of the Greens. The major parties, on the other hand, conduct expensive campaigns with large paid staffs and so usually acquire debts in elections. In 1983 the Christian Democrats and the Social Democrats voted together to pass a new federal law that will increase the payments to 5 DM per vote. Even though they would benefit from the increase, the Greens in the Bundestag opposed the majority vote on the grounds that it would mean taking more money from the taxpayers to prop up the unresponsive, unprogressive, and largely corrupt major parties.

The grassroots structure of the Green party is somewhat complicated and is presented in Appendix A. In general, it is a pyramid structure with some crucial distinctions. Power resides—at least theoretically—at the base (die Basis), which directs the upper levels; there is no apex point embodied in one leader, as the "highest" levels are two committees (the national executive committee and the national steering committee), whose functions are primarily administrative; and the base is directly connected to the top in many respects without having to go through intermediary levels. For instance, delegates to the Greens' national assemblies, at which key issues are voted on and the three party speakers as well as the national executive committee are selected, come directly from the local groups (at a ratio of one delegate for every twenty members) rather than being chosen by the state-level party.

The Greens' structure has worked quite smoothly except for one area of contention at both the state and federal levels: the relationship and "pecking order" between the two highest committees and the *Fraktion* in the legislative body. The problem is greater at the federal than state level and was a dominant theme at the Greens' annual congress in Duisburg in November 1983, by which time the rapport between the eleven-person national steering committee and the twenty-seven parliamentarians had become extremely strained, for reasons we discuss in Appendix A. Due to the heavy workload and the impending debate in the Bundestag on deployment of the Pershing II and cruise missiles a few days later, the parliamentarians failed to prepare a group report on their work, as requested. They were made to wait until 10:00 P.M. to speak, and then their attempt to present individual reports was cut off after the first one. Many of the older Greens told the parliamentarians they were shocked at the treatment and the contempt that was being encouraged among the grassroots toward the supposedly elitist parliamentarians. In his customary role of mediator, August Haussleiter, addressing the assembly, compared the Greens' entry into the Bundestag with the assault on the Bastille as a triumph at the forefront of the "nonviolent ecological revolution." He granted that the avant-garde role of the *Fraktion* must be watched critically, but added that their difficult work requires the understanding and cooperation of the grassroots.

In contrast to the major parties, who report to the public on their doings only infrequently, often just before an election, the Greens are committed to relaying privileged information that usually does not get outside the forums of power. Indeed, they have become skilled communicators. All levels of the party produce a flood of printed material—on recycled paper, they hasten to add. There are two main types of publication: reports from the Green *Fraktion* in legislative bodies, and reports on projects, actions, and issues from the party.

The Green *Fraktion* in the Frankfurt city council, for example, issued a 450-page report on their first two years in office titled *What Have the Greens Done on the City Council?* The cover photograph featured an elderly couple looking assertively from their apartment window over a banner they had hung: "Finally, planning for people!" The report included textual presentations, photostats of official letters from the *Fraktion* to the government, photostats of newspaper accounts, and numerous photographs. The focal points were nine issues or clusters of issues. Also included were discussions and a list of all the legislation they had proposed. A summary was published in a four-page pamphlet. The price of the unabridged report was 15 DM ($6) with a 30 percent discount to bookstores, citizens' movements, and Green members, but most Green publications are distributed free of charge.

Most of the Green *Fraktion* groups in the state legislatures produce monthly bulletins that are distributed through many networks. Similarly, the Bundestag *Fraktion* issues the monthly *Green Bulletin,* which is usually about fifteen pages long. The Green *Fraktions* in all legislative bodies also publish pamphlets and reports on special issues.

Publications of the party include newsletters at the local and county level published at two- to six-week intervals. Nearly every state and city-state party produces a monthly or bimonthly newspaper or magazine, often featuring a cartoonlike mascot: a crocodile in Bremen, a horse in Hannover, a beaver in Hamburg, a hedgehog in Berlin. The most ambitious of these state periodicals is the *Green Hesse Journal,* a magazine that often runs to more than forty pages; it sells for 2 DM (80¢). The cover of the issue following the election in September 1982 featured the Greens' friendly version of the state lion lounging happily in a hammock strung between one pillar of the state legislature building and a tree. (The professional quality of the Hesse Greens' publications and press releases is largely due to Jutta Ditfurth, a journalist and city council member in Frankfurt.)

The national party publishes a weekly newspaper, *Die Grünen (The Greens),* in Munich, home of August Haussleiter, who is the managing editor as well as one of the six content editors—three in Munich and three elsewhere. Haussleiter laughingly informed us that when the editorial meetings extend past midnight it is he, at age seventy-eight, who has the most energy. He also told us proudly that *The Greens* is the only party newspaper that breaks even financially strictly on subscription income—4.80 DM (about $2) per month. The Christian Democrats' newspaper receives funding from corporations, and the Social Democrats' newspaper operates with a large deficit even though it receives donations from labor unions. *The Greens* is produced entirely with voluntary labor and is controlled to a great extent by the grassroots, who often send the newspaper up to seventy letters per day.

More than 10,000 copies of *The Greens* are printed every week and each issue brings forty to sixty new subscribers.* More than 7,000 of their weekly copies bear a four-inch-high title in green ink proclaiming *The Greens* and their "four pillars." Another 3,000 copies are published under the name *Die Unabhängen (The Independents)*, which was formerly the title of a newspaper from Haussleiter's ecological organization in Bavaria, the Union of Independent Germans (AUD), which became part of the Greens. Some subscribers in conservative areas prefer to receive the Greens' newspaper under a more discreet heading, and others find they can better spread Green ideas to new people with this neutral packaging. The content in both versions is identical.

The national headquarters in Bonn produces a monthly bulletin, *Grüner Basis Dienst (Green Grassroots Service)*, as well as frequent *Pressespiegel*, that is, collections of photocopied newspaper articles about the Greens. There are also plans for a national party magazine. As of fall 1982, *Moderne Zeiten (Modern Times)*, a German radical-left magazine that has covered the Greens extensively, was vying for the contract, but many Greens insisted that the new magazine be an independent publication of the party. They pointed out that the national party has experience in successful commercial publishing with books such as *Die*

---

*American readers of German who wish to subscribe may write to *Die Grünen*, Postfach 20 24 22, 8000 Munich 2, West Germany.

Zukunft des Sozialstaats (*The Future of Socially Responsible Nations*, 1983), an anthology.

The strategies and options open to the Greens as a political party in West Germany are circumscribed to some extent by their nation's dark inheritance. Contemporary historians have noted that the Germans have learned many lessons from the Nazi era but not necessarily the right ones. The following examples illustrate how the specter of the past is used and confused in response to the Greens' grassroots ideals and political actions:

- Direct voting (rather than the double-list system now used in West Germany) is considered dangerous since it was manipulated by the Nazis during their rise and reign of power. The government reminded the Greens of this in May 1983 in refusing their proposal for a national direct referendum on deployment of the Pershing II and cruise missiles. (Polls at that time showed 74 percent of the public opposing deployment.) Heiner Geissler, Minister for Family and Youth and Secretary-General of the Christian Democrats, went so far as to claim that the pacifists of the 1930s paved the way for a military government and so were responsible for Auschwitz!

- The term *Bewegung* (movement) has Nazi connotations since Hitler called his scheme the National Socialist movement and appealed to certain traditional values and classless idealism. Hence the ecology movement, anti-nuclear-power movement, peace movement, etc., are called citizens' "initiatives" (*Bürgerinitiativen*). The Greens have to proceed very gingerly in presenting their concept of a Green movement that is larger than the party and will lead to a new society.

- Symbols are also problematic since the Nazis used them so successfully. We found the Greens' logo, sunflower, and graphic style on the posters quite striking and effective, so we were surprised when the party's general manager, Lukas Beckmann, spoke of them in a very offhanded manner. We asked him whether the Greens use symbols to express the deep meaning of their concepts beyond words:

> No, that's too dangerous. Symbols generally contain a great deal of energy. If I lived in The Netherlands, I might have no problems

with symbols, but it is very difficult here to know beforehand how the German codes will be read, how the German soul will receive symbols. We have no problem with the sunflower, but because of the historical situation here it's better to transmit ecological politics through humans than symbols. Our graphics were simply selected from suggestions by different artists.

• A spiritual dimension to a political movement is extremely suspect, as we discussed in Chapter 2. When the Greens speak with reverence of a subtle connection to the Earth and nature, older Germans are reminded of the Nazi teaching that German soil is sacred, as is her "superrace" of citizens.

• Because of Hitler, strong leadership is not trusted in principle. Hence people who are too charismatic, too effective, too noticeable, too creative in their theories, or too sought after by the media are often attacked and to an extent devoured by the Greens. Of course, much of this is just garden-variety jealousy, but it can be called "politically correct" in the context of post-Nazi Germany.

• Since Hitler manipulated women by lauding the "sacred" role of German mothers, many Marxist feminists today are uncomfortable with programs in the Greens and elsewhere that focus attention on the rights of mothers. (German Marxists have developed elaborate theories about the roots of fascism. Some German Marxist feminists even consider Adrienne Rich's book *Of Woman Born*, Bantam Books, 1977, fascistic because it explores the dynamics of motherhood in powerful, far-reaching ways!) Marxist-oriented feminists within the Greens prefer to focus on demands for full employment of women, rather than alternatives needed by mothers, such as part-time jobs, job-sharing, and neighborhood cooperatives. Gisela Erler, a Green feminist in Bavaria, told us that the Marxist-oriented feminists within the Greens generally ignore the dual economy and support an industrialized culture.

In spite of the shadowy parameters in German politics, the Greens do use symbols in their actions, speak of the spiritual dimension of life, cultivate a broad-based movement, and press for direct referendums on major issues. Their major constraint within the legislative bodies, however, is the fact that they are a very small minority party. They do not have the power to get their bills passed, or in most cases to block unwise bills proposed by the major parties. Their principal function is to serve as the political voice of the citizens' movements within the city councils, county assemblies, state legislatures, and the Bundestag—as well as to channel inside information out to the citizens' groups.

The strategic importance of their opposition role depends on the proportions of representation in the legislative body of the Christian Democrats, the Social Democrats, and the Free Democrats. (The Free Democrats, or FDP, are a small liberal party comprised mainly of professionals and small-business people who were long in coalition with the Social Democrats until fall 1982 when they switched to the conservatives, a surprising move that sent many of their members into the SDP and the Greens.) The conservative sweep that accompanied Kohl's victory in March 1983 brought a CDU majority in most legislative bodies. However, in some cases their proposals could be blocked if the small FDP *Fraktion* voted with the Social Democrats. (In certain local areas their old coalition still held.) In other situations the SPD needed both the Free Democrats and the Greens to outnumber the right. Often the major parties and the FDP vote together in solidarity with old-paradigm values, and the Greens are the sole opposition.

In the small number of cases when the Greens have managed to get a bill through a legislative body, their temporary allies have been variously the left or the right. For example, the Greens on the Freiburg city council proposed that the city stop salting the streets during winter, except when truly necessary, because it was killing trees. The Christian Democrats voted with them while the Social Democrats opposed the measure on the grounds that the protection of jobs, including those of street-salters, is more important than ecological concerns.

The most fear-provoking arrangement for the major parties was one in which each lacked a majority so that the Green *Fraktion* was the deciding factor. This occurred in Hamburg from June to December 1982 and became known as "the Hamburg situation." Because such unpredictability was perceived as potentially dangerous by the German public, the city's newspaper published the agenda of the city council every day and reported its actions closely. Thomas Ebermann, who served in the Green *Fraktion* then, told us it was in fact a very positive period:

> In restaurants, bars, or anywhere you went people were very well informed about what the city council was doing. There was a lot of involvement. Especially because of this situation, there was cooperation and the council always reached a consensus on the major issues such as the budget and industrial financing. Only in discussions about nuclear-free zones in Hamburg was there dissent.

Perhaps the most difficult situation for the Greens developed in the Hesse state legislature between the elections of September 1982 and 1983. The Social Democrats needed the Greens in order to outnumber the Christian Democrats, but the working relationship between the first two went from tenuous to extremely estranged. The Social Democratic party is considered by many Greens to be the "Yes . . . but" party, as in "Yes, nuclear power is dangerous and costly . . . but perhaps we should continue building plants only until 1990." The head of the Social Democrats in Hesse, Holger Börner, is generally pro-growth and anti-ecological, so he made it difficult to find common ground. The SPD initially expected the Greens to vote with them, but the Greens repeatedly asked for compromises on the Social Democrats' growth-oriented budget and energy policies. Conversely, even when the Greens proposed bills that were close to certain traditional SPD positions, they refused to vote with the Greens and thereby lose face.

A split developed within the Green *Fraktion* in Hesse about how much cooperation could or should be offered. The fundamentalists (or fundamental oppositionists) said none was possible in that situation. Meanwhile, the frequent dissents of the Greens proved, as far as the two major parties were concerned, that the Greens were "animals," incapable of conducting politics. While many Greens feel that the antagonism was unavoidable in Hesse, some disagree. The Baden-Württemberg Greens, who have good working relationships with the other parties in their state legislature, generally believe that if the Hesse Greens were more skillful politicians, they would not have missed the opportunity to split the SPD. Thomas Ebermann of the radical-left Hamburg Greens, who often find common ground with the left wing of the Social Democrats, called the fundamentalists "silly"

Greens. Jo Müller, of the Bremen Greens, published an article called "Against Fundamental Opportunism," charging that the fundamental oppositionists tend to fall in love with themselves as a movement and forget the goals of the Greens.

During the summer of 1983 the Social Democrats in the Hesse legislature voted with the Christian Democrats to dissolve the legislature and call for new elections in late September—even though the SPD realized that the right might increase their number of seats. The Social Democrats preferred risking a clear CDU majority than having to answer the challenging questions of the Greens on various issues.

Within that hostile and frustrating context, a member of the Green *Fraktion* conducted a symbolic action that sent shock waves through the West German public. At a reception on 2 August in the legislature to which U.S. military officers had been invited, Frank Schwalba-Hoth, a twenty-seven-year-old former student of theology, threw some of his blood, carried in a small plastic bag, on U.S. General Paul S. Williams, Jr. Schwalba-Hoth said at the time that it was "blood for the bloody army" and was "for Vietnam, Chile, and El Salvador." West German television showed his act nearly every hour for the next two evenings and added that the entire Green *Fraktion* in Hesse had voted to approve this action beforehand.

The effect of Schwalba-Hoth's act on the election was widely discussed, and the Greens' national steering committee was split over whether to endorse it. Twenty percent felt it was violence, but the majority's statement declared that the act had sprung from powerlessness and helplessness in the face of U.S. policies preparing for war in Central America and in Europe and that the act had not been directed toward the person of Paul S. Williams but against the general's much decorated uniform as representative of a ruthless system. Many other Greens, however, agreed with Kelly, Bastian, and von Ditfurth, who spoke out strongly against the action on the grounds that nonviolent action means never abusing the dignity of any person.

In the Hesse election of 25 September 1983 the Greens disappointed the left and the right by winning 5.9 percent of the vote and again entering the legislature. Since this election had been perceived by numerous political observers as a test of whether the small party would merely fade away, the results delighted Greens all over West Germany. Many felt the public was willing to overlook the Greens' tactical errors, such as the blood-throwing, because of their strong and commonsense stand on the issues. On the same day as their Hesse victory, the Greens displaced the Free Democrats as the third-ranking party in the Bremen legislature, causing many political analysts to assert that the Greens have now stabilized as the third most important party in West German politics.

The Hesse election also caused the CDU/FDP coalition to lose its majority, which was interpreted widely as a vote of no-confidence for Kohl's policies, while the Social Democrats increased their total votes by 5 percent. The number of Green seats decreased from nine to seven, but the Social Democrats' fifty-one seats (compared to forty-three for the CDU and nine for the FDP) gave them a ruling majority only with the cooperation of the Green *Fraktion.* That such a situation would recur after the election had been the SPD's worst nightmare. However, both the Greens and the Social Democrats moved surprisingly smoothly toward reconciliation. The Green *Fraktion* in Hesse—with a nudge from the larger party—decided by a three-fourths majority to offer the SPD "continual cooperation," which was a victory by the "realists" over the "fundamentalists." Subsequent polls indicated that the majority of Hesse citizens wanted the Social Democrats to work with the Greens and create a stable government. Not only did the majority of the SPD at their statewide congress that fall opt for "serious negotiations" with the Greens, but even Börner himself delivered a two-hour speech in favor of such cooperation.

The Hesse Greens requested that their negotiations with the SPD be held in an auditorium so that the public could attend. The negotiations spanned several months, throughout which the national Green party was far from united over the matter. The "fundamentalists" continued to insist from the sidelines that no deals should be made, while some of the more extreme "realists" seemed bent on achieving an agreement at any cost to Green ideals. A mediating role between these two camps was attempted by one of the Hamburg Greens, since they had successfully maneuvered through a similar situation in

1982. At one point, even the Greens' national steering committee advised against continuing the negotiations because the sacrifices outweighed the rewards. Nonetheless, agreement over a three-year period of "cooperation" between the Greens and the SPD was finally reached. Among the concessions the Greens won from the SPD were the following: no new nuclear power plants, a safety study of nuclear power plants to be conducted by *Öko-Institut,* no new freeway construction, no night flights on Runway West (requested by the adjacent communities), no discrimination in government jobs because of one's political orientation *(Berufsverbot),* funding for shelters for battered women, and the establishment of a professorship in Women's Studies at the University of Frankfurt. In general, the Greens are eager to demonstrate to the public that they are capable of forming a responsible partnership that can function effectively as a majority government. Such proven ability would aid the Greens in the federal election of 1987, when they would like to win enough seats to create a "Hesse situation" in the Bundestag. Looking forward to that goal, Jo Müller, a leading advocate of the "realist" position who thinks like a shrewd Chicago ward politician, told us simply, "It's better to have a Green minister in the government than to have Green *Berufsverbot.*"

The Greens, though a very small *Fraktion* everywhere, often proposed half of the bills and "applications," that is, oral declarations, of a legislative session. The third form of parliamentary action in West Germany is the formal presentation of questions to the government, something the Greens do frequently. One of the common projects of the Greens is to focus public attention on budgetary decisions of city councils and state legislatures. In some cities the Greens hold public hearings on the budget to which they invite numerous citizens' groups and the press.

At the state level the Baden-Württemberg Greens have been the most successful at getting legislation passed. Like the Greens in the state legislature of Lower Saxony, these Greens see their role as educating the other parties about the necessity for change. The "ecological reformist" Greens in Baden-Württemberg are aided by a liberal political culture in that state (although there are some very conservative areas in the countryside) and by a tradition of somewhat gentle politics. For example, during the German revolution of 1918 the king assembled the Swabian people before the palace in Stuttgart (now the capital of Baden-Württemberg) and explained that there seemed to be a revolution in the rest of Germany so he had to leave them. Then everyone walked him to the train station and waved good-bye. Such was the Swabian revolution!

The press is kinder to the Greens in Baden-Württemberg than elsewhere, but Wolf-Dieter Hasenclever told us that the main cause of the Greens' successes there has been their strategy of engaging in dialogue with the other parties—as opposed to simply making declarations in the legislature—and treating opponents like human beings rather than enemies. He feels the Greens have not only produced a number of ecological laws and guidelines but have affected the thinking of the other parties in several key areas.

At the national level, the Greens were in the Bundestag for only one hundred days before the summer recess in 1983. They introduced numerous issues—such as opposition to the census, opposition to nerve gas and nuclear deployment, numerous ecological concerns, and women's rights—and presented a much higher proportion of questions to the government than did the other parties. However, their inquiries were often ignored by the bureaucracy, as Petra Kelly explained with frustration:

> We present the questions and what happens is that we receive letters from the government stating things like "Questions 1–4 cannot be answered because they are secret; Question 5 has already been answered; and Question 6 is something we cannot answer because of national security." Rather than accepting this, we should find a way to communicate to people that the government refuses to answer even basic questions, such as those on deployment. We should do something, literally *do* something. The next step is to take action in the Bundestag to make it a real forum for the nation.
>
> As it is, the other parties reject our proposals and try to show that what we ask is far too radical, yet they know we must vote for many of theirs because there is some good in them. This is our dilemma, which we are unable to communicate to the people outside who say to us, "Why did you vote that way?"

How to make government responsive, then, is the ongoing question for the Greens at all levels. They are concerned that both major parties, especially the Social Democrats, have attempted to co-opt the Green issues, to "put on a Green coat" for the purpose of winning votes, as we discuss in Chapter 7. However, monolithic, old-paradigm parties have no intention of encouraging the sort of structural changes called for by a holistic analysis. They find the tiny Green party threatening precisely because the need for such structural change and decentralization is increasingly irrefutable. Perhaps that is why a group of American professors visiting West Germany on a government-sponsored program during the summer of 1983 were told repeatedly in lectures by both Christian Democratic and Social Democratic politicians that the Greens are "very dangerous."

Chapter 7

The First Four Years– An Evaluation

Few West Germans feel neutral toward the Greens. The two million people who voted for them in the federal election of March 1983 and the hundreds of thousands more who have voted in state and local elections since then believe that the Greens are a necessary voice in government—that they are the personified bad conscience of government as well as ecological guardians of the future. Other citizens feel the Greens are probably right about some issues but are too radical in general. Still others scorn the Greens as disrupters of the status quo who lack an understanding of political and economic necessities. Finally, much of the radical left finds the Greens not radical and disruptive enough, criticizing their "bourgeois" goals and tactics in leftist publications.

Since winning seats in most of the legislative bodies in West Germany, the Greens have become the political voice of the citizens' movements in the forums of power and a conduit for privileged information from those forums to the movements. They also have fundamentally affected the content of political debate.

143

For example, it was the tiny Green party that early on identified some of the major issues—ecological damage and the presence of 5,000 nuclear missiles—that the Establishment parties were compelled to address in the federal election in March 1983. Prior to the Greens' entry into the Bundestag, ecology was hardly considered a bona fide political topic. A discussion of *The Global 2000 Report* (Penguin Books, 1982)—which was commissioned by President Carter but sold more than three times as many copies in West Germany as in the United States—was attended by only one-tenth of the parliamentarians. As we have mentioned in previous chapters, the Greens have achieved more tangible successes at the local and state levels than in the Bundestag, but all of their *Fraktion* groups have introduced fundamental questions concerning government policies that have never been raised before.

This deep reassessment of the government's goals and actions has not been limited to elected assemblies. The Greens are changing the entire political culture of West Germany. In just one of their "theaters" of action, the peace movement, it was the rallying calls of the Green party—to refuse the new missiles, to withdraw from NATO, to adopt nonalignment, to work toward a bloc-free "Europe of the regions"—that urged the larger movement far beyond anger over deployment of the Pershing II and cruise missiles to exerting "such pressure on the Establishment that the entire system has been put in question," according to the weekly newsmagazine *Der Spiegel.* Other political commentators have agreed. The Munich daily newspaper *Süddeutsche Zeitung* predicted that the peace movement "won't leave the republic unchanged," as it has propelled the country into a "long-overdue re-evaluation." Not all citizens in the heterogeneous peace movement endorse the entire Green peace program, of course, but, thanks to the Greens, West Germany's role in NATO is for the first time a primary topic of public discussion.

In invigorating and transforming the political culture, the Greens have changed not only what should be discussed but also who should discuss it: women as well as men, and ordinary citizens as well as entrenched party politicians. When the Greens upset the traditional patriarchal "balance" by electing to the Bundestag a *Fraktion* that is more than one-third women—and uppity ones, at that—the old-paradigm politicians were unable to contain their anger. Petra Kelly, as well as many of the other Green women, told us of the not-so-subtle reactions in the national assembly:

> Because our small *Fraktion* has recently increased the number of women in the Bundestag, a great many of the male parliamentarians are hostile to the Green women who get up to speak. They always display laughter, or aggression, or disdain and derision. In addition, the microphone was always tuned to the male voice, which made women's voices sound very shrill. So we have achieved a small victory in getting the microphone retuned when a woman is about to speak.
>
> I have noticed that it is the Christian Democratic men who make the most unkind, obscene, and discriminatory remarks. When Green women have gotten up to speak, those men have said that we are whores, that we are cheap, that we should get off our ass and work—things like that. It's the most ugly, chauvinist language. When I get up and quote from a whole range of women, including Rosa Luxemburg, they completely stop listening to me. They either laugh or hold up their newspapers. And when I suggested to Mr. Kohl that perhaps he should read up on what Rosa Luxemburg said about peace and feminism since he probably is not familiar with it, he simply stared at me as if in a drunken stupor. He really cannot cope with it. I think all of this is a fantastic confrontation with the system because the Green women are bringing entirely new cultural values into the Bundestag.

While the Greens have exasperated the guardians of old-paradigm politics they have also inspired many other groups. They have empowered the citizens' movements in numerous ways, and the rippling effects of their electoral victories have inspired the growth of the new politics throughout the global Green network. They have brought into politics more than a grassroots, nonauthoritarian style and future-oriented approach; they have incorporated what the German philosopher Ernst Bloch called the principle of hope.

In spite of their many successes the Greens are faced with serious problems, not all of which they are addressing effectively. A major problem is that the issues the little party identified and fought for are being co-opted by the big parties.* In a few cases the Christian Democratic government has derailed the Greens' momentum by taking action that, although sorely inadequate, lays an issue to rest as far as most of the public is concerned. For example, the Greens called for immediate legislation banning all gasoline in West Germany that was not lead-free because the emissions from leaded gasoline have been linked by scientists to rapidly spreading diseases that now afflict 80 percent of the spruce trees and 50 percent of the firs in many areas, including the Black Forest. Friedrich Zimmermann, Kohl's Minister of the Interior, first said that banning leaded gasoline would be impossible. Later, under pressure from conservative forest-owners who had listened to the Greens' arguments, he announced that West Germany will switch to lead-free gasoline in 1985. The CDU thereby appears to be responsive while two more years of damage—some of it irreparable, according to foresters—will be visited upon the few remaining forests of Germany.

It is the Social Democrats who had the most to lose from the Greens' successes. In fact, they lost exactly the number of seats in the Bundestag, twenty-seven, that the Greens gained in the federal election in March 1983. While the Greens are at odds with much of the SPD program, their commitment to social responsibility in the evolution of a new politics attracts many disaffected voters from that party. Relations between the Greens and the SPD have been positive and cooperative in many town councils and in such state legislatures as Baden-Württemberg and Lower Saxony, but at the federal level there has been no love lost. Helmut Schmidt, the former head of the SPD, complained to the newspaper *USA Today* that the Greens get "too much publicity in the United States" and "are not that important." Egon Bahr, a specialist on defense issues in the SPD, told the *New York Times*, "The Greens ask interesting questions—but they do not give interesting answers."

In an effort to come up with the sort of "interesting answers" that might salvage their own position, the Social Democrats developed a taste for ecological issues and even for

*The Greens also discovered, to their dismay, that the Green symbols, slogans, and color were co-opted by a private group in Switzerland who printed and marketed a "Green" calendar in late 1982 that included a Nazi slogan.

opposition to the Euromissiles, jumping onto a bandwagon that was already rolling. Their long-overdue, last-minute shift on deployment was particularly irritating to the Greens. Deployment was by then practically certain and the SPD lost nothing in belatedly playing to the three-fourths of the public who oppose it. They are ready to move on to the next big issue, as their secretary-general Peter Glotz declared: "1984 will be the year of the economy."

Because public outrage over industrial pollution is increasing, it is likely that both major parties, especially the Social Democrats, will incorporate bits of the Greens' ecological perspective into their economic programs. But whether or not the major parties co-opt the Greens' economic proposals, a shifting of the political spotlight to economic measures is not going to serve them well at this time. The Greens' Economic Program, although insightful and pragmatically creative in many parts, is in an embryonic stage of development. The party lacks a clearly articulated model of an ecological economy, both at the micro- and macro-level, and for the most part lacks even comprehensive theoretical visions such as the one presented, for example, by the American economist Herman Daly in *Steady-State Economics* (Freeman, 1977). The Green party has "working groups" at all levels on the economy, as well as on numerous other issues, but progress in this area is particularly difficult since the Marxist-oriented Greens consider economics their turf and usually maneuver successfully to further "workerism" proposals at the expense of a unified, partywide effort to develop a radically new ecological economics. One practical step the Greens have taken is to establish basic learning projects on ecology and economics at the regional level, groups in which they bring citizens together to discuss and develop new forms of employment. In the pilot study for such projects, Roland Vogt and other Greens have begun to work with residents of Rhineland-Pfalz, where military-related jobs comprise one-third of the employment in many areas.

In addition to the danger of being co-opted on some issues and overrun on others by the big parties, the Greens face a major tactical problem: whether to enter into a coalition with the Social Democrats or function as a tiny but completely independent minority party. Understandably, the Greens have taken one day at a time since entering the Bundestag, but by now they have acquired a sense of what they can and cannot do on their own. They must determine their role at the federal level. Petra Kelly estimated for us that 30 percent of the Greens oppose any coalition; 20 percent favor nearly any type of coalition; and 50 percent would support a coalition if specific conditions about fundamental issues were agreed to by the SPD. Even if agreement were reached on which course to pursue, the Greens would still face the enormous task of determining—in a grassroots democratic fashion, of course—acceptable conditions and then negotiating them with the SPD. One can say, at this early stage, that they are proceeding wisely by maintaining their independence while testing the waters through offering official cooperation with the Social Democrats in state legislatures. The Greens may very well find that their beyond-left-and-right orientation is ultimately incompatible with SPD partnership, especially on such issues as ecologically responsible labor demands, decentralization, and "soft" energy paths.

Internally, the Greens face even more problems. The sparring between the Group Z members and the rest of the party has resulted in a growing sense of psychological weariness, felt most acutely by the visionary/holistic Greens and least by those Marxist-oriented Greens who seem to thrive on "conflict politics." In the Bundestag *Fraktion,* for example, friction from this source frequently abounds, as Petra Kelly related:

> The former Communists became critical of Marx, left their tradition and came to us—but many never really left behind their loyalty to that group. In times of crisis it is stronger than their loyalty to the Greens, and it is sometimes brutal. They make everything subservient to it and refuse to look at the cause of a conflict, convincing themselves instead that it is another group who is causing them to struggle. Sometimes they create an artificial struggle that does not even exist.

However, even Kelly stated emphatically on "Meet the Press" that the journalist Robert Novak's thesis that "the Marxists are taking over the party" was nothing short of "shocking." She explained, "The Marxists who have turned Green have become emancipatory ecological members. We also have very conservative members. So the Green party is a collection of people who, on the main issues, have a consensus." The Greens understand very well that their success lies in that consensus drawing from the entire political spectrum. The conflicts within the party—some of which are quite fierce—are not a matter of "taking over" but, rather, of debating the direction of the Green party.

The area of economics, as we have noted, is one in which the Marxist-oriented Greens often exert a good deal of influence. The parliamentarian Waltraud Schoppe told us that some feminists on the committee that wrote the Greens' Economic Program (with grassroots approval) wanted to include a holistic/feminist analysis of technology and economics in a patriarchal society, specifically the ways in which male-oriented technology expropriates women and nature. This perspective is acknowledged by many Greens at the grassroots level, but because it is unacceptable to most Marxist thinkers, male and female, the association of woman and nature was kept out of the Program by the Marxist-oriented members of the committee. However, since then, a Green women's group has prepared a statement of this feminist perspective, which they hope will be included in the next version of the Economic Program.

In terms of mobilized forces, the overall "fight" is unevenly matched as the Group-Z people are in frequent contact to discuss goals, strategies, and tactics, while there is no parallel group among the visionary/holistic Greens. With so much at stake in the evolution of the party's politics, we asked several of the latter why they have no caucus. We were told that there once had been such a discussion group but that the members had dissolved it, not wanting to become drawn into "*cadre* politics" like the radical left. While this may be admirably idealistic in some sense, it hinders the evolution of innovative Green proposals, which are sorely needed in such areas as economics. We were bemused to hear several holistic Greens assure us, implicitly or otherwise, that he or she is *the* visionary thinker in the Greens. A plurality of independent "geniuses" is healthy for the party, yet we could not help but wonder what they could achieve together in ongoing discussions.

In the early years of the party, a joke among West German

politicians was that the Greens were like tomatoes: "They start out green and become red." We asked Rudolf Bahro how far he feels the radical-left Greens could go in furthering their positions:

> They cannot push anything; they can only block. No group without a concept can take over a party. Instead of a concept, they have only old patterns of socialist behavior and a lot of tactical skills. In Hamburg there is no possibility of creating the foundation necessary for a new society; they think it is very radical for us to merely defend our little space on the merry-go-round. This is because they have a very deep psychological layer of defeatism.

We also asked Bahro whether tactical skills are the major contribution of the radical-left Greens to the party: "No, there's something else. They are militant in what is mainly, but not always, a good sense. There are a lot of soft people in the Greens without much juice in them. Their politics alone would not work."

The radical-left Greens thought their close work during their Communist years with certain factions in the trade unions would enable them to deliver a sizable volume of workers' votes, but that has not been the case. Most West German workers distrust assurances that decentralized modes of renewable-resource energy production and industrialism would create rather than destroy jobs. A group of factory workers demonstrated this in September 1983 by beating up some ecological activists who were staging a public protest. (The workers who have come over to the Greens have generally contacted the party themselves because of such concerns as storage of chemical weapons in their area or the unwanted development of their neighborhoods.)

Since the Marxist-oriented Greens help little at the polls, even alienating many voters, most Greens believe that their leverage within the Green party is limited. However, two recent developments may help to ameliorate the situation if they develop sufficiently: one is that observers feel the Group-Z Greens may finally be softening their opposition to several core Green concepts and proposals; the other is that the new constellation of "eco-liberals" within the party (drawing from the visionary/holistic faction, the "ecological reformists," the "fundamentalists," and the "realists") may mount a successful tactical challenge to the Marxist-oriented faction. At this time, neither group is suggesting a divorce. Rather, the strange bedfellows will press on like partners in an unsatisfactory marriage who hope things will somehow get better, all the while complaining about how awful the other is.

One problem all wings of the party have in common is sexism, even though it is far less rampant than in other parties. The fact that it is not taken seriously by most Green men is ironic because no other problem is so damaging that it costs votes, keeps people from joining the party, keeps many Green members from actively working within the party, and keeps certain party officials—even at very high levels—from giving their best effort to party work. Several Green women in the Bundestag *Fraktion* told us that they feel they must keep some distance from the patriarchal style of politics there and hence from part of the work process. One woman parliamentarian told us, "I spend as little time here as possible because the dynamics are unpleasant. My main identification is as an activist in the anti-nuclear-power movement." (The citizens' movements are well known for the active roles and leadership of women.) Another parliamentarian, Gabi Potthast, agreed that the situation is destructive.

> To go into patriarchal politics and adapt to their ways is self-rape. One must protect oneself and become indifferent to a lot that goes on around her. Men confuse person and function. I act in a function without identifying with the function. Women must learn to *use* the function. Right now, you could say that women are simply not considered a political factor in power politics.

The adversary—some say obviously macho—style of politics that prevails in the Greens' Bundestag *Fraktion* arose largely by default. After the extremely hectic campaign for the federal election, a mere two weeks intervened between the selection of the new parliamentarians and their stepping into the stressful demands of public life in Bonn. With no concrete, comprehensive plans for an alternative mode of operating, they simply slipped into the familiar, patriarchal patterns. Once the competitive system was in place, challenging it became extremely difficult, especially because the parliamentarians were largely strangers to each other with no accumulated trust among themselves. (See Appendix A for an account of how competitiveness and patriarchal values figured in the response to a sexual harassment incident in the Bundestag *Fraktion.*) At the state level, the dynamic is similar. Several male legislators and party officers told us there is no great desire on the part of Green men to change their patriarchal attitudes in politics.

At the local level, however, we heard more hopeful responses. Beate Orgonas, a member of the five-person executive committee in Baden-Württemberg, told us that women in many of the grassroots groups in her state have succeeded in beginning to create a new political style.

> It works because those people are neighbors or acquaintances or friends so they know and trust each other. Since many of them were apolitical before, they are more open in their expectations. The men don't really understand that they are using a particular style; the women have to show them. When men begin to make a psychologically violent argument, women interrupt them and say, "Stop talking that way. I will not answer you," or "I am afraid to answer you." They teach the men to listen better, to be more patient, and to be aware if someone is having trouble expressing himself or herself.

We asked Orgonas if the men are cooperating mainly because they *need* women in the party to swell the ranks and she replied, "No, those men are changing because they *want* the women to be in their local chapters. They want to work together, not be like the other parties."

In the Greens' local party in Nuremberg, an "emancipation group" of women and men meets regularly to work on transforming the political style. Klaus Peter Morawski, a Green member of the city council, told us that they discuss the male-dominated, aggressive style and the cultural sources of violence, especially violence against women. The men are encouraged to develop listening skills and patience, while the women are encouraged to develop more assertive speaking styles. During its first year, the group was composed of twelve women and eight men.

The local party in Bonn has also devised means to address the patriarchal style of politics. Lukas Beckmann told us the women have identified a number of oppressive behavior patterns, and they all raise their hands whenever a speaker perpetrates one of the patterns, indicating that he should stop speaking. Beckmann called the process "very interesting" and said that he and the other men are seeing things in new ways. We judged that moment an opportune time to show him a one-page article we had been distributing to various Greens: "Overcoming Masculine Oppression in Mixed Groups" by the American author Bill Moyers of the Movement for a New Society. (We had taken with us the Livermore Action Group's booklet for the International Day of Nuclear Disarmament, 22 June 1983, which contains an abridged version of the article). Beckmann loved it. He immediately began to laugh at Moyers's description of "some problems for men to become aware of," such as the following:

• Speaking in capital letters: giving one's own solutions or opinions as the final word on a subject, often aggravated by tone of voice and body posture

("Oh, yes! We have this in our group!" Beckmann exclaimed.)

• Restating: saying in another way what someone else, especially a woman, has just said perfectly clearly

• Self-listening: formulating a response after someone's first few sentences, not listening to anything from that point on, and leaping in at the first pause

("Yes, we have that, too!" he said with a chuckle.)

• Putdowns and one-upmanship: "I *used* to believe that, but now. . . ." or "How can you possibly say that?"

• Seeking attention and support from women while competing with men

• Avoiding feelings: intellectualizing, withdrawing into passivity, or making jokes when it's time to share personal feelings

"Incredible!" Beckmann concluded with delight. "We talk about all these things in our group. I'm going to have this article translated and sent to all the Green groups in Germany. In fact, I'll leave the reverse side in English so we can use it in our international work!" We smiled, willing to overlook the aspersions some Greens had cast upon the budding feminism of this "ladies' man." After all, the enthusiasm of converts has been known to accomplish impossible tasks.

One can conclude that postpatriarchal politics, like so much else in the Green party, works best at the small-scale, grassroots level. In the rest of the party's structures the women reported variations on an adage familiar to American women in public and professional positions: "A women must be twice as good as a man to be thought half as good." Emilie Meyer told us the two Green men on the Freiburg city council generally support the two Green women, but when they don't want to they say the women are not competent politicians. In general, the situation was not improving so the Green women called national assemblies in June and August 1983. They discussed how to work more closely with the "autonomous" women's movement, which they consider their major constituency, and "how to integrate more fully into the Greens without letting the party structure assimilate us so that our imagination, ideas, and experiences are not muffled." Addressing that problem is obviously an enormous task. Gisela Erler, a Green activist in Bavaria, typified the dissatisfaction felt by many Green women: "The way it is now women have to do double work: work on the top-priority Green issues and then go back into their Green women's groups and figure out 'Now what does this mean for women's politics?'"

Another internal problem faced by the Green party is the battle-scarred principle of rotation. As we discussed in Chapter 2, most Greens feel a one-term-only rule will eventually replace mid-term rotation. However, it is unlikely that the Greens can resolve the situation they have constructed without hurting people and causing resentment, especially among the *Nachrücker.* Those people have disrupted their lives to move to Bonn, or state capitals, and participate as assistants for two years while they await their turn to become parliamentarians. West German law requires employers to rehire parliamentarians in their former jobs, but no such guarantee protects the *Nachrücker.* With the new provision allowing a parliamentarian to remain in office for the remaining two years of her or his term if the home state gives a 70 percent vote, many *Nachrücker* are sure to feel cheated. Moreover, the compromise solution of the 70 percent vote has left disgruntled most of the people who strongly support rotation as well as those who strongly oppose it. The party adopted the rotation principle in various city councils, then state legislatures, and finally the Bundestag without testing it throughout a complete cycle and considering all the implications. This issue is sure to continue draining a good deal of time and energy from more important topics.

The most serious internal problem the Green party faces is what humanistic psychologists have termed "bad process." In the American peace movement, for example, it is used to describe the dynamics of an affinity group that does not communicate well and function well together. In many respects this can be said of the Greens. At the federal level and somewhat at the state level—especially among elected officials—we sensed a lack of bonding and trust; instead, there is a sense of "every man for himself." This dynamic was evident during the Green parliamentarians' trip to Washington, D.C., in July 1983. They began in their usual way, that is, stressed and almost frantically overloaded with tasks. There was no time in Bonn to discuss the goals and processes to be used on the trip; neither was preparation sufficient in Washington, as it fell largely on the shoulders of one person, Barbara Jentzsch, an Austrian journalist. During the small demonstration in front of the White House, the Green parliamentarians held a banner and pictures of the Berrigans and Martin Luther King. When the German television crew crooked their fingers, three of the parliamentarians simply dropped their pictures, left the group in the middle of the peace action, and tended to their personal media profiles. At the press conference that followed, uncoordinated, slightly disjunctive, and individualistic pronouncements prevailed. A few days later, Katherine Graham, publisher of the *Washington Post*, hosted a luncheon to which she had originally invited Gert Bastian and Petra Kelly, plus a reporter. The entire delegation managed to get invited and then competed with each other to answer the questions Graham asked of her original guests. Graham finally left before dessert, saying it was impossible to conduct the interview. The Greens thereby managed to alienate probably the most powerful woman in American media.

When the Greens returned to Bonn, they held a press conference but allotted no time for a private evaluation of the trip.

Instead they became caught up in the next whirlwind of tasks and crises, hoping that the hard feelings accumulated during the trip would simply fade away or be suppressed. This pattern of struggling through unsatisfactory process and rarely evaluating it is widespread in the Green party. The custom in the American peace movement, for example, of holding a brief evaluation of process at the end of every meeting seems to be unknown. (Of course, the process is even worse in the German Establishment parties, but there the participants are not *supposed* to feel that constructive, humane standards have been met; they are merely to fall into step behind the authoritarian leadership.)

We shared with Rudolf Bahro our observation that the Greens are blocked in many ways by a lack of trust. He agreed and added:

> Considering the structure of West German bourgeois society, it's amazing how much better relations are inside the Greens than outside. Yet there is a dark side to the important negation of bourgeois authority that arose in the sixties. There are a lot of unfulfilled needs for self-realization, so the very kind of competition we want to abolish thrives within the party. There is a great deal of jealousy toward anyone who emerges.

We asked Bahro whether part of the problem might be that the Green party has neglected to develop structures and processes that encourage bonding and conflict resolution—that is, to align their own actions more closely with the new cultural values expressed in their programs. He explained the difficulty:

> The Green party has developed with the pretense that it is the political arm of a movement and a new culture. But that culture hardly exists; it is in the embryonic state. There is a stream of humanistic psychology running through society now, but this, too, is merely part of the emerging culture. The Greens in West Germany are more closely related to the new culture than are political forces in any other country, but it is to the party's disadvantage that its own development is more advanced than the countercultural network. For example, there is only a very small communitarian movement. We now must also do the sort of more fundamental work that should have preceded the party.

Petra Kelly also spoke of the fundamental work the party must do internally:

A change of consciousness has begun, and to further it the Greens must become a spiritual movement, not in any fixed religious sense but in the sense of transforming certain values and conserving other ones such as solidarity and tenderness. We must be able to communicate this among ourselves and to the outside. At the moment none of us here in the soulless Bonn environment [in the Bundestag *Fraktion*] is living by it very well. We are all caught up in a painful and terrible process of finding ourselves as new persons in an old society, and before we find ourselves, we may all be rotated.

Some parliamentarians are not optimistic that such higher work will ever be compatible with political structures. Gabi Potthast told us she has experienced "humane politics" in the women's movement, although there are certainly exceptions, but that she has observed a stark contrast since entering the Bundestag *Fraktion:*

> We are trying to bring the holistic view into politics, but I think it is not really possible in a party. It is not possible in power politics specifically because it requires trust. Power politics is close to sadism because you're not allowed to show weakness, to say "I've got problems" without the others poking into your wound and twisting their fingers around. In power politics there is a lust to destroy; many people get energy by beating others down. It is they who are blocking postpatriarchal process.

A number of the Green parliamentarians respond to the stress and the internal struggles by using alcohol or tobacco rather than healthful means of stress reduction. There are plans to establish a center near Bonn where the Green *Fraktion* could go to relax together and learn group dynamics, stress reduction, and effective communication. Martha Kremer, who, as Petra Kelly's assistant, has observed the dynamics of the Bundestag *Fraktion* at close range, observed:

> There is an enormous amount of intelligence and creative ability in those people, but the group is held back because real communication among them doesn't exist. If they would ever take time to go together to an intensive workshop on that and would move beyond competition, they could become an incredibly effective force in the parliament.

Some Green parlimentarians describe the situation as "like being in a war," and a few frequently consider resigning. On 9

January 1984, Gert Bastian sent an open letter to his Green colleagues stating that he would leave the *Fraktion* unless conditions improved in three areas. First, he charged that Group Z has come to wield too much influence, especially in furthering "a violence-oriented and anti-American politics." (Contrary to some of the coverage in the American media, Bastian did not accuse the Marxist-oriented Greens of taking over the party; he specifically addressed their opposition to two Green positions—nonviolence and the even-handed treatment of both NATO and the Warsaw Pact in disarmament efforts.) Second, he asserted that the work structure of the *Fraktion*—an "office community" of parliamentarians and *Nachrücker* who would support one another in solidarity—has turned out to be a hopeless failure, resulting in an extremely competitive, inefficient, and costly system. Third, he observed that the positive spirit of the first few months had been supplanted by power struggles, intrigues, opportunism, and cynical contempt for idealistic positions—all of which made parliamentary work very difficult. In response to the letter, which received a great deal of media attention, the *Fraktion* postponed its regular agenda and discussed for one and a half days the problems Bastian had identified. They also established a committee to make recommendations, although there was a great deal of anger within the *Fraktion* at his publicly calling attention to the problems. On 9 February, Bastian resigned from the Green *Fraktion,* announcing that he would remain in the party and would function as an independent parliamentarian working for the peace movement. There is no doubt that the resignation of such a prominent Green parliamentarian hurt the party. Bastian demonstrated that he hoped such damage would be temporary, however, by stating that he would return to the Green *Fraktion* if conditions improved.

In the Hesse state legislature the Green *Fraktion* hired a therapist in 1983 who specializes in group dynamics to work with them. At the local level, however, we saw no efforts, such as workshops or conferences for all the Green city council members of a region, to relieve the internal and external stresses of public life—especially those inherent in trying to conduct new-paradigm politics within a largely resistant old-paradigm context. Green elected officials at all levels told us of the contradictions they encounter as a party of nonviolence in power politics. They sometimes find themselves acting more aggressively than they want, and they experience even the minimal amount of hierarchy necessary to function effectively in politics as a block to creativity and a source of "structural violence." The work load is so heavy and the pace so hectic for Green legislators that their jobs tend to consume their lives. One man in the Hesse state legislature declined to run for a second term because "I just want to be able to read a book again—and to spend some time with my girl friend!"

One more internal problem aggravating their progress is the tension and mistrust that have arisen between the Bundestag *Fraktion* and the grassroots. (Closely related is the strain between the Bundestag *Fraktion* and the party's national executive committee, which we discussed in Chapter 6.) Roland Vogt told us, "The desire for harmony in the Greens is so strong that the people at the grassroots level, who maintain that they wish to be informed of Green operations in the Bundestag, do not really want to hear about our problems and conflicts." The grassroots does, however, expect a constant level of attention for the most part, as Petra Kelly explained:

> The local groups expect us to be in our home districts every weekend, which, of course, is impossible. Many local groups have experienced a surge in membership since our election to the Bundestag. They now put a new kind of emphasis on local issues, even to the extent of my own home group in Nuremberg saying that I should not make the trip to Washington, staying with them instead to work on local issues. They say that now we are in the Bundestag our concern should be Germany first—but I say we are an international movement and our concern should be the human race first.

Pressure from the opposite direction, by the way, also causes Green parliamentarians to focus on home-rule issues, as Kelly related:

> On a global scale many groups want our advice and assistance. But all the groups who horribly overestimate us, thinking we can solve their problems, actually cause our group to be quite provincial. Some of us say, "We have our own problems, so don't bother us now because we couldn't possibly help you." That loss of priorities is very dangerous.

The Greens have problems because they have fears, insecurities, ambitions, desires, grudges, regrets, rivalries, mistrust, self-doubt, and defense mechanisms. They also have deep friendships—sometimes romantically problematic—courage, perseverance, and genuine idealism. That is to say, they are complex, intelligent human beings who are struggling to create a new milieu that supersedes their past conditioning, both personal and political. They are succeeding in some areas, failing in others. They are finding their way.

Evaluating the Greens' prospects for the future again reminded us of the saying "Two Greens, two opinions." Establishment politicians regularly predict that the Greens will fail to win 5 percent of the vote in the 1987 federal election, thereby losing all their seats in the Bundestag, and Helmut Schmidt assured an American journalist that the Greens will not last as a party for more than eight years. A more impartial source of divination is *Trend-Report*, a West German future-oriented newsletter based on an analysis of trends similar to that used by John Naisbitt to compile *Megatrends* (Warner Books, 1982). The research group, Trend-Radar, concluded that there is a greater than 50 percent probability that the Greens will become a well-established party in the Bundestag, a less than 50 percent probability that they will remain largely extraparliamentary, and a less than 30 percent probability that they will soon dissolve. Trend-Radar determined the characteristics of the Greens to be the following:

- They facilitate the dissolution of men's-club politics; they support female, and hence holistic, thinking.

- They try out process politics; there is permanent learning.

- They test flexible forms of organization, which causes delicate problems with communication and voting.

- They redefine power; holding office is not seen as a sign of superiority but as "holy sacrifice."

- Emotions, intuition, and a new balance between play and seriousness have entered politics.

- They are talented media professionals and have a good communications network.

- Collective self-organization is an important source of the Green movement.

- They have begun a transformational process that transcends left-right thinking, and that momentum for transformation is crucial to their success.

- They have reintroduced morality into politics and attempt to develop a new morality.

- Although they have taken votes from the Social Democrats in the past, the Greens will win many votes from the Christian Democrats as well in the future.

Few of the Greens we spoke with envisioned becoming a majority party. An exception was August Haussleiter, who predicted somewhat playfully, "I would say that by 1996 we will have an absolute majority, that there will then be three Green parties: the left Greens, the liberal Greens, and the conservative Greens." Other Greens, such as Helmut Lippelt, who is a teacher, feel the Green party will always remain a small "teaching party" of eight to ten percent; such an elitist role as "philosopher kings" is abhorrent to many Greens however.

On the minds of many Greens is the question of whether they can again win the more than two million votes in the federal election of 1987 they need to keep their seats in the Bundestag. Both of the major parties are seeking ways to defuse the influence of the Greens, whose internal problems are, at the same time, causing them considerable damage. A couple of Greens suggested that it wouldn't be a bad thing for the Greens to lose an election or two so that they would take time to rethink a number of key issues as a party, but Rudolf Bahro told us:

> The future of the party depends on whether it really becomes a political arm and the means of protection for the emerging culture. If we don't remain in the Bundestag in 1987, we will have to realize that this approach of being a party will not work, and we will have to find other democratic means to achieve our goals. Conversely, we may win close to ten percent and the party may

become more and more conventional. There is the danger that we will become just one more institution.

Other Greens fear too much compromising, even in the early stages of their federal success. Petra Kelly warned about such a path:

> The Green party is now at a very critical point. On one hand, it has achieved everything it hoped for in the last few years. On the other hand, it could lose it all very quickly within the next two years by literally trying to find ways to make a little influence here, a better life there, and losing sight of the larger goals. As for our work in the Bundestag, if we would just successfully address four basic points—ecology, nuclear power and weapons, health, and the exploitation of women—the entire existence of the party would be justified. Getting people to reject the idea of deterrence must be a major goal for us. If the Greens end up becoming merely ecological Social Democrats, then the experiment is finished—it will have been a waste.

There is no sense in the party at this time, however, that the Greens are finished. On the contrary, their triumphs in September 1983 in Bremen, where they replaced the Free Democratic Party in the legislature, and in Hesse, where they won votes from the entire political spectrum, have established them in the eyes of many political analysts as the third-ranking party in West Germany. Their membership continues to increase, and their programs continue to evolve. During the "hot autumn" of peace actions in 1983, a distinguished participant, the Nobel laureate Heinrich Böll, spoke for many West Germans when he told a journalist, "The Greens are always my hope."

Part Two

Global
Green Politics

Chapter 8

The Worldwide Green Movement

A close look at the current political and economic scene reveals that the Green critique applies not only at local and national levels but globally as well. In fact, the major problems we face today are global in nature. Whether we examine international politics, the armaments debate, food policy, international finance, or communications, we are faced with a finite, densely populated, globally interdependent world. Recognizing the dynamics of the global community and its embeddedness in the global ecosystem is essential, hence the need for global Green politics—in other words, the application of the Green perspective to the whole Earth and the entire human family.

A dramatic event in the raising of this global consciousness was the publication of *The Global 2000 Report* commissioned by the Carter Administration and published in 1980. Largely ignored by governments but carefully studied by the Greens in West Germany, the Report gave a detailed and frightening picture of our dwindling global supply of natural resources, continuing increase of the global population, persistent inequality, and maldistribution of wealth. The awareness of global inter-connectedness was further sharpened by the two reports of the Brandt Commission. The first, *North-South: A Program for Survival* (MIT Press, 1980), attracted worldwide attention to the fact that international relations had to be understood not only in terms of East and West but also—and even more important—in terms of North and South, that is, of the relations between rich industrialized countries and poor Third World countries. The second report, *Common Crisis* (MIT Press, 1983), pleaded once more for a new economic world order. These reports attempted to make the public acutely aware that the finiteness of energy and natural resources is a dominant factor in world politics and introduces additional volatility and tension into international relations, North-South as well as East-West.

The starting point of Green politics, the protection of our natural environment, is as valid for the entire biosphere as for local ecosystems. The effects of industrial pollution today are no longer local but global. Sulfur and nitrogen oxides emanating from coal-fired plants are carried over large distances by atmospheric currents and fall to the earth as acid rain, destroying trees, the fauna of lakes, and other forms of life hundreds of miles away, often in countries other than that of the polluters. Smog disperses throughout the Earth's atmosphere and may severely affect the global climate as it traps the sun's heat. A recent EPA report on this so-called greenhouse effect, published in September 1983, gave a stern warning. Meteorologists speak of a nebulous veil of pollution encircling the entire planet.

This pollution of the global ecosystem is caused by modern forms of industrialization that, for better or worse, have made the world ever more interconnected. We now have a global transportation system and a global communications network producing a ceaseless flow of information about events around the world. We have a global system of tightly interlinked economies, which is extremely sensitive to changes in any part of the system. American presidents have repeatedly found it impossible to carry out economic sanctions against the Soviet Union because such sanctions were felt by parts of the American population as quickly as by the Russians.

Intertwined with the global system of economies is a global

network of financial systems in which the concept of money is becoming ever more abstract and detached from economic realities. The value of money can be distorted almost at will by the power of large institutions. The widespread use of credit cards, electronic banking and funds-transfer systems, and other tools of modern computer and communications technology have added successive layers of complexity. The deposit you make in your bank can be sent several times around the world before you have a chance to write your first check. Therefore, it is almost impossible to use money as an accurate tracking system of economic transactions.

Because of this tight interconnectedness at multiple levels, a global approach to economics and politics is urgently needed. The existing global politics cannot solve any of our major problems because it is a politics of dominance, undifferentiated growth, an escalating arms race, continuing exploitation of nature and of people, destruction of the biosphere, and perpetuation of the grossly unequal distribution of wealth. The principal agents of today's global exploitation are the large transnational corporations. The assets of these giants exceed the gross national products of most nations; their economic and political power surpasses that of many national governments, threatening national sovereignty and world monetary stability. The nature of these large corporations is profoundly inhumane in many respects. Competition, coercion, and exploitation are essential aspects of their activities. The main motivation for these activities lies not in the immorality of individual corporate executives but rather in the fact that the demand for continuing growth and expansion is built into the corporate structure. Thus the maximizing of profits becomes the ultimate goal, to the exclusion of all other considerations. There are no laws today, national or international, that can effectively address these giant institutions; the growth of corporate power has outstripped the development of our international legal framework.

In their continuing efforts to expand and grow, the giant transnational corporations are extremely careless in the way they treat the natural environment, to the extent of creating serious threats to the global ecosystem. For example, Goodyear, Volkswagen, and Nestlé are now bulldozing hundreds of millions of acres in the Amazon River basin in Brazil to raise cattle for export. The environmental consequences of clearing such vast areas of tropical forest, which normally produce so much oxygen that they are called the lungs of our biosphere, are likely to be disastrous. Ecologists warn that the actions of the torrential tropical rains and the equatorial sun may then set off chain reactions that could significantly alter the climate and living conditions throughout the world.

The exploitative actions of giant transnational corporations are by no means limited to those originating in capitalist economies. Those with headquarters in the Eastern bloc and operating in the context of Marxist economies are mirror images of the capitalist corporations in their structures and activities. Eastern-bloc transnationals talk about royalties instead of profits and report to government commissars instead of shareholders, but they are organized on the same global scale and participate in the same global resource wars, motivated by the same obsession with open-ended growth.

As transnational corporations intensify their global search for natural resources, cheap labor, and new markets, the environmental disasters and social tensions created by their unbridled pursuit of growth becomes ever more apparent, especially in the Third World where the exploitation of people and of their land has reached extreme proportions. The disastrous consequences of global agribusiness may serve as just one illustration. In Central America at least half of the agricultural land—and precisely the most fertile land—is used to grow cash crops for export while up to 70 percent of the children are undernourished. In Senegal vegetables for export to Europe are grown on choice land while the country's rural majority goes hungry. Rich, fertile land in Mexico that previously produced a dozen local foods is now used to grow asparagus for European gourmets. Thus an enterprise that was originally nourishing and life-sustaining is now perpetuating world hunger. The goal of the transnational agribusiness corporations is to use their global resource base and labor force to create a single world agricultural system, a global supermarket in which they would be able to control all stages of food production and distribution.

The Greens have clearly recognized the disastrous effects of transnational corporate exploitation, and hence they always insist on solidarity with the Third World. Global Green politics will involve a thorough redefinition of the concept of development. The development of Third World countries can no longer be equated with economic growth, measured in terms of GNP, since repeated experience has shown that high rates of growth do not necessarily ease urgent social problems. New emphasis has to be put on self-sufficient economies, reducing dependence of the Third World on the northern hemisphere, enhancing South-South cooperation, and incorporating social and cultural goals into the development process. The Green principle of grassroots democracy implies, furthermore, that a group in one country should not design development strategies for other countries. Instead, Third World people may be helped to design their own paths of development, starting from their own cultural roots and from taking pride in their cultural heritage. Finally, there is an urgent need for social, cultural, and spiritual development in our industrialized countries. All countries are developing, finding themselves merely at different stages of the process.

Another central aspect of Green politics is the reconceptualization of strategies of war and peace by shifting from the current high-tech approach to more human-based systems for defense and conflict resolution, as well as adopting the concept of social defense described in Chapter 3. Since today's nuclear weapons threaten to extinguish life on the entire planet, the new thinking about peace must necessarily be global thinking. In fact, the technologies of modern electronic and nuclear warfare have brought about the most deadly form of global interconnectedness, creating a potential global battlefield that includes even outer space. In this situation it is frightening that most of our politicians, led by the American president, still seem to believe that we can increase our own national security by making others feel insecure. Green politics recognizes the dangerous fallacy of this fragmented and simplistic way of thinking. It recognizes that in the nuclear age the entire concept of national security has become outdated, that there can be only global security. This recognition found impressive support in the recent report of the Palme Commission, *Common Security* (Simon & Schuster, 1982), with a powerful introduction by Cyrus Vance, which stated unequivocally that the concept of global security must replace the outmoded notion of national security. It is exactly this position of the international peace movement that is likely to become one of the strongest expressions of global Green politics.

The notions of national security and defense lie at the very basis of another concept that is increasingly being recognized as unworkable in today's world—that of the nation-state. As Leopold Kohr foresaw as early as 1957 in *The Breakdown of Nations* (E. P. Dutton, 1978), the current nation-states are no longer effective units of governance, being too big for the problems of their local populations and, at the same time, confined by concepts too narrow for the problems of global interdependence. Gerald and Patricia Mische argue persuasively in *Toward a Human World Order* (Paulist Press, 1977) that the central confining concept today is that of national security. The present national-security policies—viewed in terms of monetary, resource, and weapons competition—no longer enhance the security and welfare of citizens but, on the contrary, diminish them by suppressing individual human development and dehumanizing society. This connection has been recognized very clearly by the European Green movement.

National-security imperatives render heads of state powerless to reorder their priorities toward an emphasis on human needs and development and, paradoxically, make them unable to resolve even the urgent problem of human survival. According to the Misches, national-security thinking, more than anything else, demands centralization. Replacing the notion of national security with that of global security would make resources and talents now consumed by national-security goals available for resolving local and regional problems. To realize the liberating power of such a shift of emphasis, we have only to remind ourselves that today nearly half of the world's scientists and engineers work for the military-industrial complex. If this tremendous potential of human creativity and imagination could be redirected, the centralized national-security states could become decentralized and effective at local and regional levels. What we need, then, is a shift from the current world order, based on national interest and national security, to a new one based on human interest and global security.

The current industrial systems produce very similar dilemmas around the world and, not surprisingly, similar human reactions. Thus the emergence of Green politics, guided by a fairly uniform set of principles, is a global phenomenon that will become increasingly visible during this decade. In accordance with its principles of decentralization and grassroots democracy, the global Green movement grows from below, manifesting itself first locally in the form of Green alliances and coalitions, and subsequently in the formation of national Green parties. At the same time a set of global citizen-based networks is gradually emerging, which distributes information about ecological and human-rights issues around the world. Examples of the activities of such global networks are the extremely effective campaign for human rights waged by Amnesty International, the worldwide raising of ecological awareness by Friends of the Earth, and the "softening up" of Establishment thinking accomplished by the Club of Rome.

At this stage, it would seem that the best strategy for the development of global Green politics would be to proceed as suggested by the slogan "Think Globally, Act Locally." Green movements and political parties will continue to grow from their grassroots, while global networks, distributing information about local developments and integrating local activities into the global vision, will continue to develop and expand. So far, the local Green organizations and the various emerging global networks have not been much in contact with one another. But as they develop and expand over the coming years they may well collaborate effectively for the implementation of global Green politics.

The origins of the global Green movement can be found in several influential studies and books published during the early 1970s, which gave stern warnings of environmental destruction and raised ecological awareness around the world. The Club of Rome's *Limits to Growth,* the British *Blueprint for Survival (The Ecologist,* 1973), and E. F. Schumacher's *Small Is Beautiful* were germinal works of this kind. Schumacher, in fact, became the prophet of the global Green movement, emphasizing the importance of appropriate technology, "good work," and the human scale in all enterprises and institutions. Schumacher had a broad vision going far beyond environmental protection. He recognized the limits of the Cartesian paradigm, stressing especially the need for reintroducing the notion of quality into our lives, and he was motivated by deep spiritual concerns.

During the 1970s citizens' movements, most of them environmentally oriented, merged into political parties in various countries around the world, from the Green parties in Belgium—the first to win seats in a national parliament—to the Values party in New Zealand. The Green movement has been strongest in the highly industrialized countries where the environmental problems are most urgent and most visible, and its success has depended largely on the electoral systems in those countries. Wherever there is a system of proportional representation, Green representatives have been elected locally, regionally, and in some cases nationally.

The first Green party was the Values party of New Zealand, whose history is very curious and rather sad. It was founded in the late 1960s and presented itself from the very beginning as a true Green party long before the ideas were fashionable, emphasizing not only environmental issues but also values and spirituality, and situating itself clearly beyond left and right. The electoral system in New Zealand is the same as the British and American system—a majority vote is required in a given electoral district in order to win a seat in the legislature. The Values party never gained any seats in national elections, but by 1972 it had established itself as a serious factor in the political dynamics of New Zealand. During the following years it worked out a detailed program that became the first statement of Green politics. It was presented as the 1975 election manifesto of the Values party, titled *Beyond Tomorrow,* and became an inspiration for ecologists and futurists around the world. The program explicitly stated, several years before the European Green programs were formulated, the need for a steady-state population and economy, new industrial and economic relations, ecological thinking, human-centered technology, soft-path energy systems, decentralization of government, equality for women, and rights of native peoples, as well as for valuing the traits traditionally considered feminine: cooperation, nurturing, healing, cherishing, and peace-making.

In the national election of 1975 the Values party captured close to 5 percent of the vote, which marked the culmination of its development. During the following years it began to decline, due to internal bickering. At the same time a new party appeared on the scene and began to draw support from the Values party. This new party called itself Social Credit because of its initial focus on the control of banks and of credit, but soon it began to take up Green issues. In the 1978 election their charismatic leader won a seat in one district, while the Values party, disunited by squabbles, did poorly.

Subsequently the arguments within the Values party escalated into a full-blown crisis during which its members debated whether the party should identify itself as a party on the left. In 1980, they took this step and declared themselves a Socialist party. This led to a major breakup and accelerated the party's decline. For the 1981 election the Values party did not even run any candidates, and since then it has virtually disappeared. Its early flowering, great inspirational force, and subsequent fading away will remain a fascinating chapter in the history of Green politics. Perhaps the Values party arrived on the political scene before its time, unable to sustain its initial momentum without the support of a global Green movement.

In Europe the first breakthrough for the Green movement came with the 1979 campaign for the election to the European Parliament, which gave Green parties in several European countries the first opportunity to introduce their political ideas to the general public. The European Parliament, which has its headquarters in Strasbourg, is one of the institutions of the Common Market (European Economic Community, or EEC), founded twenty years ago in order to facilitate the political unification of Europe. Like the United Nations, it has little actual political power but serves as a forum for the exchange of ideas and coordination of European politics. The representatives to the European Parliament were previously appointed but beginning in June 1979 they are elected every five years in each member country. Elections are based on proportional representation in each country, except for Britain where the far less democratic system of "winner take all" (similar to the electoral system used in the United States) is applied both to national and European elections.

For the Green movement, the 1979 election was extremely significant. As a European election, it was perceived by the public as less important than national elections and thus it was easier for the voters to take risks with new ideas. A further advantage was that for the European election each party needs only one list of candidates, instead of the different lists for each electoral district in national elections, which makes it much easier for a small organization to run. Roland Vogt recalled for us the 1979 campaign:

> We had a little house in Bonn between the two giant parties, little money, and many volunteers. The main work was done in the regions. The three to five people in the office in Bonn had to coordinate and do press work. I had three functions—candidate, office manager, and press secretary—and sometimes when I was out of town I had to do everything by phone.

With the grassroots campaign, run on a shoestring budget, the Greens raised a common voice against overindustrialization (particularly the EEC's heavy investments in nuclear power) and for an ecological and regionalized Europe. Similar campaigns were conducted in other European countries, notably by the two Green parties in Belgium. Although none of the Green parties gained any seats in the European Parliament in that election, their campaigns had a considerable impact on public opinion and a few of them did far better than anybody expected. In West Germany the Greens won 3.2 percent of the vote (approximately 900,000 votes), which entitled them to receive approximately $1.3 million from federal funds.

Since the 1979 European campaign the emergence and rise of Green parties has been progressing swiftly, but because of the decentralized nature of their organizations it is not easy to keep track of developments around the world. Green parties and alliances are now being formed not only in Europe but in most industrialized countries, notably in Canada, Australia, and Japan, and there is interest in Green politics in several Latin American countries. In most of those countries Green political work is taking place at the local level. In Japan, for instance, there are Green parties in several cities.

The first Green party in North America was formed in British Columbia (B.C.) in February 1983. Within a few months Green parties had sprung up in most Canadian provinces and in November 1983 they sent representatives to a federal congress in Ottawa to work out the constitution of a federal Green party. All but two provinces were represented. After a long and lively discussion about centralized versus decentralized structures, the Canadian Greens decided to reverse the traditional structure of Canadian political parties, in which a centralized federal party maintains representation in the provinces while remaining distinct from the provincial parties. Instead, the Greens, following the principles of decentralization and grassroots democracy, founded a federation in which the provincial parties will play the primary role and which will grow only gradually into a federal party. The role of the Green federation will be to coordinate the Green movement by acting as a clearinghouse, helping people to get in touch with each other, representing the Canadian Greens internationally, and maintaining contacts with the national and international media.

We discussed the strategies, hopes, and problems of the Canadian Greens with two founding members of the B.C. party, Wally Thomas, a sixty-two-year-old professor of medicine, and Adrian Carr, a twenty-nine-year-old geologist, who is the president of the B.C. Greens. Carr was in very high spirits during our telephone conversation, which took place a few days after the birth of the federation of Canadian Green parties and just a few days before the birth of her own baby. She told us she felt the Green party of British Columbia, one of the most ecology-conscious provinces of Canada which also has a strong feminist tradition, would be a model for the other provincial parties. The B.C. Greens are attracting support from both sides of the political spectrum, but probably less from the conservatives than from the socialist New Democratic party, which used to be on the forefront of new ideas but is now no longer able to attract young people. Carr told us that a recent opinion poll showed that one-third of the B.C. electorate is looking for a new alternative party.

So far, the Canadian Greens have not yet had a chance to discuss issues and work out a political program at the federal level, and Carr expects that controversies are bound to arise once they get down to this discussion. However, both Carr and Thomas told us that frictions between radical-left and liberal or conservative Greens have not been a problem and are not likely to arise as strongly as they did in West Germany. At present, anyhow, the Canadian Greens are in a very positive and constructive phase. They have not yet been able to win seats in any election, but they look toward the future with confidence.

It is evident that much of the inspiration to form Green parties in Canada and in other parts of the world has come from Europe, which is the center of the global Green movement. The European Green organizations and alliances were formed by ecologists and other citizen activists, most of whom were liberal, conservative, or apolitical. Eventually some of the Green ideas were taken up by various groups on the left who saw the need to go beyond traditional Marxism to solve the social and ecological crisis. When the Green organizations became Green parties, each had to decide whether to include those Marxist groups. For example, the Belgian Green parties proceeded successfully without the radical left, while the German Greens included them, as we have discussed. In other countries the Green and Marxist groups attempted to merge but were unable to agree. In both Austria and Switzerland there are two Green parties differing in their political positions and unable to merge into one party "beyond left and right." This inability was the main reason why the Austrian Greens failed to pass the critical 5-percent hurdle in the 1983 national election. In Britain the peace movement is identified with the left, and the Ecology party (the British Green party) has not yet been able to establish itself as the "peace party."

In some other countries where Green parties have not yet emerged, Green positions are advanced by so-called radical parties who place themselves clearly on the left of the political spectrum but differ from the many other Marxist splinter groups in their insistence on nonviolence. In The Netherlands there are two such parties, the Political Party of Radicals (PPR) and the Pacifist Socialist party (PSP), both of which have seats in the Dutch national parliament. The PPR is more ecologically minded than the PSP with strong positions on nuclear power, the arms race, and environmental protection. In fact, they are often referred to as the "ecologists," even by the PSP. The political program of the PSP represents a Marxist analysis in terms of left-right thinking, but the party also calls for democratic process and feminist values. The PPR is currently going through an identity crisis, wanting to leave behind its image as a party on the left and develop an identity "between red and green." Attempts within the PPR to form a truly Green party have recently been strongly encouraged by a national opinion poll that showed that 12 percent of the Dutch population would vote for a Green party if one existed. This result can be expected to increase the crisis within the PPR and to put pressure on many Dutch activists to form a Green list or alliance in The Netherlands.

The Italian Partito Radicale, founded more than twenty years ago, is a small party that has become very visible because of its unorthodox and highly imaginative style. In the 1983 national election they won 2.2 percent of the vote and twenty seats in the Italian parliament. They focus mainly on social issues. Abortion was their principal issue for a long time and now, having helped to make abortion legal under some circumstances in Italy, they have taken up the cause of world hunger as their main issue. The Partito Radicale is leftist without being rigidly Marxist. They are antimilitarist, antinuclear, and emphatically nonviolent. Above all, however, they are highly autonomous and idiosyncratic. Hence the European Green parties have found it very difficult to collaborate with them. "Contacts with the Partitio Radicale never worked very well," complained François Roelants of the Belgian Green party Ecolo. "They are very autonomous and don't want to commit themselves. They don't feel responsible for global programs. They may support us, or they may not; they do what they feel like doing."

There is no genuine Green party in Italy, although the Italian ecological movement is quite strong and has many faces. Especially remarkable is the fact that the Italian Communist party joined the movement through its Recreational and Cultural Association (ARCI), a large labor organization originally concerned with the working and leisure conditions of its members. ARCI is now increasingly taking up environmental concerns, particularly through its special branch, the Environment League, founded in 1979. In February 1983 the Environment

League held a congress titled "Thinking Globally, Acting Locally," which produced quite an extraordinary document, a thorough revision of Marxist thought along ecological lines. Besides such environmental groups associated with political parties there is also an ecological umbrella organization in Italy called Green Archipelago, which is not engaged in electoral politics.

As we shall discuss, relations between the European Green and Radical parties, that is, the two Dutch parties and the Partito Radicale, are generally friendly, but there are deep ideological differences between the two camps. As a result, the European Greens excluded the Radical parties from the common Green platform for the 1984 European parliament campaign.

The first self-styled Green representatives to be elected to a national parliament were those from the Belgian Green parties: Agalev (representing the Flemish, or Dutch-speaking, part of the population) and Ecolo (representing the Walloons, or French-speaking Belgians). The old antagonism between the Flemish and the Walloons continues to dominate Belgian politics and society, but we were pleased to discover that the two Green parties are working together closely and harmoniously and, in fact, are growing together more and more. When we visited the press office of Ecolo opposite the impressive (and hermetically sealed) glass complex of the European Economic Community headquarters in Brussels, we mentioned that we had an upcoming appointment with Dirk Janssens, a member of the executive committee of Agalev. The Ecolo press secretary, Jean-Marie Pierlot, readily picked up the phone and invited Janssens to join us.

Agalev—a Dutch acronym for "to go and live differently"—was the name of one of the citizens' groups from which the party was formed in the mid-1970s. It was first an environmental lobbying group but ran independently in the national elections of 1978, after its members had found out that the "greenish" politicians whom they had supported did not live up to their promises once they got elected. In 1979 Agalev won 2 percent of the vote in the European Parliament election; Ecolo, which had a more developed organization, surprised everyone by winning 5 percent. Their programs at that time were still quite vague and rather naïve, as they themselves admit today. In the general election in 1981 both Green parties got into the Belgian national parliament, Agalev with two seats in the lower house and one in the senate, and Ecolo with two and four seats, respectively.

The Belgian Green parties, who gained national representation two years earlier than the Greens in West Germany, went through the inevitable initial stresses and crises away from the television lights of the international media and have now reached a certain political maturity. Two of the leaders with whom we spoke, François Roelants of Ecolo and Dirk Janssens of Agalev, are actively engaged in organizing the coordination of the European Green parties. Roelants, who also leads an ecological association independent of Ecolo, told us there has been a lot of deeper reflection within the Belgian ecology movement since the early days of the European Parliament campaign. As a consequence, the ecological perspective was enlarged beyond environmental concerns to include many social issues. "Ecology, as we understand it today," he explained, "is a global philosophy. There is a vision in ecology; we are not just protectors of the birds and the bees."

In comparing the Belgian Green parties to the German Greens, we noticed foremost the absence of internal tension between a Marxist and other factions. Roelants explained that the Belgian Greens did not feel the need to work with the radical left because the Belgian ecological groups received official recognition by themselves, that is, they were taken seriously by the Belgian government as discussion partners and never felt the need to form coalitions with leftist groups in order to gain political skills. The Belgian Greens are glad they have fared better in this respect than their German counterparts. On the other hand, they consider the German Greens' unification of the ecology movement and the peace movement to be an inspiring success, one that the other European Greens have yet to achieve. A further contrast with Green politics in West Germany is that feminism plays a very minor role in Belgium, as the women who represent Ecolo in the Brussels region told us. One of them, Cécile Delbascourt, said quite frankly, "This is the big gap."

Like the German Greens, the Belgian Green parties attract a lot of public attention by the imaginative use of symbols and humor in their political actions. When Agalev wanted to protest against the municipal plan to cut down some trees in Antwerp, they painted those trees with bright colors. They were told that it was illegal to paint trees, to which they replied that these trees would be cut down anyway, so why was it illegal to paint them? In this way they started an animated public debate. When the two Green parties entered the Belgian national parliament in 1981, they did so in a procession of bicycles, which may have inspired the German Greens to create their visually dramatic procession into the Bundestag two years later. Inside parliament the Belgian Greens distributed to all the representatives small flasks of water from the river Meuse, which provides drinking water for a large part of Belgium, with the note: "This is non-radioactive water. It is likely to become a rarity if the planned nuclear power station on the Meuse is built." On another occasion, half a year later, the Ecolo representatives arrived at parliament in a Rolls-Royce and distributed statements explaining that the recent increase in fares in Brussels had made public transport so expensive that it was cheaper for them to rent a Rolls-Royce for their journey to work.

The two Belgian Green parties received a great deal of press coverage for their serious political work over the last two years, as well as for their symbolic actions. A special success was the municipal election in the city of Liège where Ecolo formed a coalition with the Social Democratic party, thus becoming the first Green party participating in government. As a consequence, Liège now has a Green deputy mayor, Raymond Yans, a young intellectual whose outlook has been strongly influenced by Buddhist and Taoist philosophy and who even spent several months studying Zen Buddhism in a Japanese monastery.

The way in which Ecolo agreed to a coalition with the Social Democrats in Liège was typical of the Green political style. Whereas coalition negotiations in Belgium traditionally start at a hectic pace right after the election results are in, the elected representatives of Ecolo let it be known that they would take their time. "Tonight we celebrate," they said, "tomorrow we sleep. Then we'll start talking." And so they did. They negotiated from a position of strength slowly and thoughtfully for a whole month, keeping to their convictions and thus increasing their political leverage. They stated clearly the conditions for their participation in the city government—for example, the demand that the utility company of Liège detach itself from a nuclear power plant—and these conditions were accepted by their coalition partners. Since then Liège, a city of about 200,000 inhabitants, has become a highly interesting laboratory for Green politics. There has been a considerable rapprochement between Ecolo and the unions in Liège. For example, the unions recently accepted the Green proposal of shortening the workweek and reducing salaries (with protection of minimal salaries) in order to increase employment. This and other successes have made the city of Liège an important symbol for the European Green movement.

Belgium and West Germany are the two European countries in which Green parties have been most successful. Inspired by these successes, Green parties and alliances are now established or being formed in most European countries, notably in Austria, Britain, Denmark, Finland, France, Greece, Ireland, Luxembourg, Spain, Sweden, and Switzerland. The processes of formation and rise of these Green organizations have been quite similar throughout Europe. The parties usually began as networks and alliances of small citizens' movements and political groups formed around social and environmental issues. The antinuclear issue often served as the catalyst for these coalitions. For example, when Austria became the first country to vote against nuclear power in a national referendum in 1978, this success encouraged the growth of many alternative movements out of which, a few years later, the two Austrian Green parties were formed. The newly formed Green parties would then, typically, establish local bases and use their grassroots strength to run in local and regional elections, gradually extending and broadening their bases through electoral successes at these levels.

The international character of Green politics is apparent not only from the similar developments of Green parties throughout Europe but also from the similarities of their principles and programs. However, comparisons are often difficult because at present the programs are in very different stages of articulation and evolution. Besides their common antinuclear, pacifist, ecological, and decentralist positions, the Green parties of different countries focus on different local issues. Thus the platform of the Swedish Environment party calls attention to the discrimination against immigrant workers, the Swiss Green parties focus on excessive highway construction, and the program of the Irish Green Alliance contains the following inspired comment on the situation in Northern Ireland: "Should we not recognize that the solution to the Northern Ireland problem must lie in letting the people there implement their own wish for compromise? Have we not an urgent duty to make the Republic more the sort of country others would wish to be associated with?"

Britain and France are the two major European countries that do not have a system of proportional representation, and consequently neither country has Green representatives in its national parliament. The British Ecology party started in 1973 following the publication of the germinal *Blueprint for Survival.* It has grown slowly since then, gradually improving its results in local and regional elections without, however, gaining any district or county council seats, except for one in Cornwall in 1981. The bias of the British electoral system is well illustrated by the 1983 national election. The Conservative party won this election by a "landslide," although, in fact, fewer people had voted Conservative than at the previous election. With 44 percent of the national vote the Conservatives won 61 percent of the parliamentary seats, while the Liberal-SDP Alliance, with 26 percent of the vote, ended up with a mere 4 percent of the seats. In other words, the Alliance needed more than ten times as many votes for each seat than the Conservatives. This unequal system makes it extremely difficult for a small political party to establish a foothold in parliament, as it discourages even sympathetic voters who often think that a vote for parties other than the giants would be a wasted vote.

In spite of this tremendous obstacle, the British Ecology party is gradually expanding its influence. Their spokesperson, Jonathan Porritt, told us he was extremely encouraged by the great enthusiasm at the grassroots level, where people are motivated by the strong feeling that time is on the side of Green politics. However, Porritt also criticized himself and the Ecology party for not being able to identify themselves as representatives of the peace movement. The British peace movement is dominated by the Campaign for Nuclear Disarmament (CND), founded in the early 1960s by a group around Bertrand Russell. Although the CND is officially a nonpolitical organization, it has, in fact, strong ties to the British left. Because of this association, according to Porritt, many people with conservative backgrounds refrain from joining the peace movement. The CND is also highly centralized and hierarchically structured in rather rigid ways, which makes any fusion with the Ecology party very unlikely for the time being.

The situation in France is only slightly better. A French Green party, Les Verts–Parti Ecologiste, was founded in 1982. Since then, it has won seats in local elections, sometimes in coalition with the left, but it is not represented in the French national parliament. In fact, the whole situation in France is somewhat convoluted, as is often the case in French politics. There are two Green parties at present, Les Verts and Les Verts–Parti Ecologiste. A third—Les Verts-Confédération Ecologiste—was recently dissolved.

In addition to the national Green parties—which, it must be emphasized, are built on grassroots strength—the European Green movement is also developing networks and political organizations to facilitate the flow of information among the national groups and to coordinate Green politics at the European level. At present, there are at least two such organizations. The first, called Ecoropa, is not engaged in electoral politics but acts as a sort of European Green think tank delineating the characteristics of an ecological society, promoting ways of living and political institutions consistent with ecological principles, and emphasizing the European dimension of ecological issues. Ecoropa was founded in 1976 and is represented in most European countries; it has a general secretariat in Bordeaux, France. In West Germany, Ecoropa is represented by the E. F. Schumacher Society. From its beginning Ecoropa has also maintained close contacts with many ecologically minded individuals and grassroots organizations in the United States.

The other effort to coordinate the European Green movement has a political basis. Following the European Parliament election of 1979, which was the debut of Green politics in Europe, a committee of Green and Radical parties was formed in order to develop a common electoral platform for the 1984 campaign. Over the next few years this committee experienced many problems and frustrating sessions without agreeing on a common Green platform. According to Dirk Janssens, who played a major role, one of the main difficulties was that most of the parties involved were very young, had not yet worked out structures and programs for themselves, and never agreed explicitly on what kind of coordination was needed. There did not seem to be any disagreement on basic issues among the European Green parties, but there was a lot of discussion about finding the proper language. Questions like whether to use "ecological" or "Green" became major issues, for example.

A further initial obstacle was the fact that the chair of the coordinating committee was first held by a member of the Dutch PPR, a choice that was criticized by many people because the Dutch Radical party is not a proper Green party. The genuine Green parties felt that the collaboration of the Radical parties would interfere with their ability to agree on a minimal common program, as the Radicals have neither strong ideological links among themselves nor comprehensive programs along the lines of Green politics. The Green parties in the coordination group decided therefore to exclude the Dutch and Italian Radical parties from the discussions of the common Green platform, assuring them however that all other channels of friendly communication and solidarity between the Green and Radical parties would be kept open.

After that decision some progress in formulating the common program was made, even though we heard many complaints in different countries that the German Greens had dragged their feet at first and showed little enthusiasm for contributing sustained effort to the European coordination. In the early stages, the Belgian Agalev party did most of the work. However, gradually things improved, proposals were sent back and forth between Bonn, Brussels, London, Paris, and other European capitals, and finally, on 1 October 1983, the Belgian Greens called a meeting to hammer out the final version of the European Green platform. At this meeting a minimal common program was adopted together with the common name "the European Greens." However, it was felt by all participants that some additions, especially regarding agricultural and energy policies, still had to be made. The general feeling after the meeting was that there was no disagreement, only the need for added sections, clarifications, and more concrete formulations. At the time of this writing, the final platform is not yet available, but the preliminary platform is already an impressive document of European unity among the Green parties, and the final version promises to be a persuasive testimony of Green politics for the 1984 election.

The preamble of the Green platform states that in Europe, as in other parts of the world, militarism, the destruction of nature, and the exploitation of people do not stop at national borders. Therefore, a Green European politics is needed that will encourage the cooperation of the social, ecological, and peace movements in East and West beyond national frontiers. The aim of the common Green program is to facilitate the creation of a confederation of European Green parties for the European elections and the European Parliament, which will carry out a common Green politics.

The following section of the platform presents the Green critique of current European politics. After World War II, the creation of the Common Market and the other European institutions was accompanied by great hopes for a peaceful Europe without national borders. However, what emerged in Brussels during the subsequent decade was a bloated bureaucracy incomprehensible to the citizens of Europe and removed from all parliamentary control. Moreover, the European Economic Community committed itself to economic growth in its founding treaty and has since supported the destructive direction of industrial societies. Therefore, the European Greens reject the EEC, maintaining that it is based on competition and exploitation. They point out that not even the European Community for Coal and Steel, from which the EEC originally emerged, has been able to prevent crisis and massive unemployment in these sectors. Similarly, the European agricultural policy, which takes up about 80 percent of the EEC budget, has not been able to prevent the agricultural crisis. On the contrary, by accelerating the emphasis on industrial agriculture and food production it has contributed to the ruin of small and medium-size farms and to the poisoning of soil and food. The European Atomic Community (EURATOM), together with the European

Investment Bank (EIB) has encouraged a dangerous and anti-ecological energy policy through its enthusiastic promotion of nuclear power.

The Green platform also states that the foreign policy of the EEC has in no way fulfilled the European hopes for a peaceful future. In fact, the Greens are afraid that the European Economic Community may lead to a European Defense Community. Another superpower is the last thing they would want. They point out that the enlargement of the EEC is often discussed in strategic terms—membership of Spain and Portugal would allow NATO to establish strategic bases on the Canary Islands, and so on—and that the majority of the European Parliament has supported this militaristic tendency, for example, by proposing the creation of a European armament agency and by demanding military naval cooperation of EEC countries in the South Atlantic. In addition, the European Parliament has also supported foreign policies vis-à-vis the Third World that have virtually ignored the historical obligation of Europe. The Community, especially after the acceptance of Spain and Portugal as new members, is comprised of the very countries that exploited the peoples of Asia, Africa, and Latin America for hundreds of years as colonial powers.

The final part of the Green critique of European politics concerns the system of elections to the European Parliament. The platform points out that arbitrary barriers in the national electoral systems prevent grassroots-democratic political organizations from contributing to the reconstruction of Europe from below because they are kept out of the parliamentary process. However, the platform also notes that in spite of this considerable handicap the European Green movement is increasingly taking the form of political parties that share as their highest motive the survival of people and nature in the face of the present global threat.

The main portion of the Green platform consists of their proposals, which are presented in five sections: peace, environmental, social-economic, and Third World policies, and the Green vision of Europe's future. The starting point of the peace policy is "an emphatic engagement to prevent a third and atomic world war." The Green parties assert that the new European order they envisage must be based on friendship between peoples and ethnic groups, on nonviolence, and on freedom from military blocs. They also suggest that military concepts of defense should be replaced by civilian concepts, such as social defense, and they express the belief that the European Parliament, in close cooperation with the peace movement, should make new initiatives toward this end. Roland Vogt pointed out to us that the European Economic Community, so far, does not have a military wing, its military security being the responsibility of NATO. When the EEC was founded, the plan of a European army was rejected by the French, and since then no military branch has been developed. The Greens believe that the Europeans should turn the present state of affairs, which came about by historical coincidence, into a principle: Europe as a nonmilitary power. Vogt reminded us that the sociologist Max Weber defined the state as the only body empowered to use violence in a legitimate way. By that definition the European Economic Community is not a state because, as yet, there is no accumulation of violence in the form of a European army or police. The Green plan is to take advantage of the present situation for starting a movement in the opposite direction. As Petra Kelly put it, "We are trying to move away from a European Economic Community to a European Ecological Community." The detailed demands of the European peace platform include a Europe free of nuclear, biological, and chemical weapons; an amendment to the Geneva Convention of 1977 to outlaw nuclear weapons together with chemical and bacterial weapons; an immediate call for a European disarmament conference; and the creation of a European disarmament agency.

The section on environmental policy calls for "a policy of ecological balance, which assures the foundations of our lives and does not stop at national or European borders." The platform maintains that Europe, being one of the richest and technologically most advanced regions of the world, should be able to carry out comprehensive environmental care, and it demands democratic and responsible research and economic development aimed specifically at restoring ecological balance. The judicious use of resources "in order to ensure a humane future for our children," energy conservation, and environmentally benign energy production from wind, sun, tides, biomass, and other sources instead of nuclear technology are listed among the specific demands.

The economic, social, and labor policies listed in the European program exemplify the Greens' rejection of economies determined by quantitative growth and enumerate many demands concerning the quality of work and working conditions. These include the creation of meaningful work through ecological investments; equal rights for women and men in training, working conditions, and pay; study of the effects of new technologies on the environment and on the labor market; shortening of work time in order to redistribute the work load and create new employment; support of decentralized and economically viable units; and transitional aid for farmers who want to shift to ecological production methods. Closely connected with these demands are the Third World policies listed in the subsequent section of the program, which are based on the ideals of "a sincere partnership with the peoples of the Third World and support of their desperate attempts for a just participation in the wealth and development chances of the world."

In the last part of their program, the European Greens present their vision of Europe's future. They believe that the European nation-states are artificial units, which were created as the result of wars—that is, imposed by violent action—and have been motivated by national chauvinism, competition, and expansionist thinking. Instead of these nation-states, the Greens want to create a "Europe of the regions," that is, a Europe of "historically grown, self-determined, but mutually interconnected units." In our conversations Green politicians of various nationalities emphasized that Europe has many cultural communities that transcend national borders. These communities were formed by tradition and history; they share a common cultural heritage, are bound by a common language, and often also represent natural ecological units. Cultural communities, of course, may sometimes be more or less identical with nations, and the Europe of the regions will have to show flexibility in taking this into account. However, the European Greens feel that, on balance, regional identity is stronger in Europe than national identity.

At present, there are fifty-four regions within the EEC that form administrative units. Some of them are somewhat artificial units, others are natural ecological regions, and yet others represent cultural communities. The Green plan is to start from these existing regions and let the inhabitants define their limits themselves (the Greens prefer to use the term limits rather than borders). This might involve the merging of two or more regions, sometimes across national borders. Until the final structure of the Europe of the regions is established, the present nation-states would act as temporary federations of regions. To approach this goal, the European platform demands decentralization of political and economic decision-making structures, disentanglement from existing European institutions, and the recognition and support of the cultural variety of historically grown European regions.

Among the Greens in West Germany there is still no consensus on their European politics. Many of their members, especially those with radical-left backgrounds, are structually conservative in that they feel the existing structures of the EEC should not be rejected outright. However, the concept of a non-military, decentralized Europe of the regions is the official Green position, in West Germany as well as in the other European countries. The idea of a regionalized Europe has resonated especially strongly in Belgium which, perhaps more than any other European country, is an artificial unit composed of three cultural groups—Dutch-speaking Flemish, French-speaking Walloons, and a small German minority. As the saying among the French-speaking Belgians goes: *"La Belgique n'est pas une nation mais une notion."* ("Belgium is not a nation but a notion.") For many Belgians their state has no real significance and the Green concept of ecological and cultural regionalism seems very natural to them.

In March 1984, the European Greens plan to hold a congress in Liège, where their common platform for the European elections is to be adopted by an assembly of Green delegates. The Liège congress will represent the culmination of several years of European coordination and will be a demonstration of unity of great symbolic value for the European Green movement. The immediate future goal of the Green parties is to gain at least ten seats in the European Parliament. François Roelants explained to us that this would be a very significant number. A group of ten Green representatives would be large enough to form committees and could be politically effective in numerous ways. Roelants told us that if Ecolo got into the European Parliament, its representatives would also represent the interests of the Ecology party, who will not get in because of the slanted British electoral system. The long-term goal would be, according to Roelants, to create an international Green network with a global perspective.

In the process of developing a common Green politics for Europe, the success of the Greens in West Germany has been a tremendous inspiration to the other Green parties. As Michel Delore, of Les Verts–Parti Ecologiste, expressed it, "They have helped us to believe in the future of an ecology party." As we visited offices and headquarters of Green organizations around Europe, we noticed that many of them use the sunflower logo of the German Greens, combined with various slogans in their own languages, and several of the Green parties have modeled their programs after that of the Germans. At the same time, all Green parties realize that their historical context, cultural idiosyncrasies, and local conditions are different from those in West Germany, and their structures and programs have to differ accordingly. Indeed, these differences were quite apparent to us, often in very delightful ways, in the many restaurants, pubs, offices, and homes throughout Europe where we discussed Green politics with women and men who expressed themselves within their own cultural contexts and yet were united by a common vision.

The coordinating efforts of the European Green movement together with those of other ecological networks, such as Ecoropa and Friends of the Earth, are beginning to transcend the boundaries of Europe and to result in contacts with Green movements at the global level. For example, there will be a meeting of Green groups from industrialized countries and Third World countries in Italy in the fall of 1984 with the aim of initiating a Green North-South dialogue. Thus Green politics, a politics of thinking globally and acting locally, is slowly becoming a political reality for the entire human family.

Part Three

Green Politics
in the
United States

Chapter 9

The Green Alternative – It *Can* Happen Here

The roots of Green ideas in American culture reach back to our earliest origins. For more than 20,000 years Native Americans have maintained a deeply ecological sense of the subtle forces that link humans and nature, always emphasizing the need for balance and for reverence toward Mother Earth. Spiritual values are inherent in their politics, as they were for the many colonists who came to this land for the protection of religious pluralism. The Founding Fathers of our government, who were familiar with the federal system of the Iroquois nation, created a democratic federalism that reflects the shared values comprising national identity but entrusts extensive powers to the states and to the people's representatives, who can block the designs of federal authoritarianism. The young nation spawned a network of largely self-sufficient communities that flourished through individual effort and cooperation—the barn raisings, the quilting bees, the town meetings. Yet local self-sufficiency and self-determination eventually gave way to control by such huge institutions as the federal bureaucracy, the military establishment, massive corporations, big labor unions, the medical establishment, the education system, institutionalized religion, and centralized technology.

The inability of our centralist "dinosaur institutions" to address the multifaceted crisis we face is stimulating the growth of the Green alternative in this country. Not only do we—like the other polluted, nuclearized, economically imperiled societies—see the writing on the wall but we also have an outpouring of books and articles that, taken together, are unique in the world for the breadth and depth of the new-paradigm solutions they propose. Stimulated by the civil rights, feminist, counterculture, ecology, anti-nuclear-power, and peace movements—and especially by the rise of the holistic paradigm in science and society—visionary thinkers in the United States have been brainstorming in print for the past decade, each contributing to the evolution of a coherent view that could guide an ecologically wise society free of exploitation and war.

We do not need to wait for someone to synthesize those ideas into a massive tome. The basic concepts of new-paradigm politics can be found in a representative selection, such as the following: in economics, *Steady-State Economics* by Herman Daly (Freeman, 1977), *The Next Economy* by Paul Hawken (Holt, Rinehart & Winston, 1983), *The Politics of the Solar Age* by Hazel Henderson (Anchor/Doubleday, 1981), and *The Challenge of Humanistic Economics* by Mark Lutz and Kenneth Lux (Benjamin/Cummings, 1979); in politics, *Rethinking Liberalism* edited by Walter Truett Anderson (Avon Books, 1983), *Beyond Adversary Democracy* by Jane Mansbridge (University of Chicago Press, 1980), *Human Scale* by Kirkpatrick Sale (Putnam, 1982), and *New Age Politics* by Mark Satin (Delta Books, 1979); in science, *The Reenchantment of the World* by Morris Berman (Cornell University Press, 1981) and *The Turning Point* by Fritjof Capra (Bantam Books, 1983); in futurism, *Seven Tomorrows* by Paul Hawken, James Ogilvy, and Peter Schwartz (Bantam Books, 1982), *An Incomplete Guide to the Future* by Willis Harman (Norton, 1979), *Beyond Despair* by Robert Theobald (Seven Locks, 1981), and *The Third Wave* by Alvin Toffler (Bantam Books, 1981); in feminist theory and activism, *The Anatomy of Freedom* by Robin Morgan (Anchor/Doubleday, 1983) and *The Politics of Women's Spirituality* edited by Charlene Spretnak (Anchor/Doubleday, 1982); in Black history, *The Other American Revolution* by Vincent Harding (Center for Afro-American Studies, UCLA, 1981); and in global perspectives, *Building a Sustainable Society* by Lester Brown (Norton, 1981), *On the Creation of a Just World Order* edited by Saul Mendlovitz (Free Press/Macmillan, 1975), *Toward a Human World Order* by Gerald and Patricia Mische (Paulist Press, 1977), and *Person/Planet* by Theodore Roszak (Anchor/Doubleday, 1978). It is true, however, that these works are not widely known as a body and that the visionary thinkers do not always agree. Moreover, the concrete, practical side to most of their theories has not been developed.

We do have years of experience, though, in certain kinds of holistic political practice. The ecology and peace movements have discovered their common ground, the feminists have held ecofeminist conferences and peace actions, and countless networks working toward comprehensive, nonviolent social change have developed. Most of these people are working with a "big picture" orientation, rather than single-focus problem solving. They are among the fifteen million adult Americans who, according to recent studies by the research institute SRI International, are basing their lives fully or partially on such values as frugality, human scale, self-determination, ecological awareness, and personal growth. In addition, the holistic health movement seriously challenges the mechanistic approach of the medical establishment. Many churches are now reinterpreting the Scriptural charge to "have dominion over the earth," reading it as a call to stewardship rather than exploitation, and some are even going beyond stewardship to deep ecology. Numerous positive steps have been taken toward realizing that our existence is part of a subtle web of interrelationships—yet these fall far short of creating an effective political manifestation of the new paradigm.

We believe it is essential that Green ideas enter the American political debate at all levels. Currently the Democratic and Republican parties struggle fruitlessly to apply outdated and irrelevant concepts and priorities to our burgeoning crisis. They are unable to respond effectively to changing conditions such as the end of the fossil-fuel age and the growth of global interdependence and so are leading us toward disaster. As the quality of life in this country declines and hardships in the Third World increase, the old-paradigm parties are losing credibility. Ronald Reagan was elected president with only 28 percent of the eligible vote; hopelessness and fearful apathy carried the majority. Behind the rhetoric of both parties, it is apparent that one of their shared functions is to remain nonideological, to diffuse dissent rather than standing for a coherent program.

To consider the possibilities for Green politics in the United States, we should first reflect on the lessons from West Germany—with the understanding that Green politics here, as in other countries, must grow from our own cultural and political tradition and from our current situation.

First, moving into electoral politics put a great deal of stress on the Green movement, although it brought many advantages. Because of the demands of campaigning and the critical scrutiny of the press, the Greens needed fully developed positions on scores of issues almost as soon as they declared party status. Once they won seats in the legislative bodies, a great deal of their attention shifted from evolving responses and comprehensive positions to internal power struggles and ongoing debates on legislative strategy. The stress on the Green legislators themselves is generally intense since the grassroots constituency demands attention, the party's governing bodies expect results, and the working relationships within the *Fraktion* groups are often uneasy and distrustful. In addition, the media are always waiting for any misstep. Hence a movement's entry into electoral politics should be preceded by a great deal of preparation and attention to the predictable problems—if it is to be undertaken at all.

Second, the presence of the Marxist-oriented faction within the Greens has increased the political awareness of many ecologists and provided a valuable ongoing critique of Green ideas—but at what cost? It cannot be said that the radical-left Greens have advanced the development of *radically Green* political thought. On the contrary, they have often put the brakes on that process and created endless struggles. In hindsight, perhaps some of the strife could have been avoided, although that is difficult to say. In this country many "alumni" of the New Left have come to realize various limitations of Marxist theory, and are sincerely seeking new options for nonviolent social change. Fringe groups on both the left and the right, however, with well-defined political philosophies that overlap only somewhat with Green ideas would probably make a more negative than positive contribution in the long run to the growth of Green politics in the United States.

Third, while the Greens officially oppose all exploitation including that of women by men and include a number of proposals on women's issues in their programs, neither feminist analysis of major problems other than sexism nor postpatriarchal practices are actively encouraged. Hence many women stay out of the party, and the Green analysis of several issues is not as comprehensive as it could be. Moreover, the Greens' political style is often built around competition, aggressive strategies, and dominance—quite at odds with their principles. These problems could be avoided, or at least lessened, by seeking truly holistic, that is, all-encompassing, analyses from the beginning and by incorporating a postpatriarchal style of politics, such as many groups in the American peace and anti-nuclear-power movements have done.

Fourth, the rotation principle for elected officials has proven to be more trouble than it is worth for the Greens in West Germany. Corruption by the system may be as large a threat here as there—we certainly have our share of egotistic, unresponsive politicians—but other means should be devised to address it. If a Green movement were to field candidates in the United States, those individuals should be able to serve a full term, whether that be two, four, or six years. Placing a limit such as one or two terms is a possibility, but then the movement would forfeit the eventual power of seniority positions on legislative committees. A more important practice would be to rotate internal positions of power (which should be as decentralized as is practical) on a staggered schedule so that no more than one-third or one-half of an elected committee is new and the continuity of experience is unbroken.

Fifth, politics is about how people treat one another as well as the power relationships among groups and classes. The self-aggrandizing mode of some Greens and the detached, self-protective mode of others have often blocked the kind of unified action that would best serve their political goals. When fear is the core motivation for personal behavior—fear that there is not enough recognition, enough attention, enough appreciation, enough acceptance, enough love to go around—then the creative energy of the group is constricted and the practical expression of Green ideals remains out of reach. Individuals in a Green movement must share a commitment to personal development (which means *work*) toward wisdom, compassion, and a deep understanding of the essential oneness of all beings or else the larger transformation of society will never be achieved. If such values are not actively accepted as guiding principles, the political work of "saving the world" often results in miserable interior lives and uncomfortable interpersonal relations, as many German Greens could testify.

Sixth, conflict within a movement is unavoidable because of the range of opinions on strategy, tactics, short-term and even long-term goals. The challenge is not to deny conflict but, rather, to deal with it creatively and positively. Green politics in West Germany often entails one faction's or group's temporarily conquering another, which leads to resentment and blocks the synthesis of good ideas. American Greens would have at their disposal a number of techniques for incorporating the best of conflicting proposals in "win-win" (rather than "win-lose") solutions, such as the methods presented by the Harvard Negotiation Project (see *Getting to Yes* by Roger Fisher and William Ury, Penguin Books, 1983).

Seventh, trust and bonding are positive elements in Green groups at local levels, but are generally absent at state and national levels. Members of the Green *Fraktion* in state legislatures as well as the Bundestag are usually strangers thrown together and then submitted to numerous and unrelenting pressures. The estrangement that results could probably be lessened or avoided if all newly elected representatives in a party or movement went on a weekend retreat together in between their election and taking office. The aim would be to get to know each other as multifaceted persons rather than potential adversaries. Such retreats should be repeated, perhaps seasonally. In addition, ongoing attention to group dynamics should be an inherent, not peripheral, part of the political process. Frequent evaluation is essential. Also, stress reduction techniques should be shared and practiced.

Eighth, perseverance and flexibility are essential. The Greens failed to win the 5 percent of the vote necessary for representation in the European Parliament election of June 1979, again in the Bundestag election of March 1980, and again in several state elections. In response they continued to develop their programs and organize broad-based support among the citizens' movements and the general public.

Ninth, perhaps the most important lesson from the German Greens is that we do not have to hide our deepest longings and highest ideals to be politically effective. Entering politics usually means having to tone down or even give up a visionary goal in order to be more pragmatic or safe. The Greens have shown us that an undaunted call for an ecologically wise, nonexploitative, peaceful culture in which spiritual values are honored does resonate with people. A call to move beyond the old mechanistic ways of thinking to deeply ecological concepts that more closely follow nature's ways is not, after all, political suicide. What we require are thoughtfully developed positions and good organizing.

If Green politics is to develop in this country, we first must develop a coherent view. By that we mean a coherent world view, which would give rise to a set of values and ethics, which in turn would lead to a political analysis (for example, an analysis of the power relationships among corporations, the military, the government, the unions, and the professions), from which would emerge specific programs and strategies. Next we would have to articulate this view effectively in public and mobilize the response. A core problem of new-paradigm politics is that accessible language sufficient to present the long-term goals dynamically and persuasively has yet to be developed. Finally, we would effect change—either within or outside of the electoral system, or both.

The power of Green politics lies at the grassroots level, but we believe a national organization is also necessary to encourage and sustain the people involved, as well as to benefit from the media attention. We suggest five possible forms of such an organization, not as a rigid plan but merely as a basis for discussion.

• A Green Network

Since the ecological view of reality is one of a network of relationships, the network structure would be especially appropriate. Networks tend to be nonconfrontational and to require little commitment, so they have succeeded in attracting many people during the past decade and introducing them to political thinking.

A Green network would link existing decentralized groups and networks of groups in such a way that they could address the political system. They could engage in political discussions and educational activities and exchange creative suggestions for living by Green ideals and values.

There are already a number of social-change networks around the country pursuing such activities. They are a necessary first step in the building of a political movement, but in our view they are insufficient. Their limited functions do not translate easily into the activities necessary for political actions, and they carry no responsibility to formulate programs and carry them out. They are, in short, not politically empowering, but they provide a good entry level for many people.

• A Green Movement

Such a movement would be a national membership organization that would formulate a coherent view and present proposals to the two parties at all levels. It would act as politically as a party, and might include a fund-raising political action committee (PAC), but would not run candidates for office. It could select "shadow cabinets" at all levels of government to comment publicly from the Green perspective on the actions of cabinet members, state officials, and city councils.

A Green movement could be effective in persuading legislators through paid lobbyists (pooling resources of organizations would increase the currently small number of Green-oriented lobbyists), volunteer work in campaigns, and the delivering of large numbers of votes through endorsements. The movement could receive ideas from the grassroots level and present them directly to legislators, as well as suggest practical proposals to local chapters and relay information and models among them horizontally. It could also hire professional organizers to enlarge the movement and could support a think tank in conjunction with forming a consortium of Green-oriented research institutes.

Although a movement would require greater commitment than a network to social change and to the process of (nonviolent) struggle, it would be more effective. It would also be more open-ended, dynamic, and welcoming toward innovation than a party. Hence it would have a broader appeal, both ideologically and in the variety of people it would attract.

• A Green Caucus Within the Movement

The caucus would be an arm of the larger Green movement that would work with, and sometimes directly provide Green candidates for, both the Republican and Democratic parties. This part of the movement would concentrate on electoral and legislative strategies at all levels. The Green elected officials would present new-paradigm politics in the forums of power and could use the media attention to the advantage of the movement.

This option would avoid a split between those Greens who favor entering electoral politics and those associated with citizens' movements who feel that is an error. However, the caucus would have to walk a fine line between sincerely cooperating with the major parties and standing firmly for Green principles and the long-term vision for society. Most of our elected officials probably would be afraid to embrace Green ideals because they owe their electoral victories to campaign contributions from corporations and other monolithic institutions. The caucus would have to proceed on an item-by-item basis in the legislative bodies and would encourage dialogue between the mechanistic, growth-oriented and the ecological, qualitative points of view.

• A National-Membership Green Caucus Instead of a Movement

This option would allow people to indicate when joining the Green caucus whether they wished to be affiliated with the group in the Democratic or Republican party. Like the caucus within a movement, this option would be much less expensive to form and operate than a party. However, the danger exists that Green ideas would be co-opted and adopted only to a superficial degree by the major parties. Moreover, working conditions for the Green caucus within the parties might be difficult if the other politicians did not trust colleagues whose first allegiance is to another group.

This option would probably alienate some Green supporters who disapprove of entering electoral politics directly, but it would provide good insider experience. The possibility exists, of course, for American Greens to form their own party if coalition within the major parties is found to be impossible. However, the cooperation must be attempted sincerely, not with constant threats from the Greens to bolt for the door each time a problem arises. Americans are pragmatic people. Before supporting a Green party, they would want to be shown convincingly that working along Green lines within the old-paradigm parties is impossible.

• A Green Party

If organized intelligently, a Green party could have a broad base and would legitimize the movement. It would require leaders with different qualities from those in caucus work and, unfortunately, an enormous amount of money. At the mention of a party, one thinks of national media exposure, speeches in Congress, extensive secretarial and support services, and access to classified or at least behind-the-scenes information. All of that follows only if one's candidates get elected. The high cost of campaigns in this country makes it extremely difficult to win unless a candidate attracts money from corporations or other monolithic institutions, which would be unlikely for the Greens. On the other hand, if a party's presidential candidate appears on the ballot in thirty states and wins over 5 percent of the vote, and if the party will run in at least ten states in the following election, the Federal Election Commission awards matching funds through a formula based on the number of votes. John Anderson, for instance, won 7 percent of the vote in 1980 and later received about $6.5 million (much less than what his campaign had cost).

Unlike the German Greens, the American party would not receive the governmental payment of $1.40 per vote, which has yielded *die Grünen* such a sound financial basis. Similarly, our efforts would not bring us the legislative seats they have won because we lack proportional representation in our system of government. To win hundreds of thousands of votes means nothing unless one can beat the big-money candidates at district and state levels. Winning votes up to the time of the first major success is not only expensive but also extremely difficult because third parties are perceived as losers by most of the American public, who are not inclined to waste their vote. The inevitable early losses could be demoralizing to party members.

Another consideration is that Green ideas might become rigid within a party framework. The ecological truth that all living systems are in process has not yet found a place in politics, so the public expects fixed positions. Many a politician impresses voters by reminding them that his political positions have not changed one iota in the past twenty years. Meanwhile, biological conditions and economic and social constellations changed at extraordinary rates, but reality is ignored in favor of the comforting illusion of stasis. Denying change is still one of the biggest ruses in party politics, and people with consistent but evolving positions are suspected of lacking competence.

Just as we believe a network to be an insufficient political form for Green ideas, so we believe that moving into electoral politics prematurely would be an error. Considering the political system and traditions in this country, a bipartisan caucus is probably the shrewdest choice, although Green candidates could run at the local level as Independents. However, whether or not a caucus or party evolves later the soundest starting point is a well-organized, grassroots, national Green movement that develops a coherent view and comprehensive programs to present to law-makers and the public. The structure should respect local and regional autonomy within a framework of shared values and should have only the minimal amount of national coordination necessary to present the movement as a potent element in American politics.

Combining ecological concepts with the realities of the American governmental structure, we suggest five strata of organization for the Green movement: local, bioregional, state, macroregional, and national. Three are familiar, but the "new" concept of regionalism has been quietly emerging—from its long but dormant role in American history—as a major focus in ecodecentralist politics. Bioregionalism has taken on a deeper meaning than mere localism, one more akin to the Native American sense of abiding respect for the natural forces and the surrounding life forms, the survival of which we now understand to be essential for our own. Peter Berg, director of Planet Drum Foundation (see Appendix C), defines a bioregion as both a geographical terrain and a terrain of consciousness, both a place and the ideas that have developed about how to live in that place. In *Reinhabiting a Separate Country* (Planet Drum Foundation, 1978), he wrote:

> A bioregion can be determined initially by use of climatology, physiography, animal and plant geography, natural history, and other descriptive natural sciences. The boundaries of a bioregion are best described by people who have lived within it, through human recognition of the realities of living in place. All life on the planet is interconnected in a few obvious ways and in many more that remain barely explored. But there is a distinct resonance among living things and the factors which influence them that occurs specifically within each separate place on the planet. Discovering and describing that resonance is a way to describe a bioregion.

To date, at least twelve bioregional congresses have been formed, such as those of the Great Lakes area, New York State, and the Ocooch Mountains of southwestern Wisconsin. Scores of smaller groups are also active throughout North America, located, for example, in the Slocan Valley in British Columbia, the Rio Grande, the Sonoran Desert in Arizona, the Ohio River Basin, Cape Cod, the High Plains of Wyoming, the Kansas River

Watershed, and the Hudson River Valley. The extremely varied nature of their activities is demonstrated by bioregional periodicals, which feature articles ranging from interviews with octogenarian residents to information on local watershed systems to reports on "natural provision enhancement projects" (restoring the economic base of a community through reforestation, cleaning a river for salmon production, and so forth) to innovative political theory. As bioregional journals are generally energetic and avant garde, many of their enthusiasts would agree with G. Pedro Tama, editor of *Siskiyou Country* in northern California, that "the underground press of the sixties and seventies is rapidly becoming the bioregional press of the 1980s." The first continental gathering of bioregionalists, the North American Bioregional Congress (see Appendix C), will be held near Kansas City in May 1984; it is being coordinated by David Haenke of the Ozark Area Community Congress, along with a council of other Green-oriented activists.

Ecodecentralists believe bioregions are the answer to "Decentralize to what?" They want us to see where our water, our food, our energy, and our products really come from and to understand the natural carrying capacity of our area in order to develop an economy in balance with the ecosystem and minimize dependence on imported food and fuel. Many bioregionalists such as those at the Center for Studies in Food Self-Sufficiency in Burlington, Vermont, and the late Peter Van Dresser, whose book *Development on a Human Scale* was a pioneering work, have been conducting research on economic self-sufficiency.

The most fully developed bioregional organization is probably the Ozark Area Community Congress (OACC), founded in 1976 and based on the principle of "political ecology," by which the Congress means that political consciousness must be bioregionally oriented and must operate as an extension of natural or ecological laws. The Congress, which considers itself an alternative representative body for the Ozarks, is committed to achieving regional self-reliance and sustainable economics by using renewable resources and respecting the integrity of the environment. By late 1983 OACC had held four congresses, attracting not only scores of regional enterprises and groups but also participants from national and international organizations. OACC maintains ten standing committees—peace, feminism/human rights (Mother Oak), water, energy, agriculture/forestry, health, communication/education, economics, communities, and spiritual/cultural—which implement the principles in the OACC Green Platform as well as various resolutions. One of the core groups, New Life Farm, publishes several OACC brochures on water quality, regional seasonal diet, and the Ozark Regional Land Trust; posters of the regional geohydrology and the subtle signs of the seasons; maps; a bioregional directory (the Green Pages); and a booklet on the Native American cultures of the Ozarks. Not all bioregional organizations are rural, however. In fact, most of them span cities, suburbs, and country areas, and some are predominantly urban such as the Lower Hudson Estuary Group, which is gathering information on the natural systems there, and the Reinhabiting New Jersey group.

The concept of macroregions reached a broad audience through Joel Garreau's book *The Nine Nations of North America* (Avon Books, 1982) and now even Madison Avenue designs advertising campaigns stressing regional themes and speech patterns. However, bioregionalists dismiss Garreau's divisions as too rooted in old-paradigm thinking and lacking a sense of deep ecology. Using the bioregionalists' concept of soft borders, it would be possible to divide North America into macroregions such as the northeastern woodlands, the Appalachian highlands and Piedmont, the southeastern coastal plain, the Caribbean, the Great Lakes area, the prairies, the Ozark highlands, the Great Plains, the Rocky Mountain range, the Great Basin, Mex-America, and the Northern Pacific area. These are merely our suggestions*; a Green movement would generate its own macroregional structure and might wish to consult Planet Drum Foundation, whose staff is working on a biopolitical map of North America.

The form in which bioregional consciousness might manifest itself in government is a favorite topic among bioregionalists. Some view their movement as the means to evolve a quite radically decentralized future. Like the German Greens they

---

*Our delineations of the macroregions draw upon similar areas identified by Carl Sauer in *Man in Nature: America Before the Days of the White Man,* which was published in 1939 and has been reissued by Turtle Island Foundation in Berkeley.

consider the nation-state to be inherently dangerous, aggressive, and ineffective. They maintain that the association of security with large size, which unfortunately is deeply engrained in the collective consciousness of our patriarchal cultures, must be discarded in the face of evidence that bigness has led to big exploitation, big wars, and big suffering. A representative of this position is Kirkpatrick Sale, who has been researching bioregionalism for his forthcoming book *Centrifugal Force: The Bioregional Future.* He believes that many of the crises we face are the result of ignoring bioregional realities. In the newsletter of the E. F. Schumacher Society of America (Fall 1983), Sale expressed a position that closely parallels the philosophy of the German Greens:

> We finally comprehend that if there is to be salvation for this world, it will come through the development of bioregions into fully empowered, politically autonomous, economically self-sufficient social units in which bioregional citizens understand, and control, the decisions that affect their lives.

Other activists believe that bioregionalism will lead to ecologically wise organizations responsible for everyday self-government, wielding increasing degrees of influence over the "professional government." A third idea, developed by Peter Berg and other bioregionalists, is that state borders could be redrawn to reflect ecological imperatives, preserving a system of federation even while radically restructuring it. Projections for possible governmental structure, however, are less compelling to most bioregionalists than the here-and-now work of developing ecologically wise ways of thinking and being. The need for a new ethic is a core motivation for the bioregional movement, as Berg states: "There has to be a transition from Late Industrial Society toward shared values, goals and understandings that fit in with rather than contend against the regenerative process of the biosphere. We need to begin building a dwelling in life instead of on top of it."

At all five levels the Green movement could organize study groups that would gather information, discuss Green perspectives, and formulate Green proposals to present to lawmakers

and the public and to incorporate into a comprehensive program. Applying the holistic world view entails asking fundamental and interrelated questions currently absent from the political
dialogue in America. In particular, questions of sustainability
and long-term goals must be raised. We are recklessly living off
future generations, abiding by irresponsible policies simply because the "future" to our presidents means the next four or
eight years, to our business community it means the next few
financial quarters, to our labor unions the next contract term,
and to most people the next decade or two. A Green perspective
encourages finding our place in the ecosystem, realizing that our
very existence depends on the continuity of interdependent living systems. If we bankrupt those systems through greed and
stupidity, we destroy the life supports for ourselves and our
descendants, thereby severing the human chain of generations
that has spanned millions of years.

With sustainability as the key to their proposals, the various
Green study groups would formulate public policy statements.
We do not attempt such an ambitious task here but, rather, present suggestions of Green responses to several current issues:
energy, employment, national security and conversion of the
arms industry, healthcare, and school prayer. With these examples we wish to illustrate three principles of Green thinking.
First, there is a wealth of already published Green-oriented
ideas that can be tapped and synthesized in solving our problems creatively. Second, measures must be ecologically sound
and socially responsible; they must, in short, have a future.
Third, one cannot successfully address particular problems—
such as the danger of the arms race, the enormous defense
budget, or the unemployment problem linked to conversion—
without responding to their interconnected nature. Green solutions, like the laws of our ecosystems, are based on systemic
interrelationships.

Walter Truett Anderson, editor of *Rethinking Liberalism,* has
observed that our glittering consumer society is as precarious as
the glittering court of prerevolutionary France. The United
States comprises 5 percent of the world's population and uses
approximately 30 percent of its energy. Our enormously powerful and expensive military forces exist, as Secretary of Defense

Caspar Weinberger reminded Congress in his annual report for fiscal year 1984, not only to protect us but "to protect access to foreign markets and overseas resources." Once our multinational corporations expropriate those resources, usually on terms that cause great hardship over time in the Third World, they—in cooperation with the big labor unions, who seldom look beyond the immediate issues of wages and growth—produce for us planned obsolesence; toxic products; polluted air, soil, and water; and manipulative advertising campaigns to convince us that the quality of American life has everything to do with having and little to do with being.

Do we need to continue being the energy hogs of the global community—or could we drastically reduce our consumption with some rational planning and very little sacrifice? According to Arthur Rosenfeld, a physicist with the American Council for an Energy-Efficient Economy, the United States could practically *export* oil if we would simply retrofit our buildings and homes (an occupation that would create many new jobs) and manufacture only energy-efficient cars and large appliances, none of which would require spartan living. He emphasizes that our televisions, blenders, hair dryers, and so forth, use nothing compared to the energy that goes through the roof and walls. Hunter and Amory Lovins, of the Rocky Mountain Institute, have determined that economically justifiable uses of electricity, an extremely expensive form of energy, amount to only 8 percent of all delivered energy in the United States, as in most other industrial nations. Since that 8 percent is already supplied twice over by existing power stations, why do both the Democratic and Republican administrations continue to lead us down the "hard energy path" (nuclear reactors, coal plants, offshore oil drilling, expanded strip mining, and synthetic-fuel projects)? Why has government-supported research on the soft energy path (passive and active solar heating, passive cooling, small hydro dams, wind power, solar cells, cogeneration, liquid fuels from farm and forestry wastes, and means of energy efficiency) nearly ground to a halt? Why are there few tax incentives and low-interest loans to encourage the use of such sources? Why are our engineering colleges training our future technocrats only in the hard energy path as if there were no tomorrow? And why do *we*, the technopeasants in the voting booths, go along with such irrational policies when we know that corporate campaign contributions and influence are behind them?

Many communities have decided not to go along anymore. For example, the citizens of Fitchburg, Massachusetts, mobilized themselves in 1979 for rapid and extensive weatherization of their town. Using $95,000 in seed grants from three federal agencies (ACTION, HUD, and DOE), they established local training centers and recruited five hundred volunteers for the three-month project. By spending an average of $73 per house, or $102,200 for the program, they saved 150 gallons of oil per household the first winter, or $600,000 for the town. The Lovinses report that at least twenty other communities have adapted the techniques pioneered in Fitchburg.

Another example of grassroots progress in energy usage is the thousands of inexpensive solar greenhouses built by the Hispanic community in the San Luis Valley of southern Colorado. Averaging less than $200 each for construction, mostly from scavenged material, the solar greenhouses not only provide most or all of the space heating but extend the families' growing season from three months to year-round. Other renewable sources of energy, such as wind power and geothermal heat, are being used in the Valley as well, and the local bankers are now reportedly hesitant to extend loans on any *non*solar building. The Lovinses have written extensively on the enormous savings our country could realize if the renewable-resource, resilient technologies were not handicapped in the market by the huge federal subsidies and favorable policies for nuclear power and fossil fuels. They call for free competition among *all* energy technologies (see "The Fragility of Domestic Energy" by Amory and Hunter Lovins in *The Atlantic Monthly,* November 1983).

Suppose small-scale, worker-owned businesses will predominate and labor-intensive rather than capital-intensive investments will be made. The fact remains that there are not going to be enough jobs to go around. It has been estimated that 40 percent of the current white-collar jobs could be eliminated by computerization, and the current push to modernize American industry ("reindustrialize America") probably will mean more automation. If the remaining jobs were redistributed so that everyone worked half-time for nearly the same pay as now while machines did most of the production and business operations, many people would develop serious personal problems because self-esteem and identity are intertwined with the job ethic in our culture. This is true especially for men, who often dread retirement. Given our circumstances, is it not time to encourage an ethic of ecology and self-realization? There will always be plenty of *work* to be done in an ecodecentralized, nonexploitative society: community service to increase direct control of numerous activities and decrease government bureaucracy, lifelong education, care of our elderly, care and education of young children, bartering of goods and services, neighborhood food and other cooperatives, community structures for societal and individual rites of passage, and participatory cultural programs. Why should any of these be devalued if they are not monetarized as jobs? Beyond the need to secure necessities, what motivates us to work? What human and ecological values should be expressed in the inevitable restructuring of work? Shall we measure our society's progress in providing opportunities for self-development by the basic human needs index proposed by the United Nations Environment Program? Shall we consider the comprehensive physical quality of life indicator proposed by the Overseas Development Council? Or shall we cling to the GNP as our sole measure of well-being, one that rewards the shrinking pool of job-winners and transforms everyone else into unproductive, idle dependents of the government?

It is the issue of jobs that has stumped the peace movement in considering conversion of the weapons industry. How can we scale down the huge military-industrial complex, and hence the defense budget, without creating more unemployment and increasing our vulnerability? A Green response, while mindful of the long-term goal of a nonviolent, demilitarized world, would address this immediate problem from many directions.

First, real threats to our security do exist in this world, yet our government could adopt a new policy that includes restructuring the military to rely more on human power than on firepower and more on simple weaponry than on complex, high-tech devices, as James Fallows suggests in *National Defense* (Random House, 1982). The defense budget, which now consumes nearly one-third of our tax dollars ($260 billion in 1984), could be cut by 40 percent through reducing the surplus, dangerous, and interventionist elements of U.S. forces, as the Boston Study Group demonstrates in *Winding Down: The Price of Defense* (Freeman, 1982). Similar analyses have been developed in *The Baroque Arsenal* (Hill & Wang, 1981) by Mary Kaldor and in *Reforming the Military*, a booklet edited by Jeffrey Barlow and published in 1981 by the conservative Heritage Foundation. In addition, we could conduct *serious* negotiations with the Soviet Union for bilateral reductions of nuclear weapons, and urge other nations to join us in stabilizing the Third World by giving 1 percent of our GNP directly to citizen-controlled development programs. We could also conduct serious studies of social defense and the eventual establishment of zones throughout the world that would have only defensive weapons, as well as scenarios for achieving and maintaining a demilitarized world.

In *Toward An Alternative Security System* (World Policy Institute, 1983), Robert Johansen delineates seven policy models for the global system: a nuclear-war-fighting capability, a policy of mutually assured destruction, a minimum deterrent posture, a defensive weapons system, a peace-keeping federation, defense through civilian resistance, and a policy of global security. The seventh model is in harmony with Green politics, as it incorporates some of the features of conventional defense, a peace-keeping federation, and social defense but emphasizes the fact that no one country in the increasingly interdependent global community can be secure any longer unless everyone is secure. This policy model stresses long-term interests over short-term advantages and advocates greatly expanded positive incentives rather than negative military threats to influence other nations' security policies. It incorporates human rights in the positive image of peace so that securing the basic rights and basic needs of all people becomes as important a guideline in decision making as securing the institutions of the state. Since the nuclear and environmental policies of "foreign" governments affect each of us, this model teaches that, rather than "my" and "their" governments, the realistic view is one of "my immediate" and "my more distant" governments. Finally, it shifts the most vital line of defense away from new generations of nuclear weapons toward a new code of international conduct to restrict the use of military power.

With such a security policy, a large portion of the people now developing and building weapons would not need to do so. The Mid-Peninsula Conversion Project in Mountain View, California, estimates that two million jobs are linked to defense contracts, so the displacement from a shrinking arms competition would be sizable. The traditional response of the left to such a situation is to create huge government-supported work programs, while the right would have those workers fend for themselves in the "free" market. Conversion specialists offer a third alternative. They help defense-oriented factories and businesses develop "alternative use planning" by encouraging the formation of joint committees of workers and management. They discuss switching from the production of weapons to that of products such as light-rail vehicles, commuter aircraft, and alternative energy systems. The only industrial planning in this country at the national level, so conversion specialists maintain, is strictly defense planning. If the federal government offered the same kind of financial inducements, for example, loans, tax breaks, and contracts, to converted companies as it does to defense-oriented companies, conversion would flourish. A Green perspective would link certain criteria to those financial incentives: the new product or service would have to be socially necessary; production would cause minimal damage to the environment; distribution would be limited largely to the macroregion and adjacent ones (to avoid the demands of long-distance transportation and fuel); the business would be democratically operated* and at least partially employee-owned; and the scale of the operation would be appropriate, that is, no larger than what would benefit the people affected.

A Green response to the problem of conversion incorporates awareness not only of ecological balance and socially responsible production but also of the dignity and creativity of the individuals in the workforce. Therefore, an auxiliary conversion

*See *Workplace Democracy and Social Change*, ed. Frank Lindenfeld and Joyce Rothschild-Whitt (Porter Sargent, 1982), for analyses and first-person accounts of new systems of work and participation.

program should be available for those weapons makers who wish to leave their old firms and develop their own businesses. Since the defense industry provides no products or services to sell to our society, the workers involved—scientists, engineers, managers, secretaries, steelworkers, and assembly line workers—are actually receiving federal grants as their salaries. Those salary grants could be continued during a transition period of perhaps three years as part of a voluntary program that would encourage some of the workers to develop new businesses by attending seminars, workshops, and courses on sound business practices that are nonexploitative and ecologically wise; study of successful and failed businesses in their area would be emphasized. Some people would take job-training courses or college degree programs. Some might want to form cooperatives or neighborhood cottage industries, while others would create more technological enterprises. Once a group had developed a comprehensive business plan for the first several years of operation, it could apply to the government for a low-interest seed loan. Among the criteria for judging the business proposals would be the Green-oriented considerations cited above. The program would include information-sharing networks for people developing and operating similar types of businesses. Such a flowering of self-organized, self-determined businesses all over the country would also create jobs for unemployed people other than the former weapons makers because businesses utilize numerous service operations. In addition, small companies tend to be labor-intensive rather than spending huge capital outlays on automation.

This dual program would facilitate conversion among both types of workers: those who do not wish to leave the security of their current place of employment and those who wish to create their own enterprise. Our suggestions are merely preliminary and would require a great deal of development, but they do address the essential issue largely overlooked by the peace movement, that lowering the levels of armaments—even temporarily with a freeze on research and production—will never come about without creative, sound programs for conversion. No American president is going to agree to any proposal in Geneva or in our Congress that would substantially increase the unemployment rolls. If we are serious about de-escalating the arms race, every community with a defense contractor should begin developing proposals for partial or full conversion. If we are equally serious about sustaining life on Earth, those proposals must be ecologically sound and socially responsible.

On the issue of healthcare, do we want to devise government-supported and/or private schemes that merely increase everyone's access to mechanistic, invasive, dehumanizing medical practices—or shall we emphasize a holistic model of health that takes into account the interactions and self-organizing dynamics of the body/mind system? Studies have demonstrated that many symptoms of disease are indeed expressions of dis-ease, that is, negative states of mind relating to one's self-concept or personal perceptions. Relationships with family and friends, for instance, have been established as an important factor in health: disconnected or partially isolated people are statistically less healthy. Often illness is manifested, consciously or unconsciously, as an escape route out of stressful, unpleasant situations (see *Getting Well Again* by O. Carl Simonton, Stephanie Matthews-Simonton, and James Creighton, Bantam Books, 1980). With the striking disproportion between the cost and effectiveness of modern medicine, would it not be wise to emphasize "wellness" and healthy life-styles through health education and promotion programs?

A Green response to the rising tide of interest in holistic medicine would encourage that movement to avoid the pitfall of "victim-blaming" in analyzing illness and be truly holistic by giving proper weight to *all* the factors that contribute to ill health: not only inner dynamics, but also environmental factors (such as exposure to lead, asbestos, or toxic chemicals), employment conditions (such as stressful, tedious, or demeaning tasks), and societal phenomena (such as competitive situations, impersonal city life, and the threat of nuclear holocaust). A Green movement would promote a systems view of health, defining health as an experience of well-being resulting from a dynamic balance that involves the physical and psychological aspects of the organism, as well as its interactions with its natural and social environment (see the chapter on "Wholeness and Health" in *The Turning Point* by Fritjof Capra).

The poisoning of our biosphere has been so extensive that even wisdom about the self-organizing and self-healing powers of our organism is not going to preclude the need for a great deal of medical care in the future. A Green perspective would perserve those sensible and successful treatments that have been developed by conventional medicine but would integrate them into a larger framework of holistic healthcare and healing that actively involves the patient. This framework would also include freedom of choice by allowing access to a range of therapeutic models and techniques, such as acupuncture and homeopathy, that have long and successful traditions in other countries. The American Council of Life Insurance, which is hardly a radical group, published a report in 1980 predicting that in fifty years "osteopaths, acupuncturists, massage therapists, and ethnic healers" will have roughly the same status and earnings as the traditionally trained allopathic doctors.

Perhaps the most immediate issue in healthcare today is the question of how we shall pay for it. Some states and communities have taken transitional steps toward a more balanced, less profit-hungry system. For example, in 1983 the state of California initiated a reform of the medical and insurance payment systems. It is generally agreed that hard decisions lie ahead, such as whether a large sum of money should be spent on one coronary operation or on providing good primary care to a great number of people. In addition, we are most likely going to experience an increase in degenerative diseases such as hypertension, arteriosclerosis, cancer, and many geriatric ailments, which are significantly related to environmental stress factors. A Green perspective would encourage comprehensive programs of healthcare, that is, "package plans" that integrate biological, psychological, social, and environmental approaches to diagnosis and healing.

Is the Green respect for spiritual values served by prayer in the schools? Only if it honors the pluralism of the American tradition. A Gallup poll in September 1983 found that 81 percent of the American public favor school prayer. We doubt that the percentage would be so high if the imposition of one particular kind of prayer were specified. Most people want to desecularize our culture and let a rich spiritual life grow. Why not have our children begin their school day with five minutes of silence, which they could pass in contemplation and, if they wished, in offering a prayer to God, Goddess, the cosmos, or their favorite tree? And why have them sit in isolation during those moments? If they stood and joined hands in a circle and closed their eyes, they might experience a "body parable" of our essential unity—a relevant teaching from preschool through graduate seminars.

The network of issues a Green movement would address is far more vast than this brief sampling. It might initiate a Constitutional amendment to change our system of representation in legislative bodies to a proportional one, such as West Germany has. The 5-percent hurdle would keep out fringe groups but allow into our government a great deal of creative political thought, which is not forthcoming from the old-paradigm parties.

If a Green movement is to become a political reality in this country, it will have to overcome several initial problems, both internal and external. The first is the issue of who may become a member. Green politics attracts people who have been searching for a way to transform new-paradigm understandings into political practice, people who were previously somewhat apolitical but now realize that single-issue citizens' movements are inadequate by themselves, and political people who were dissatisfied with their old party or movement and now embrace Green ideals. Unfortunately, in nearly every country where a Green movement has been established, it has also attracted opportunistic persons from unsuccessful political groups on the right and the left who enter the new movement with hidden agendas and dishonest tactics. Identifying and banning them are difficult for two reasons: Individuals from any political background *may* sincerely change their thinking and adopt Green politics, and a diversity of opinions within the framework of Green goals and values should be honored. However, persons who undermine the progress of Green political development by repeatedly trying to impose their own incongruous priorities should not be allowed to ruin the movement. One of the first orders of business during the movement's founding stage should be the creation of a statement of principles and goals, more detailed than the "four pillars," to which all members would adhere. Although allegiance to such a declaration would not preclude the possibility of dishonesty, it would clarify the movement's expectations of its members. If infiltration actually occurs, additional means would have to be devised to address it.

A second internal problem is that the movement may be heir to unconstructive personal attitudes that should be addressed. As Green politics attracts a broad spectrum of citizens interested in developing possibilities beyond the limits of left and right constructs, it is important that people actively work at recognizing the positive aspects of all proposals and perceiving the genuine concerns behind them. A Green movement could avoid a failure-prone posture by tapping the enormous amount of ethical, moral, and spiritual power that is inherent in Green ideals. The struggle is not to smash "bad guys" or to fight for short-term gains for one group or even one class but to effect systemic change that will yield a better life for all people, all our partners in nature, and all the generations that may follow us.

Another destructive attitude might be negativity toward people with leadership abilities. In an effort to find more democratic models than the traditional pyramid structure, many of us experienced the "tyranny of structurelessness" in political groups in the early 1970s where unofficial channels of information, and hence control and power, developed to fill the void. Groups in the feminist, peace, anti-nuclear-power, and ecology movements since then have found small steering committees and well-defined positions—such as facilitator, note-taker, correspondent, agenda-maker and timer, and process-watcher—to be effective. These positions are rotated not to thwart potential monsters in our midst, but to encourage as many people as possible to take a central role and develop leadership skills. Competent leaders are essential for the success of a movement. They should be supported and encouraged at all levels.

Numerous other internal problems may arise, as we discussed earlier. Certainly one of the major challenges will be to arrive at agreement among a broad spectrum of members on the key principles, such as the extremely complex issue of decentralism. As Kirkpatrick Sale demonstrates in *Human Scale,* the decentralist impulse has been a stubborn, if minority, position within American politics since the beginning. Its era of greatest success was the late nineteenth century, when the Populist party achieved electoral victories from Texas to the Carolinas, even gaining control of the North Carolina legislature in 1890 and passing laws for local self-government through county autonomy. The first two decades of this century, however, saw the triumph of the centralized government's power through federal laws such as the Income Tax Amendment, the Federal Reserve Act, the Prohibition Amendment, and the Selective Service Act. Still, the decentralist spirit did not disappear. The Agrarian movement of the 1920s and 1930s, the cooperative movement, and various "home-grown radicalisms" joined to found the journal *Free America,* which existed from 1937 to 1946 with this creed:

> *Free America* stands for individual independence and believes that freedom can exist only in societies in which the great majority are the effective owners of tangible and productive property and in which group action is democratic; in order to achieve such a society, ownership, production, population, and government must be decentralized. *Free America* is therefore opposed to finance-capitalism, fascism, and communism.

With decentralist values reaching so far back in the American tradition, how did we end up with the huge monolithic institutions that control most of our economy, politics, healthcare, and culture today? Sale explains:

> The centralizing tendency has always existed in this country alongside the decentralizing—for every Anne Hutchinson a Governor Winthrop, for every Jefferson a Hamilton, for every Calhoun a Webster, for every Thoreau a Longfellow, for every Debs a Wilson, for every Borsodi a Tugwell, for every Brandeis a Frankfurter, for every Mumford a Schlesinger, for every Schumacher a Galbraith.

Some Green-oriented thinkers in this country are strict, almost abolutist, decentralists. They maintain that the general lack of corruption in the federal government would also prevail at local levels if local government was made the focus of our system. Centralists, on the other hand, insist that impartial inspections and investigations, civil rights, control of acid rain, equitable allocation of resources, and countless other matters must be handled by a strong federal government. It is likely that a Green movement would opt for neither of those either-or positions but, rather, for a holistic both-and approach: appropriate governance. Green politics in this country would support a great deal of decentralizing in government, the economy, and energy production. At the same time, it might well support accountable, responsive federal power to safeguard the shared values of an ecological, nonexploitative society. For instance, our federal government would determine that air pollutants must not exceed a certain level beyond which serious diseases result, but would leave the means of compliance up to each state to determine. Of course, the false decentralism of the Reagan Administration is a farce, because it demands, for example, $260 billion from us in 1984 alone to feed a bloated defense budget and then sends only a relatively small amount of our tax dollars back to the states, leaving them unable to address our problems adequately. In addition, the federal government has persistently increased its proportion of tax revenues from sources that overlap with those of cities and states, for example, gasoline tax. Much of our tax money that is allocated for the poor goes instead to intermediary federal bureaucracies, causing many people to wonder whether direct grants to poor families, administered at state or local levels, might not be more efficient. The tensions between the desire for autonomy and the reality of interdependence are but one conflict a Green movement would have to reconcile creatively. Mark Satin, editor of *New Options*, suggests that people are decentralists in their hearts but centralists in their heads. Like the German Greens, who call for a global federation to address issues of ecological balance and peace, he feels, "We'll always need a referee."

One of the external problems a Green movement will face is that several groups will probably claim to be the national Green party or movement with little justification.* The Citizens party, for example, considers itself the American counterpart of the

---

*The "International Green Party" led by Randy Toler claims to have twenty thousand members, five million supporters, and close affiliations with Petra Kelly (which she denied unequivocally in several press conferences during her American lecture tour in September 1983), but many people suspect that it is scarcely more than a one-person conceptual art project!

West German Greens. It received an endorsement from a few of the Greens in its early stages and prints their symbol, the sunflower, on its material along with its own, the fir tree. However, the politics of the Citizens party is less Green than socialist grafted with some environmentalism. For example, its leaflets blame our problems solely on corporations rather than pointing out the entire web of interrelated causes and the need for decentralization and structural changes in our economy.

Apparently, the discrepancy went unnoticed by the Citizens party until its convention in San Francisco in September 1983, which featured keynote addresses by three German Greens: Rudolf Bahro, Hannegret Hönes, and Christine Schröter. After those speeches, a guest delegate, David Haenke, was able to convince seventeen of the scores of delegates to form a Green caucus in order to introduce and encourage Green ideas in the party. The caucus was denied a permanent, nonvoting seat on the party's executive committee, but was accorded a Green column in its newsletter, *Citizens Voice*. In an article Haenke wrote at the convention for the daily newsletter there, he told of being pointed toward the door after identifying himself to a member of the Citizens party as "a political ecologist who was not and never had been a leftist." Haenke reminded party members that, unlike in the West German Green Party, the "decentralist, conservative right and the rest of the political spectrum" were missing and would probably not be welcome in the Citizens party. Although the party has achieved some admirable successes at the grassroots level, it is our feeling after attending the Citizens party's convention that many people are members because it is currently the only national organization that addresses even a few of their desires for a new politics. Whether the Citizens party could actually become Green in the true sense of the word after such a firmly rooted founding in a different political tradition is questionable.

Another external problem about which a Green movement should not be naïve is possible harassment by a reactionary fringe group that regularly denigrates the Green party in West Germany via its European chapters. This group is known variously as the National (or International) Democratic Policy Committee, the National Caucus of Labor Committees, the U.S. (or European) Labor Party—or, most commonly, as "the Lyndon

LaRouche people." They were identified as being the disrupters at lectures Petra Kelly gave in New York, Washington, and Los Angeles in September 1983, shouting from the audience that she is a "whore" and a "Nazi." The Los Angeles lecture was held on the campus of the University of Southern California, where the audience behaved in exemplary fashion: They chanted in unison "Out! Out! Out!" at the handful of disrupters, who, as is their usual pattern, were scattered throughout the assembly. The police were on hand, but their services were not necessary.

Such annoyances, however, are hardly the major external problem a Green movement will face. To achieve their goals, American Greens will have to accomplish a dynamic expansion of their ideas into mainstream consciousness. The extent of this problem was expressed to us by a high-level bureaucrat who has experience in both state and federal government. We asked him to read this chapter of our manuscript, and he responded: "When I think about some of the idiocies of old-paradigm politics, I get really angry. And when I read about these Green ideas, I think, 'Right, this is probably the way we should go.' But then I consider how far these ideas are from the way policy-makers think, and I drift off and end up thinking about some of the really great football games I've seen in my lifetime." What to say? Without dismissing the enormous challenge of getting from here to there that all idealists *and* realists face, we can take heart in the successes of the German Greens. Many of the very same policy-makers in West Germany who insisted not long ago that Green proposals are utterly impossible are now adopting and implementing some of them.

Another problem in applying Green ideas is that, despite their frequent complaints, people are in the habit of letting the monolithic agencies and institutions make decisions for them. The Green ideal of self-government and participatory democracy requires involvement, time, and effort. Combining such hindrances with the inevitable personality conflicts, one may wonder whether there is any hope for mobilizing Green forces of change.* The answer lies in whether enough of us come to

---

*See *Nothing Can Be Done, Everything Is Possible* (Brick House, 1982) by Byron Kennard for a witty dose of reality, as well as inspiration, on the possibilities for social change.

realize, as the German Greens have, that the matter at hand is survival.

Not everyone will be willing to look directly at such a stark fact, either because of psychological defense mechanisms ("I don't want to know how bad things really are") or because of seemingly irrational, yet usually self-serving, defense of the status quo. For example, books such as *Global 2000 Revised* by Julian Simon and the late Herman Kahn argue that because some of the projections in *The Limits to Growth* and similar reports were incorrect, we should ignore all warnings from ecologists and proceed with full-speed-ahead industrial growth and use of resources. It should be obvious that no amount of quibbling over the specific year in which we will deplete various minerals, ores, and fossil fuels can alter the fact that we are living in a biosphere with a finite amount of physical resources. Pretending that the human race is somehow above the dynamics of the ecosystems, of which we are a part, is sheer hubris and will lead to a fall of catastrophic proportions.

Although an effective Green movement in the United States will not manifest itself automatically, its potential far outweighs the possible problems. There are literally thousands of groups and periodicals that are working along the lines of Green politics. The Networking Institute lists 2,000 such organizations, and New Options, Inc. lists 1,600 change-oriented periodicals. From these two resources we contacted more than 500 groups and selected a representative list of one hundred, which appears in Appendix C.* In our opinion, these groups are working with means and goals that are consistent with Green politics; together their membership is over 2 million. If a Green movement is to develop in this country, many of the organizers will probably come from these and similar groups. Moreover, we hope that local Green groups will contact these organizations for resource material in the various areas we have delineated.

When we were in the final stages of writing this book, peo-

---

*We have limited the list to organizations in the United States, but there are also many Green-oriented groups in Canada, such as the Vanier Institute for the Family in Ottawa. Interested persons can learn of them by contacting the Green Party of British Columbia (see Appendix B).

ple began to learn about Green politics, beyond the media distortions, through the speeches and interviews of several German Greens who made lecture tours of the United States. In public forums we also shared our research on the Greens and our ideas for Green politics in this country, which were met with a great deal of enthusiasm. Many people asked us, "When? Where? How?" *As soon as we do it. In our own towns and cities. By expressing Green ideals to a broad cross section of groups and individuals and inviting them together.*

The first gathering might be a fund-raising picnic or fair or party at which Green values and goals could be discussed and community groups working in beyond-left-and-right modes could display material. Local groups might then decide to establish task forces for projects such as weatherizing the homes and buildings in a community as Fitchburg, Massachusetts, did, thereby taking their first step on the soft energy path. The Green organization might wish to conduct a "goals and futures project" to consider various scenarios for the future of their town, developing such policy-making tools for their local government as an agenda of long-range, intermediate, and short-term goals, along with analyses of issues and planning for legislative policies. The Institute for Alternative Futures (see Appendix C) has assisted numerous towns and regions with such "Year 2000 Projects," and their director, Clement Bezold, has edited a helpful anthology, *Anticipatory Democracy* (Random House/Vintage Books, 1978). In conjunction with such a project, the local Greens might establish study groups on various issues who could gather information and develop Green proposals to be discussed and refined by the larger group—incorporating the wisdom of our elders and the fresh insights of our children—and then present them to officials and community groups. One of the central aims of grassroots Green politics is to make the question "How do I live?" a key issue in social activism, that is, to make everyday life the focus.

The local groups could send representatives to bioregional and eventually state and macroregional meetings as well, but it is important as the grassroots level develops to have some coordination at the national level. The business of a founding convention would include developing a statement of principles, deciding on the structure for the movement, suggesting guidelines for the process of a meeting, deciding on a name (some people feel "Green" is too narrowly associated with environmentalism in this country), and establishing a newsletter by which to convey ideas and inspiration among the local groups. Such decisions would require a great deal of preliminary work, of course.

Several people interested in building a Green movement have suggested that an assembly could be held in late 1984 or early 1985. We have prevailed upon the staff of *New Options*, the newsletter of Green politics in the United States, to serve as a temporary clearinghouse for information about the development of a movement: Green Movement, c/o *New Options*, P.O. Box 19324, Washington, DC 20036. They welcome reports from local Green groups and ideas about all aspects of the movement. In addition, they would like to hear from people interested in supporting and working on the founding convention. It is certainly possible that Green politics could grow as quickly and as firmly here as it has in other countries.

If there is an immediacy to Green politics, there is also a deep optimism that we have taken the first steps. Both the right and the left will attack our course, as the Greens in other countries have found. Perhaps the words of a courageous Green in West Germany, Rudolf Bahro, can inspire us: "When the forms of an old culture are dying, the new culture is created by a few people who are not afraid to be insecure." The carrot of "security" has been used in the past to lead people out of crisis situations into fascism when no comprehensive alternatives existed to challenge that drift with sufficient strength. Anyone who seriously examines the ecological and economic underpinnings of our system can see that we are heading for a staggering escalation of the current interrelated crises. At that point will the increasingly powerful centralized states that nuclearism is feeding enact "emergency measures" with all the repressive force the old-paradigm institutions can exert? Or will we be well on the way to building a regionalized global community that is ecologically wise, nonexploitative, and spiritually grounded? The future, if there is to be one, is Green.

Appendices

Appendix A

The Structure and Operation of the Green Party in West Germany

The fundamental unit of the Green party is the local group. The groups meet biweekly or monthly and control the membership of the party in that in many local chapters the members must approve a person's application, on the grounds of sincere acceptance of Green principles and goals, before she or he can join. Local chapters also keep the party membership records, which are sent to the national office through the county and state offices. Dual membership with another political party is not allowed. Local groups collect party dues via a sliding scale of 5 to 20 DM ($2–8) per month. Of that, usually 4 DM are sent to the state office, which in turn forwards 2 DM to the national office. The state office then distributes most of its share to the county groups. Some counties maintain offices, while others prefer to spend most of the money on projects. (In all the Green offices we visited, by the way, we never saw a filing cabinet. Instead, the Greens file records and correspondence in looseleaf binders stored on bookshelves that line the walls.)

Some local chapters permit nonmembers, such as representatives from citizens' movements, to vote on Green decisions. This policy is in keeping with the Greens' desire to cultivate a broad-based Green movement, only part of which is the political party. They wish to serve the

229

needs and concerns of the entire grassroots level *(die Basis)* including those activists who do not wish to enter electoral politics. Individual members and nonmembers send proposals or problems directly to Green officeholders or party committees at all levels. In most local chapters, however, nonmembers are barred from voting although they are invited to participate in discussions. When this rule has been challenged, it has generally been by radical-left groups rather than citizens' movements. For example, Green members in the Nuremberg chapter who had formerly belonged to Communist groups attempted in June 1983 to achieve open voting, with an eye toward packing the meetings with their ideological colleagues. However, the core group of Greens was able to narrowly defeat the proposal.

In a large city the next level of structure is the city-quarter group and then the citywide organization *(Stadtverband)*. Where the Greens have succeeded in getting onto the city council, there is also a group of Green council members and their assistants *(Stadtratsgruppe)*.

In most areas, however, the next level after the local groups is the county organization *(Kreisverband)*. In rural areas, this group, rather than the local one, may handle membership and collect dues. County-wide meetings are usually held once a month and are open to all members. There may also be a group of Greens who have been elected to the county legislature *(Kreistagsgruppe)*.

The highest-ranking body in the state—at least theoretically—is the statewide assembly *(Landesversammlung)*, which meets semiannually. In some states, this meeting is open to all members, in others to delegates who are elected at the county level with one person representing every twenty members. The assemblies vote on major policy positions, priorities, and strategies. They also select a candidates' list for elections to the state and federal legislatures.

A statewide steering committee *(Landeshauptausschuss)* is either elected by the assembly or is comprised of one delegate from each county. These people are the main decision makers for the statewide party throughout the year. They meet at least monthly to coordinate actions with citizens' movements, decide on budgetary matters, respond to proposals and problems presented by local groups or individuals, issue press releases, prepare for statewide assemblies, and so forth. The assemblies can be called either by the steering committee or by one-third of the county groups.

To carry out administrative tasks, the statewide assembly elects an executive committee *(Landesvorstand)*. This body is usually small, for example, five members in the state of Baden-Württemberg, seven in Hesse, and thirteen in Bavaria. Some states elect one to three speakers from the executive committee but others do not. A treasurer and a secretary seem to be the only indispensable positions.

At state, county, and local levels one usually finds *working groups* on a wide variety of issues. One of the functions of the statewide steering committee is to coordinate these groups through the state office and to act on their findings and recommendations. The topics are usually the same as those the Hesse program focuses on (see Chapter 6), although priorities vary in different towns and regions. However, we were surprised to find Third World working groups even in small local organizations. They investigate the source of various imported products, raw materials, and foodstuffs in their town and determine whether the local patterns of consumption are contributing to exploitation and suffering in the Third World. If so, alternative patterns and/or worker-owned sources are then sought and publicized.

The statewide steering committee also selects one person to serve on the board of the state's *Öko-Fond* (see Chapter 2), along with two Greens chosen by the statewide assembly and two non-Greens from the citizens' movements. As we explained, each state's *Öko-Fond* receives money from the "surplus" in the salaries of Green state legislators and the Bundestag parliamentarians. It then awards loans and grants to various enterprises in the larger Green movement, such as model projects for alternative energy, legal fees for environmental groups, ecological research investigations, peace camps, and publicity needs of numerous citizens' movements. A small minority of Greens feel that at least some of that money should stay within the party and be spent on developing the party infrastructure.

In those states where the Greens have won election to the legislature—Baden-Württemberg, Hesse, and Lower Saxony—there is also a parliamentary group *(Landtagsgruppe)* consisting of the legislators, their successors, and the assistants. The Greens have also won seats in the combined city-council/state-legislatures *(Bürgerschaft)* of the three city-states: Berlin, Bremen, and Hamburg. In Berlin the Greens ran as part of the leftist Alternative List (AL) and in Hamburg they ran in coalition with the AL, but in all three city-states the working partnership between the Greens and those radical leftists began to unravel during the summer of 1983, leading to various schisms.

Ideally, the state legislators work closely with the statewide steering committee and its executive committee, but this is not always the case. Part of the problem is that the legislators must spend nearly all their time addressing duties such as initiating and responding to bills, serving on countless governmental and *Fraktion* committees, dealing with the media, and responding to various Green individuals and groups. Most of the Green *Fraktion* groups at the state level see themselves as parallel to the statewide steering committee rather than responsible to it.

A somewhat rivalrous relationship between the Hesse Greens and the Baden-Württemberg Greens became apparent during our discussions of this issue with them. Several Hesse Greens, who are quite proud of the democracy demonstrated by their lack of a speaker and "stars," suggested to us that the best known of the Baden-Württemberg legislators, Wolf-Dieter Hasenclever, a former speaker of the party there, controls not only the *Fraktion* but the entire state party. Several Baden-Württemberg Greens dryly responded that a powerful man on the Frankfurt city council and a few others exert a great deal of influence over the Green *Fraktion* in the Hesse legislature. (We did hear complaints from Hesse Greens at the county level that the Frankfurt people carry too much weight in the state party.) The Baden-Württemberg Greens charge that such covert control is less democratic than the openly acknowledged influence of a popular elected official such as Hasenclever.

On the national level one finds a similar structure along with an exponential increase in the problems and the intrigue. Theoretically, the highest level body in the entire party is the national delegates' assembly *(Bundesdelegiertenversammlung)* held annually in November. Delegates are elected not by the state parties but directly from the grassroots level of local or county groups; currently, every twenty members are represented by one delegate. This assembly votes on political issues and policy decisions. Sometimes special national assemblies are also called, such as the one at Sindelfingen in January 1983 to finalize the economic program for the national election in March, and the one at Hannover in June to establish working groups at the national level.

The ongoing business of the party is conducted by a national steering committee *(Bundeshauptausschuss)* consisting of forty members. They are elected for a two-year term but may step down after one year. The number of delegates a state is allowed to send to this body corresponds to its membership. It meets approximately every six weeks. Sometimes the national steering committee is called upon to solve a problem or to endorse a particular action within the Greens, which usually entails much debate. However, its two main functions are to serve as the link between the grassroots level and the national executive committee, and to channel information from the grassroots level to the Bundestag *Fraktion* and back. The delegates are required to follow the "imperative mandate" of their state organizations when voting on an issue, although they may express personal disagreement with their state party's position. Proposals and problems are sent to the national steering committee both by groups and by individuals.

A small administrative body, the national executive committee *(Bundesvorstand)* meets two or more times during the six-week intervals between the meetings of the national steering committee. These eleven people are elected for two years by the annual delegates' assembly. To win a seat a candidate must receive an absolute majority. From this committee the delegates elect the three speakers of the party. As of the November 1983 assembly the speakers were Wilhelm Knabe, Rebekka Schmidt, and Rainer Trampert.

The national executive committee was the focus of attention of the party and the media until the Greens entered the Bundestag in March 1983. The members we spoke with denied that being pushed out of the spotlight by the *Fraktion* in Bonn has been a concern, although other Greens disagree. One of the radical-left members of the committee dismissed such suppositions with the favorite Marxist rebuttal: "That is a psychologizing of the situation."

After twenty-seven of the Greens became federal parliamentarians, with all the privileges that entails, the three speakers of the national executive committee requested that the party "professionalize" their own positions by paying them salaries and providing secretaries. In truth, the members work very hard, enduring relentless schedules of marathon meetings. An even more important concern, though, was the question of to whom the Bundestag *Fraktion* should be responsible. As the paramount standing body of the party and the channel for both state and grassroots concerns, the national executive committee felt the *Fraktion* in Bonn should be clearly under their control and should follow the "imperative mandate" channeled through the party structure. Several parliamentarians, however, felt their responsibility was to the state that had elected them.

In the first few months after the election of the Bundestag *Fraktion*, the national executive committee established a watchdog group of three people to periodically visit Bonn and report back to them. The parliamentarians claimed such a system was not useful as there is so much activity going on within the Bundestag *Fraktion* that no one can grasp the entire picture on periodic visits of a few hours. The national executive committee also convened the Hannover assembly in June to establish working groups on various issues that would send their findings and proposals to the *Fraktion* via the executive committee. The national executive committee was miffed to learn later that several parliamentarians wanted the *Fraktion* to establish its own working groups to suit the demands of the legislative system more closely. This question of control and responsibility was one of the major issues addressed, although not effectively, at the national delegates' assembly in Duisburg in November 1983.

The national executive committee also hires the general manager *(Bundesgeschäftsführer)*, who has been Lukas Beckmann since the founding of the party. He is assisted by Eberhard Walde. The manager conducts the party's business with a staff of eight people in a two-story house in Bonn, identified as the national headquarters by a small sign bearing the party's logo and a sunflower. The unimposing architecture and the bicycles chained to the fence along the garden stand in wry contrast to the high-rise that is the headquarters of the Christian Democrats and the modernistic grouping of "functional" boxes that houses the Social Democrats. Both declare their presence with huge initials thought to be an eyesore by many people.

On the other side of Bonn, the Green parliamentarians were assigned to a high-rise office building that is part of the government complex. Most of them taped over the air-conditioning vents, opened their windows, and hung posters on the walls. Still, they consider the building an oppressive environment. The *Fraktion* stationery optimistically shows vibrant sunflowers overgrowing the boxlike government buildings on which the dove of peace has lighted.

The *Fraktion* group currently is composed of twenty-eight parliamentarians (twenty-seven Greens plus one person from the Alternative List in West Berlin), the twenty-eight *Nachrücker,* about thirty specialist assistants, and about twenty secretaries. Most of the parliamentarians do not have a secretary and share the office tasks with their assistants. The group has a business manager, Michael Vesper, and a parliamentary manager, Joschka Fischer, who maintains direct communication with the president of the Bundestag and keeps track of the Greens' turns to speak there.

The *Fraktion* group spends an inordinate amount of time in meetings, as well as in the Bundestag sessions. The parliamentarians and their successors meet weekly—often for eight hours beginning in the evening! They also hold all-day sessions during crises. Like all bodies within the Greens, the *Fraktion* tries for consensus but operates according to majority rule.

In addition to serving on standing committees in the Bundestag, the parliamentarians and their successors are organized into working groups. These meet weekly and are clustered around the following topics: business and finance; women and society; rights and community; disarmament, peace, and international affairs; and the environment. In addition, the fifty-person staff meets regularly to discuss issues in working conditions and salaries. The women's group—parliamentarians, *Nachrücker,* specialist assistants, and secretaries—meets to discuss sexism within the *Fraktion* group. They also explore the possibilities of developing a new style of politics in the *Fraktion* to replace the patriarchal one that was established quickly in the beginning. The staff focuses on the division of labor that makes men "official" and women "supportive."

The women's group played a central role in a "sex scandal" that was featured in German and American newspapers in August 1983. A fifty-three-year-old male Green parliamentarian entered the office of a twenty-six-year-old female specialist assistant, a biologist, and grabbed her breasts. Shaken, she told him to leave. She then went to other women in the *Fraktion* group to warn them, only to learn that he had made similar assaults on several other women. She composed a letter calling for a meeting of the women's group to discuss the problem but not mentioning the man by name. (She told us she was able to pursue a course of activism rather than stunned silence because of her experience working in a campaign against sexual harassment at McGill University in Montreal in 1978–80.) A reporter for *Bild am Sonntag,* a newspaper with standards similar to those of the *National Enquirer,* is believed to have stolen a copy of the letter from the mailboxes and asked around until he had ascertained the man's identity, which appeared with a photograph and large type on the front page the next day. Several male parliamentarians were angry with the women for having addressed the matter semipublicly, if discreetly, since, as they saw it, it was merely a matter of one man's crisis. The women maintained that it was a widespread pattern in patriarchal culture and called a press conference to invite women all over West Germany to send accounts of sexual harassment in the workplace. "The Green party is not an island in patriarchal society but a part of it," stated Sarah Jansen, one of the leading activists in the women's group. "It's just that we can discuss this matter openly without fear of losing our jobs, unlike most other women."

The sensationalist publicity increased, including a cover story in *Der Spiegel,* until the man finally resigned. Most of the pressure for his resignation came not from the women, many of whom felt he should be allowed to stay, but from a few powerful men who felt competitive with the accused man and delighted in this excuse for his ouster. In fact, it was one of those men who informed *Bild am Sonntag* of the attacker's identity. Since these internal dynamics were not made public, many Greens feel the women were used because they appeared to have demanded vengeance on top of the man's public humiliation. The Green women's group did wage a successful campaign in the national media and in meetings with unions to bring attention to the problem of sexual harassment, and the Green *Fraktion* appeared responsive because it hired two women to edit a book (half documentation and half analysis) that will draw on the hundreds of accounts that have been received. However, a backlash of "feminist-phobia," according to the victim of the assault, manifested within the *Fraktion,* with several men directing sustained hostility toward her over a period of months and accusing her of having fabricated the entire incident (even though several similar complaints had been made in the man's home state as well as in the *Fraktion* group). They planted the rumor that she had orchestrated the incident in order to improve the political position of her feminist boss, who, as an activist scientist, was the logical choice among the Green parliamentarians to succeed the ousted man as head of the committee on science and technology in the Bundestag (the only committee chair that was allotted to the Greens). The men successfully blocked the feminist scientist's appointment to that chair, selecting instead a much less feminist female parliamentarian who had been working on another committee altogether. "They think only in terms of power politics here so they suspect my motivation," the woman who was attacked told us. "Those men seem incapable of understanding that someone could act out of *feelings* of being hurt and humiliated." In the final analysis of this incident, then, the *Fraktion* publicly appeared responsive, while privately a group of male parliamentarians operating with patriarchal values had eliminated a male competitor, branded his victim a liar, and penalized her feminist boss.

Unofficial concentrations of power are sometimes a problem within the Greens, but their avowed position is to keep power decentralized. That is why Green rules forbid anyone to serve on more than one body within the party. This is in contrast to the major parties, in which the speaker of the Bundestag *Fraktion* is also the speaker of the party, and several entrenched members each control various operations.

For the same reason, the Greens generally prefer leadership by committee rather than by individuals. They elected three speakers of the *Fraktion* for a one-year term: currently, Marieluise Beck-Oberdorf, Petra Kelly, and Otto Schily. However, like so much else in the Greens, these selections did not come about without a struggle. Schily, who is very popular with the left for his role of defense attorney for terrorists during the 1970s* and is considered by some people more a "radical liberal" than a Green, received the highest number of votes, followed by Kelly and then Beck-Oberdorf. Schily then suggested that he be the speaker for the *Fraktion* and the two women could be his assistants, or vice-speakers! Men as well as women successfully opposed Schily's plan on the grounds that it violated basic Green principles; they voted instead for Roland Vogt's counterproposal for a triumvirate. In many other respects, however, the *Fraktion* did slip into conventional and often patriarchal forms and styles. For reasons no one could explain to us, the three speakers in the Bundestag are the same people who preside over the *Fraktion* meetings, which is a centralizing of power that easily could be avoided.

*Terrorism is antithetical to Green principles, and we found no support for it among the Greens as a political tactic. However, we were surprised to encounter a general sympathy among many Germans under forty for those individuals who had become terrorists in the mid-1970s because of "frustration" with the political options then.

Appendix B

Addresses of Green Parties

ALÖ
Mohrstrasse 10
A-5020 Salzburg
Austria

BELGIUM:
Agalev
Onderrichtstraat 69
B-1000 Brussels
Belgium

Ecolo
Rue Basse Marcelle 26
B-5000 Namur
Belgium

CANADA:
The Green Party of British
   Columbia
214-1956 W. Broadway
Vancouver, B.C. V6J 1Z2
Canada

FRANCE:
Les Verts
52 rue Faubourg Poissonnière
F-75010 Paris
France

Les Verts–Parti Ecologiste
Cité Fleurie

65 Boulevard Arago
F-75013 Paris
France

GERMANY:
Die Grünen
Colmantstrasse 36
5300 Bonn I
West Germany

IRELAND:
Comhaontas Glas
15 Upper Stephen Street
Dublin 2
Eire

LUXEMBOURG:
Dei Grëng Alternativ
Boite Postal 2711
Luxembourg

SWEDEN:
Miljöpartiet
Box 22096
S-10422 Stockholm
Sweden

UNITED KINGDOM:
Ecology Party
36/38 Clapham Road
London SW9 OJQ
England

Appendix C

One Hundred Green-Oriented Organizations in the United States

New Values/Old Values

Association for
  Community-Based Education
1806 Vernon Street N.W.
Washington, DC 20009

Basic Choices
Blakeman Place
1121 University Avenue
Madison, WI 53715

Center of Concern
3700 13th Street N.E.
Washington, DC 20017

CoEvolution Quarterly
P.O. Box 428
Sausalito, CA 94966

In Context
P.O. Box 215
Sequim, WA 98382

Institute for Liberty and
  Community
Concord, VT 05824

Leading Edge Bulletin
P.O. Box 42211
Los Angeles, CA 90042

League for Ecological Democracy
P.O. Box 1858
San Pedro, CA 90733

The Networking Institute
P.O. Box 66
West Newton, MA 02165

New Age Journal
342 Western Avenue
Brighton, MA 02135

New Jewish Agenda
149 Church Street, Suite 2N
New York, NY 10007

New Options
P.O. Box 19324
Washington, DC 20036

E. F. Schumacher Society
Box 76, RD 3
Great Barrington, MA 01230

Sojourners
P.O. Box 29272
Washington, DC 20017

Twin Streams Educational Center
243 Flemington Street
Chapel Hill, NC 27514

Unitarian Universalist Service
Committee
78 Beacon Street
Boston, MA 02108

World Council of Churches
475 Riverside Drive, Room 1062
New York, NY 10115

Ecodevelopment

Abalone Alliance
2940 16th Street, Room 310
San Francisco, CA 94103

Agenda
P.O. Box 5234
Westport, CT 06881

Environmental Action
1346 Connecticut Avenue N.W.,
Suite 731
Washington, DC 20036

Friends of the Earth
1045 Sansome Street
San Francisco, CA 94111

Greenpeace USA
2007 R Street N.W.
Washington, DC 20009

Hudson Valley GREEN (Grass
Roots Energy and
Environmental Network)
P.O. Box 208
Red Hook, NY 12571

Human Environment Center
810 18th Street N.W.
Washington, DC 20006

Institute for Social Ecology
P.O. Box 89
Plainfield, VT 05667

The New Environment
Association
270 Fenway Drive
Syracuse, NY 13224

The Northcoast Environmental
Center
879 9th Street
Arcata, CA 95521

SEA Alliance (Safe Energy
Alternatives)
324 Bloomfield Avenue
Montclair, NJ 07042

Sierra Club
530 Bush Street
San Francisco, CA 94108

Solar Lobby
1001 Connecticut Avenue N.W.,
Suite 510
Washington, DC 20036

Southern Unity Network for
Renewable Energy Projects
(SUNREP)
P.O. Box 10121
Knoxville, TN 37919

Women for Life on Earth
339 Lafayette Street
New York, NY 10012

Zero Population Growth
1346 Connecticut Avenue N.W.
Washington, DC 20036

Appropriate Technologies

New Alchemy Institute
237 Hatchville Road
East Falmouth, MA 02536

Rain
2270 NW Irving
Portland, OR 97210

The Transnational Network for
Appropriate/Alternative
Technology (TRANET)
Box 567
Rangeley, ME 04970

Responsible Business and Labor

Association for Workplace
Democracy
1747 Connecticut Avenue N.W.
Washington, DC 20009

Center for Economic
Revitalization
Box 363
Worcester, VT 05682

Community Economics
1904 Franklin Street, Suite 900
Oakland, CA 94612

Co-Op America
2100 M Street N.W., Suite 605
Washington, DC 20063

The Corporation for Enterprise
Development
1211 Connecticut Avenue N.W.,
Suite 710A
Washington, DC 20036

Environmentalists for Full
Employment
1536 16th Street N.W.
Washington, DC 20036

National Center for Employee
Ownership
1611 South Walter Reed Drive,
#109
Arlington, VA 22204

The Co-Op Bank
National Consumer Cooperative
Bank
1630 Connecticut Avenue N.W.
Washington, DC 20009

Nutrition and Regenerative Agriculture

American Farm Foundation
236 Massachusetts Avenue N.E.,
Suite 610
Washington, DC 20002

Center for Science in the Public
Interest
1501 16th Street N.W.
Washington, DC 20009

The Cornucopia Project
Rodale Press
33 E. Minor Street
Emmaus, PA 18049

Rural America
1302 18th Street N.W., #302
Washington, DC 20036

Peoples of Color

Akwesasne Notes
Mohawk Nation
via Rooseveltown, NY 13683

Alternativas
P.O. Box 424
Señoral Mall Station
Rio Piedras
Puerto Rico 00926

International Indian Treaty
    Council (AIM)
777 United Nations Plaza, Suite
    10F
New York, NY 10017

Institute of the Black World
87 Chestnut Street, S.W.
Atlanta, GA 30314

League of United Latin
    American Citizens (LULAC)
400 1st Street N.W., Suite 721
Washington, DC 20001

The Martin Luther King, Jr.
    Center for Nonviolent Social
    Change
449 Auburn Avenue, N.E.
Atlanta, GA 30312

National Council of La Raza
20 F Street N.W., 2nd Floor
Washington, DC 20001

Operation PUSH
930 E. 50th Street
Chicago, IL 60615

Survival International USA
2121 Decatur Place N.W.
Washington, DC 20008

Local and Bioregional Self-Help

Action Linkage
Box 2240
Wickenburg, AZ 85358

Citizen Action
1501 Euclid Avenue, Suite 500
Cleveland, OH 44115

Community Service
Box 243
Yellow Springs, OH 45387

Conference on Alternative State
    and Local Policies
2000 Florida Avenue N.W.
Washington, DC 20009

Federation of Egalitarian
    Communities
Box 6B2
Tecumseh, MO 65760

Institute for Local Self-Reliance
1717 18th Street N.W.
Washington, DC 20009

Neighborhood Revitalization
    Project
American Enterprise Institute
1150 17th Street N.W.
Washington, DC 20036

Movement for a New Society
4722 Baltimore Avenue
Philadelphia, PA 19143

National Association of
    Neighborhoods
1612 20th Street N.W.
Washington, DC 20009

National Association for
Neighborhood Enterprise
1130 17th Street N.W., Suite 500
Washington, DC 20036

North American Bioregional
Congress
Box 129
Drury, MO 65638

Planet Drum Foundation
P.O. Box 31251
San Francisco, CA 94131

Human Needs

American Holistic Medical
Association
6932 Little River Turnpike
Annandale, VA 22003

Association for Humanistic
Psychology
325 9th Street
San Francisco, CA 94103

Gray Panthers
3635 Chestnut Street
Philadelphia, PA 19104

National Men's Organization
5512 Bartlett Street
Pittsburgh, PA 15217

Sojourner: The New England
Women's Journal of New Opinions
and the Arts
143 Albany Street
Cambridge, MA 02139

Peace and Real Security

Center for War/Peace Studies
218 East 18th Street
New York, NY 10003

Coalition for a New Foreign and
Military Policy
120 Maryland Avenue N.E.
Washington, DC 20002

Ground Zero
806 15th Street N.W., Suite 421
Washington, DC 20005

Interhelp
330 Ellis Street, Room 505
San Francisco, CA 94102

Nuclear Free America
2521 Guilford Avenue
Baltimore, MD 21218

Nuclear Times
298 5th Avenue
New York, NY 10001

Nuclear Weapons Freeze
Campaign
4144 Lindell Boulevard,
Suite 404
St. Louis, MO 63108

Peace and Common Security
(PACS)
2520 Milvia Street
Berkeley, CA 94704

Peacework
American Friends Service
Committee
2161 Massachusetts Avenue
Cambridge, MA 02140

Physicians for Social
Responsibility
639 Massachusetts Avenue
Cambridge, MA 02139

Search for Common Ground
1346 Connecticut Avenue,
Suite 1126
Washington, DC 20036

Union of Concerned Scientists
26 Church Street
Cambridge, MA 02238

Women's Action for Nuclear
  Disarmament (WAND)
P.O. Box 153, New Town Branch
Boston, MA 02258

Global Contexts

Cultural Survival
11 Divinity Avenue
Cambridge, MA 02138

The Development Group for
  Alternative Policies
The Development GAP
1010 Vermont Avenue N.W.,
  Suite 521
Washington, DC 20005

Global Education Associates
552 Park Avenue
East Orange, NJ 07017

Institute for Food and
  Development
Policy/Food First
1885 Mission Street
San Francisco, CA 94103

Overseas Development Council
1717 Massachusetts Avenue N.W.
Washington, DC 20036

Planetary Initiative for the World
  We Choose
c/o Planetary Citizens
777 United Nations Plaza
New York, NY 10017

Plenty Project
156 Drakes Lane
Summertown, TN 38483

US Association for the Club of
  Rome
1525 New Hampshire Avenue
  N.W.
Washington, DC 20036

World Hunger Education Service
1317 G Street N.W.
Washington, DC 20005

World Policy Institute
777 United Nations Plaza
New York, NY 10017

Worldwatch Institute
1776 Massachusetts Avenue N.W.
Washington, DC 20036

A Choice of Futures

Institute for Alternative Futures
915 King Street, Suite B-42
Alexandria, VA 22314

World Future Society
4916 Saint Elmo Avenue
Bethesda, MD 20814

About the Authors

FRITJOF CAPRA is a native of Austria who has lived in the United States for over ten years. He received his Ph.D. from the University of Vienna and has done research in high-energy physics at several European and American universities. He is currently working at the Lawrence Berkeley Laboratory of the University of California. In addition to his many technical research papers, Dr. Capra has written and lectured extensively about the philosophical, social, and political implications of modern science. He is the author of two international best sellers, *The Tao of Physics* and *The Turning Point*.

CHARLENE SPRETNAK holds degrees from St. Louis University and the University of California, Berkeley. She is active in the peace movement and the feminist movement and is the author of "Naming the Cultural Forces That Push Us Toward War" (*Journal of Humanistic Psychology*, Summer 1983). She is also the editor of *The Politics of Women's Spirituality*, author of *Lost Goddesses of Early Greece*, and coeditor of *Frauenzukünfte (Women's Visions of the Future)*, an international anthology published in West Germany in the *Öko-Log-Buch* series.